Additional Praise for *Whitetail Savvy*

If it is indeed true that we "Only conserve what we love . . . Love only what we understand . . . And understand only what we are taught," then Dr. Leonard Rue, by his photography and writings, has done much to greatly advance the conservation of the white-tailed deer with yet another great treatise on this magnificent game animal. *Whitetail Savvy* is a must-read for the serious student of deer.

—Robert W. Duncan
Executive Director, Virginia Department of Game and Inland Fisheries

Leonard Lee Rue III has been observing and photographing whitetails longer than most of us have lived. An award-winning writer, photographer, and educator, his books represent thousands of days spent watching deer. Leonard has seen it all, and in this beautiful book, he intricately ties it together for hunters and nonhunters alike. If you enjoy whitetails, this readable treasure is a must. The scientific and observational information is extremely interesting, and the accompanying photos are what you expect from Dr. Leonard Lee Rue III.

—Dr. Dave Samuel
Professor Emeritus of Wildlife Management, West Virginia University

If there's one person who has changed the way modern American hunters understand whitetails, it's Dr. Leonard Lee Rue III. He can not only be credited for his landmark insights on deer behavior, he pioneered such research when he became a private land wildlife manager more than fifty years ago. Rue's work, *Whitetail Savvy*, should be on every hunter's nightstand. The insights contained here are priceless for anyone who wants to truly know what makes deer tick.

—Daniel E. Schmidt
Editor in Chief, *Deer and Deer Hunting* magazine

I'm almost lost for words when I try to describe the overwhelming accomplishments of Dr. Leonard Lee Rue III. For more than twenty-five years, I have been a student of his highly acclaimed whitetail deer research. Deer hunters and wildlife professionals will find Rue's book *Whitetail Savvy* to be the best and most commanding volume ever published about the ways of the whitetail. Dr. Leonard Lee Rue III is truly an encyclopedia of knowledge!

—Denny Quaiff
Senior Editor, *Whitetail Times* magazine

WHITETAIL SAVVY

WHITETAIL SAVVY

New Research and Observations about the Deer, America's Most Popular Big-Game Animal

By **Dr. Leonard Lee Rue III**

Foreword by **Charles J. Alsheimer**

Skyhorse Publishing

Skyhorse Publishing books may be purchased in bulk at special discounts for sales promotion,
corporate gifts, fund-raising, or educational purposes. Special editions can also be created to
specifications. For details, contact the Special Sales Department, Skyhorse Publishing, 307 West 36th
Street, 11th Floor, New York, NY 10018 or info@skyhorsepublishing.com.

Skyhorse® and Skyhorse Publishing® are registered trademarks of Skyhorse Publishing, Inc.®, a
Delaware corporation.

Visit our website at www.skyhorsepublishing.com.

10 9 8 7 6 5 4 3 2

Library of Congress Cataloging-in-Publication Data:

Rue, Leonard Lee, III-
  Whitetail savvy : new research and observations about America's most popular big game animal /
Dr. Leonard Lee Rue III.
      pages cm
  Includes index.
  ISBN 978-1-62087-648-0 (hardcover : alk. paper)
  1. White-tailed deer. I. Title.
  QL737.U55 R844 2013
  599.65/2--dc23

Cover design by Tom Lau
Cover photograph credit: Lennie and Uschi Rue III/Rue Wildlife Photos

Paperback ISBN: 978-1-5107-1741-1
Ebook ISBN: 978-1-62636-531-5

Printed in China

Dr. Leonard Lee Rue III

Naturalist, Wildlife Photographer, Author, and Lecturer

Dr. Rue sold his first photograph in 1949 when he was nineteen years old and later went on to become the most published wildlife photographer in North America. He has over 1,800 magazine covers to his credit and has taken over one million still photographs. He has produced over two and a half million black-and-white photographs, and his work has been published in every major nature magazine, and most minor ones, in the country. His photographs are used in magazines, books, calendars, and advertisements, as well as for fine art prints, posters, puzzles, T-shirts, clocks, cups, caps, brochures, etc.

In 1989, in addition to doing still photography, Dr. Rue expanded his photographic knowledge and expertise into the field of videography. Dr. Rue and his wife, Ursula, operate *Rue Wildlife Photos,* a digital stock image library, and Leonard Rue Video, a stock footage library, which contains over 3,000 hours of broadcast quality Beta SP and DVCAM video footage and 1,300 species of wildlife, nature, and scenics. These are sold to companies and corporate producers for television programs and educational and advertising purposes, as well as being used in his own productions. To date he has produced twenty-three educational and instructional videos, including *Basic Wildlife Photography, An Eye On Nature, The White-tailed Deer, Birds of the Dooryard, Wolves and How They Live,* and a series on the Lenape Indians.

Dr. Rue wrote his first newspaper column when he was twenty-one and has since written over 1,500 columns for publications. He currently writes columns for *Deer & Deer Hunting* and *Whitetail Times* magazines.

As an author, Dr. Rue has twenty-nine published volumes that have sold over five million copies and has coauthored an additional seven books.

Repeatedly cited and honored with awards by the New Jersey Association of Teachers of English for literary excellence, Dr. Rue is a charter member of New Jersey's Literary Hall of Fame. He has also received the following awards:

- The Conservation Award by the Garden Club of New Jersey, 1973.
- The Golden Citation for outstanding accomplishment as an author, 1979.
- The Michael Award of New Jersey's Association of Teachers of English, for excellent writing, 1987.
- The Outdoor Writers' Association of America's (OWAA) prestigious "Excellence in Craft" award, 1987.
- The Honorary Doctorate of Science by Colorado State University in Fort Collins for his "dissemination of knowledge about wildlife," 1990.
- The OWAA Jade of Chiefs Award for conservation writings, 1997.
- A charter member of the Belvidere High School Hall of Fame, 1997.
- The North American Nature Photographers' Association's highest award, The Lifetime Achievement in Nature Photography award, 1998.
- The NANPA (North American Nature Photographer's Association) *"Fellow"* award, 1999.
- The OWAA 2005 Best Book award for *The Encyclopedia of the Deer.*
- Inducted in the New Jersey Bow Hunter Hall of Fame, 2007.

Dr. Rue's books include *The Deer of North America,* which was heralded as "a notable achievement, a distillation in easy-to-read language of just about everything known about deer"; *How I Photograph Wildlife & Nature,* a compilation of the skills and individual techniques developed during his many years as the nation's most published wildlife photographer; and *How To Photograph Animals in the Wild,* which he coauthored with his son, Len Rue Jr. Some of Dr. Rue's other books include *Way of the Whitetail, The Deer Hunter's Encyclopedia, The Deer Hunter's Illustrated Dictionary,* and *Beavers.* Dr. Rue's latest book, *Deer Hunting Tips and Techniques,* was published in 2007.

Dr. Rue writes with the authority of one who has lived with his subjects and knows their every habit, habitat, and haunt through personal research, as well as printed material gathered during years of research. Drawing from these materials stored in bulging files, research reports from many countries, and clippings gleaned throughout the years from periodicals and newspapers, and the seventeen thousand–plus volumes in his personal library, Dr. Rue's books and articles are thoroughly documented studies written in a very readable style and are well laced with his own photographs.

His first lecture was given at the age of twenty-two and, over the years, he has delivered more than 4,000 lectures and seminars for schools, professional and civic groups, and clubs. He taught outdoor education classes for years and has traveled the nation presenting wildlife travelogues, seminars on deer and the wild turkey, and, with his son Len Rue Jr., an all-day seminar on photography.

Dr. Rue, raised on a farm, has spent a lifetime studying, photographing, and living with wildlife in its natural habitats. His studies and photographic assignments have taken him throughout the world, to all seven continents—from the searing heat of the desert to the iciness of the mountain peaks, to Alaska for fourteen summers and to Africa for seven, as well as to Europe five times, Asia, the Galapagos Islands, Australia, Antarctica, and South America, in addition to his extensive work throughout the continental United States and Canada. "It's a never-ending job," says Rue. "The life sounds glamorous, but there's a lot of hard work and discomfort involved." This does not deter Leonard Lee Rue III in his pursuit of excellence—in research, in writing, in photography. Sometimes it means standing or sitting motionless by a mosquito-infested waterhole, waiting for animals to come for their evening drink, and then perhaps not getting a single photograph or frame of video footage. Sometimes it means being pursued by the very animal he intended to photograph. But, whether clambering over sleeping walruses on a beach, having a bear enter his campsite and curl up under his hammock for a nap, or being charged by a wounded Cape buffalo, Dr. Rue's life is filled with the unusual.

Whether it is as author, photojournalist, or foremost authority on wildlife, it is the same man, fascinated by wildlife and intensely concerned with interpreting its beauty and encouraging each and every person to treat it responsibly, humanely, and with an interest in both its future and our own.

Dr. Rue's driving force throughout his life has been the biblical admonition Mark 9:23:

> *"Canst thou believe, anything is possible to him that believeth."*

Personally autographed copies of *Whitetail Savvy* are available through Dr. Rue's website www.ruewildlifephotos.com

Contents

Most of our beautiful wild-flowers, like these yellow lady slippers, have been eliminated by the overabundance of deer.

Deer relish many kinds of mushrooms but avoid the amanitas, which are deadly poisonous.

Preface

Deer are enriching the lives of millions of Americans each day. For most people, just catching a glimpse of one of these graceful creatures is enough to make their day. Knowing of my lifelong interest in deer, people are eager to tell me their experiences of the deer that come in for food put out for them, of the fawn they found hidden in their shrubbery, of deer that bed down in view of their kitchen window, or of big bucks they hope to take in the hunting season. All of these people want me to respond to their experiences and tell them more about deer.

Being an obsessive observer and compulsive teacher, I love to share things I have learned about deer. I have observed and documented behaviors not yet reported in scientific journals. As a result, I've had to change my mind about some behaviors and what they signified. In this book, I have done my best to tell you what I would otherwise tell people personally. Here also, I've documented in photographs almost everything I've written, as if you were with me when the events occurred.

I have studied deer since 1939. I wrote my first deer book in 1962. In 1978, I wrote *The Deer of North America*, containing everything I knew then. I updated that book in 1989 because I had learned so much more in the intervening eleven years.

The *only* benefit that I have found with age is learning more about everything in life and especially about deer. After all, I live with them. Hunters, naturalists, and the public want to know—need to know—the basics about deer. North American deer are touching more people's lives than ever, partly because we have more deer than when the Pilgrims landed. The decisions that need to be made about deer should be made by informed people. This book is my effort to provide that information. I do not claim to have all of the answers on deer; no one can make that claim. Yet this book contains everything I've learned about deer behavior from well over seventy-four years of personal research and all that I have been able to gather from the thousands of other researchers. Sears Roebuck used to claim, "If Sears doesn't sell it, you don't need it." I don't want to go that far. But I am showing and telling you everything I know about white-tailed deer.

—Dr. Leonard Lee Rue III
August 1, 2013

Author's Acknowledgments

I want to thank all of those who have helped me in writing this book, the hundreds of deer biologists whose work I read at every opportunity, and my many friends who contributed by sharing their personal experience about deer with me. They include Wayne Trimm, who contributed the illustrations of a deer's body; Mark Stallings, who created the accident/activity time charts; Kurt von Besser, whose company, Atsko, Inc., supplied the charts on the spectrum of the deer's vision; the Boone & Crockett Club for their antler scoring charts; and Manny Barone, who did my taxidermy work. I also wish to thank Larry Kleintop, Adam Bealer, Gary Knepp, Joe Taylor, Vincent Piancone, Mike and Denise Keating, Glenn and Danita Wampler, Space Farms, Lorrie and Art Smith, Mike and Ruth Decarolis, and Helen Whittemore, who allowed me to photograph their deer and other wildlife over a period of many years. For allowing use of their photos, I thank Bill Phillips, Kevin R. Kelly, Willi Boepple, and my oldest son, Len Rue Jr. Larry Marchinton, an outstanding deer biologist, whom I have known for many years, was gracious enough to write this book's foreword. My good friend, editor, and agent Neil Soderstrom went far beyond the call of duty in making this book as readable as possible. Jay Cassell, editorial director at Skyhorse Publishing, with whom I've worked for many years; he immediately liked this concept and ensured that it became the fine book that it is. I also want to thank Skyhorse's Constance Renfrow for her outstanding editorial assistance. My wife; Uschi, made this book possible; she did all of the digital work involved in the photography as well as shooting many of the photographs. She is not only my wife; she is my partner.

I want to thank all of the folks listed above, and the scores not listed, and pray that the good Lord be with all of them and with you.

Foreword to the Paperback Edition

I knew Dr. Leonard Lee Rue III long before we ever shook hands for the first time. You see, I grew up with him. He was one of my heroes as a teenager. As a high school student I would go to the school library and devour his whitetail photos and articles that appeared in the various outdoor magazines each month. I was a farm kid who was passionate about hunting white-tailed deer, and Lennie (as I came to know him) was one of only two or three writer/photographers in the 1960s who were prolific in their writing and photography about America's favorite game animal. To me he was the best of the best.

In 1964, I purchased a copy of Lennie's first whitetail book, *The World of the White-tailed Deer* (which went through a record twenty-seven printings). It had a huge impact on me, and as the years passed I read everything I could find authored by him.

In 1981, I landed a field editor position with *Deer and Deer Hunting* magazine. One of the other field editors was Lennie Rue, who gave me an opportunity to finally meet one of my boyhood heroes. Lennie was arguably the foremost nature photographer in the world, with white-tailed deer being one of his specialties. No one else was even close. At the time, over eighty magazines had his photos on file, and it was not uncommon for his photos to be published in more than forty magazines each month.

As I struggled to gain a foothold in Lennie's world, I reached out to him in 1983 for advice. Rather than just giving me phone time, he invited me to his home. Over the course of two days, he not only opened his home to me but gave a ton of advice on cameras, writing, and where I needed to be photographing if I wanted to have a successful career in the hunting and outdoor world. Simply put, it was a "wow" weekend. But more importantly, it was the beginning of a special relationship.

Not many people can say they had the opportunity to meet and become friends with one of their boyhood heroes. I feel blessed to have been one who did. The greatest things in life are not things but rather relationships and experiences. The relationship I've had with Dr. Leonard Lee Rue III has been special. My bookshelf contains many of his books and is testimony to the impact he has had on me. What I've come to realize over the last thirty-three years is how blessed I've been to have had the chance to learn from the greatest whitetail mind of all time.

The measure of a man can be summed up by how others view him. Growing up in the Depression years, Lennie didn't have a chance to graduate high school, but he is a brilliant man. His legacy is what he's given all who love nature. Winston Churchill once said, "We make a living by what we get, but we make a life by what we give." Lennie Rue is a giver, so much so that in 1991 he finally received his diploma when Colorado State University awarded him an honorary doctorate of science for his life's work.

He certainly gave to me. Had it not been for him, I might not have pursued the incredible career I have. On more than one occasion he offered guidance and "opened doors" for me. To say he had an impact on my career would be an understatement, because much of his advice has been woven into the eight books and hundreds of articles I've written on white-tailed deer.

Having just passed ninety years of age, Lennie's accomplishments speak for themselves. God has allowed him to take hundreds of thousands of photos of white-tailed deer. In the process, he's had thousands of magazine articles published. His photos have graced the covers of over 1,800 magazines. He's had thirty books published, seven of which are on whitetails, and done over 4,500 speaking engagements. It's safe to say that no one in the hunting world will ever come close to matching what he has accomplished in his life.

This latest book, *Whitetail Savvy,* is arguably his best book to date on the white-tailed deer. The accuracy of the text, both scientifically and anecdotally, is impeccable, and his photography is a tribute to both the animal and his greatness with a camera. No whitetail stone is left unturned in the book's thirteen chapters. Simply put, it is a book every whitetail enthusiast should own. It's that good.

Charles J. Alsheimer
Bath, New York
October 20, 2016

Foreword

When I was a boy in the mid 1900s, rabbits were considered the most sought-after wild species and most hunted game animal in the United States. Now, since the tremendous comeback in numbers throughout their range, white-tailed deer are clearly the most hunted. In addition, more and more whitetails actually live in cities, towns, suburbs, and exurbs.

In recent years, the number of hunters in the United States increased significantly to 13.7 million. And it's probably safe to suggest that people who only watch, photograph, and study whitetails represent a number many times greater than the hunters.

One thing that makes male whitetails so fascinating is the unique bony adornments on their heads. If these antlers could be examined with sufficient precision, each antler, like a snowflake, would be different from every other one that existed since the beginning of time. Antlers of magnificent male deer throughout the deer family (Cervids) are revered by humans. Some scientists and other thinkers, including me, believe that "antler worship" dates back to our caveman ancestors. Proof of one's manhood and ability to provide for a mate required the taking of great—often dangerous—creatures, and antler "trophies" remained tangible proof of this capability. Because of this, many of us believe that reverence for antlers may be in our genes. Large antlers of whitetails are not as large as large antlers of other members of the deer family in North America, but for many of us, they are the most prized.

I once speculated that more books, scientific papers, and popular articles have been written about whitetails than any other wild animal on Earth. Lennie Rue asked that I read a draft of this book and write the foreword. It soon became evident to me that the manuscript contained a great many facts and observations that had never been published. While understandably heavy on northern observations, most of Lennie's observations apply to all regions of North America. Who among us ever thought to count the number of twigs or acorns it takes to feed a deer for one day? Or counted the numbers of spots on a fawn and the lateral grooves in a buck's antlers? Who else has, for nine and half hours, continuously filmed a doe before, during, and after giving birth? To my knowledge, nobody has previously reported the behavior of deer while dreaming and even waking from a nightmare. Scientists are reluctant to talk about animal emotions. Lennie is not, and I believe his detailed description of emotions is generally accurate, even if not provable. I could go on, but readers will discover this incredible wealth of information about whitetails for themselves.

The author of this book, Dr. Leonard Lee Rue III, is truly a legend. He has traveled all over North America and throughout the world photographing and studying animals. His photographs, writings, and personal research have filled twenty-nine other books. There is only one other wildlife icon of the last two hundred years that one might justifiably compare to Lennie, and that is his boyhood idol, the world famous 19th and early twentieth-century naturalist Ernest Thompson Seton. At the publication of this book, Lennie is eighty seven years young. As he approaches the stage in life where one begins pushing the log ends into embers of the campfire, this book may represent his greatest achievement.

Dr. Larry Marchinton
Professor Emeritus of Wildlife Biology
The University of Georgia

Chapter 1

Populations and Nomenclature

US Populations and Species

Today there are about forty million deer in the United States and Canada. Of these, about thirty million are whitetails and about ten million are mule deer and blacktails of the western states and provinces. It is impossible to give more exact figures because some state game departments don't estimate their deer populations. Of the states that do, all base their calculations on samples instead of actual counting, which of course would be impossible.

There are thirty-eight subspecies of whitetail found from the tropical forests of Central and South America to the boreal forests in Canada. Of those thirty-eight subspecies, only seventeen are found north of the Mexican border, and they will be my focus in this book.

A typical white-tailed buck; the very embodiment of beauty, grace and alertness.

The mule deer is the largest of our deer species. This handsome buck shows the large "mule-like" ears for which he was named.

Scientific Nomenclature

All animals, plants, and other organisms are classified according to a scientific system of nomenclature established in 1750 by Swedish botanist Carolus Linnaeus. In this Linnaean system, all organisms are given a two-word (binomial) Latinized name within an overall structure, like a family tree that traces ancestors. This system laid the foundation for the worldwide orderly designation of every creature by its universally accepted binomial name, allowing scholars throughout the world to speak the same language.

A black-tailed buck in velvet, showing the typical black-tail top.

In this binomial system, each organism has a Genus name and a species name, both printed in italics. A genus is a grouping of similar species. The genus name begins with a capital letter; the species name does not. Biologists throughout the world refer to the whitetail as *Odocoileus virginianus* (pronounced *oh-doe-COY-lee-us vir-gin-ee-AHN-us*).

Within the Linnaean system, a deer is assigned to the kingdom *Animalia* representing what is generally regarded as an animal, rather than a plant, and to the phylum *Chordata* because it has a backbone. It belongs to the class *Mammalia* because the females have mammary glands and suckle their young, which are born alive. All mammals also have a four-chambered heart, hair covering at least a part of their body, and are warm blooded (*homeothermic*), meaning they have a fairly constant body temperature regardless of the temperature of their surroundings. Deer are further subclassified into the order *Artiodactyla*, meaning "even toed" because each foot has four toes (two hooves plus two dew claws higher up the leg).

Along with cattle, deer belong in the suborder *Ruminantia* (ruminants) because they have a four-chambered stomach and chew a cud—that is, re-chewing in leisure what they swallowed quickly while browsing. Like all other ruminants, a deer is also an herbivore, feeding almost exclusively on vegetation. The deer family grouping is Cervidae, spelled without italics and pronounced *SERV-ee-dah*. In North America, this deer family also includes elk, caribou and moose.

The whitetail's genus name, *Odocoileus*, was actually a mistake when named by French American naturalist Constantine Samuel Rafinesque in 1832. Eager to give American deer their official genus name, he decided to characterize a feature on the fossilized remains of a deer he found in a cave in Virginia. However, in describing the concave ("hollow")

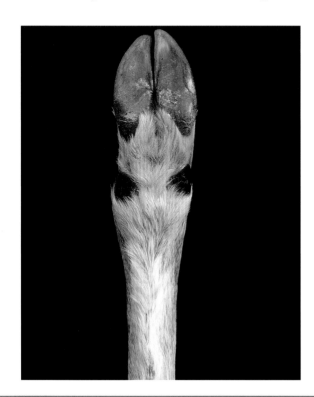

On this right front foot, typical of all deer, the two center digits serve as main hooves. Farther up are small vestigial toes commonly called "dew claws." They correspond to the human forefinger and pinky. The deer's once vestigial thumb gradually vanished through evolution.

tooth in Greek, Rafinesque should have used the term *Odontocoileus.* Although recognized as a misnomer, the genus name *Odocoileus* is still honored because original names tend to have priority. The species name, *virginianus,* of course, acknowledges the state of Virginia.

There are forty-six living species of the deer family (Cervidae) worldwide, with one specie having a very restricted range in North Africa. Deer are absent from Antarctica. They were introduced by man to Australia and New Zealand. Until recently, there were fifty one deer species, but the Asian musk deer was reclassified to its own family, *Moschidae.*

What's a Species?

Males and females of any organism are genetically linked, so they can breed and produce offspring. Occasionally, matings take place between different species, but only rarely are the resulting offspring fertile. Members of most species look alike and have similar characteristics. Variations that evolve within a species, creating subspecies, are usually the result of geographic conditions causing regional isolation of one or more populations. The response by the organism to a given environment affects its size, weight, body conformation, and color as the individuals adapt to differences in temperature, light, moisture, altitude, regional vegetation, and so on.

The white-tailed deer (*Odocoileus virginianus*) is considered the most adaptable deer species in the world, having the largest range and living under the most diverse conditions. Using "electophorensis," Dr. Michael Smith, at the Savannah River Ecology Laboratory in Aiken, South Carolina, found that the whitetail has twice as many genetic variables in its protein band as any other creature he tested. These variables have allowed the whitetail to live under most conditions and to surmount almost all challenges posed by predators and disease.

Range and Variations

The ancestor to our modern deer evolved during the late Paleocene and the early Eocene epochs about fifty five million years ago in tropical Central and North America. But *Odocoileus* has been moving northward ever since and continues northward today. The melting of the continental ice sheets of the Wisconsin Glacier, the last ice age ending about 10,500 years ago, allowed deer to inhabit most of what is now the United States. Today, global warming, land development, and a burgeoning human population have encouraged northward expansion. Here's how I know humans have helped: While

The gray wolf is a major predator of the white-tailed deer wherever their ranges overlap.

guiding wilderness canoe trips in Quebec in the 1950s, I personally saw the whitetail expand its range northward about one hundred miles in a mere ten years. There, as the virgin spruce forest was cut for pulpwood, regrowth was primarily berry bushes and young seedlings of maple, birch, and aspen that provided deer with a rich supply of highly nutritious food. Concomitant to the opening of the forest was the great reduction in the wolf population, the major predator of the deer in that area, by trapping and hunting. Since the 1960s, on my many trips up the Alcan Highway, I've witnessed an even greater northward expansion of deer—about four hundred miles in, Alberta and British Columbia. In fact, I've seen whitetails as far north as the Coal River, just a few miles south of Canada's Yukon Territory.

Whitetails inhabit every type of terrain in North America, from islands and mountains, to marshes and swamps and plains. However, they are seldom found more than a mile from a water source. Astoundingly to some people, whitetails are equally at home in suburban and urban areas as they are in wild areas. And they thrive on most agricultural lands.

The different subspecies of deer conform to four biological rules, or laws, of natural selection. One of these, called Bergmann's rule, after Christian Bergmann, states that the farther a geographic race, or subspecies, is found north or south of the equator, the larger its body mass. The larger the animal's body, the smaller the surface area relative to weight, resulting in a reduced loss of body heat. I often say, "for northern animals, bulk is better." Conversely, the hotter the habitat, the smaller the animal's body, the larger its surface area relative to weight, allowing for greater heat dissipation. Florida's Key deer (*O. v. clavium*)—our most southern deer—is our smallest subspecies. The northern woodland whitetail (*O. v. borealis*) and the Dakota whitetail (*O. v. dacotensis*) are our two most northern and largest deer.

I wrote my own "Rue's addendum" to Bergmann's rule thus: "Distance from the equator tends to result in larger members of the same species, as long as their preferred food is abundant and meets their nutritional needs; body size decreases in direct proportion to decreasing food availability." The white-tailed deer has not yet reached the limit of its northern expansion. It will continue to move northward in response to ever increasing global warming.

The second biological rule, Allen's rule, after Joel Asaph Allen, states that among warm-blooded creatures the physical extremities—ears, tails, and legs—are shorter in the cooler part of their range than in the warmer part. This rule is exemplified by the Coues whitetail (*O. v. couesi*) of southern Arizona, which has larger ears and tail, relative to its body size, than northern deer. The larger ears in southern deer help to dissipate body heat, while the shorter ears in the northern deer keep them from freezing.

The third rule, Gloger's rule, after Constantin Wilhelm Lambert Gloger, states that among warm-blooded animals, a dark pigmented pelage is most prevalent in warm, humid habitats. However, I'd like to add that dark coloration also tends to prevail in forested regions where the animals are not highly exposed to direct sunlight. Warm, dry habitat does not favor darker pigmentation, which would be detrimental because darker colors absorb more heat. The essential point is this: northern deer tend to be darker in general because of the survival advantage afforded by heat absorption of dark hair in the winter.

Official Subspecies

The following are the seventeen subspecies of the Virginia white-tailed deer found north of Mexico:

1. Virginia Whitetail (*Odocoileus virginianus virginianus*)
2. Northern Woodland Whitetail (*O. v. borealis*)
3. Dakota Whitetail (*O. v. dakotensis*)
4. Northwest Whitetail (*O. v. ochrourus*)
5. Columbia Whitetail (*O. v. leucurus*)
6. Coues, or Arizona, Whitetail (*O. v. couesi*)

7. Texas Whitetail (*O. v. texanus*)
8. Carmen Mountain Whitetail (*O. v. carminis*)
9. Avery Island Whitetail (*O. v. mcilhennyi*)
10. Kansas Whitetail (*O. v. macrourus*)
11. Bull's Island Whitetail (*O. v. taurinsulae*)
12. Hunting Island Whitetail (*O. v. venatorius*)
13. Hilton Head Island Whitetail (*O. v. hiltonensis*)
14. Blackbeard Island Whitetail (*O. v. nigribarbis*)
15. Florida Whitetail (*O. v. seminolus*)
16. Florida Coastal Whitetail (*O. v. Osceola*)
17. Florida Key Whitetail (*O. v. clavium*)

Taxonomists and Classification

The scientists who classify living things are called "taxonomists." Traditionally, the original division of the subspecies of any mammal was based on physical differences in skull characteristics, dentition, body size, and geographical locations. And there was much disagreement among the scientists, who became known either as "splitters" (those who preferred minute distinctions) or "lumpers" (those who preferred to lump closely similar creatures by discounting minor distinctions).

Today, the subspecies classifications of mammals are undergoing close scrutiny and sometimes

This is a very fine specimen of southernmost Florida's diminutive Key deer.

Whitetails have been known to bound over twenty-eight feet horizontally.

During its typical stotting gait, the mule deer lands on and takes off from all four hooves at once. This "boing, boing" gate is an evolutionary adaptation that allows rapid escape on steep mountain slopes.

revision as a result of mitochondrial DNA testing. The sub-specific classification of the deer needs this revision because of interbreeding of the subspecies where their ranges overlap—a natural occurrence. There has also been some interbreeding of the whitetail with both the mule and blacktail deer, where their ranges overlap, but the resulting offspring are usually infertile. The hybrids are further handicapped in that they carry the characteristics of both parents but lack the specialization they need to survive. Whitetails "bound," while blacktails and mule deer "stot" in order to escape predators. During stotting, all four hooves land and lift off at the same time. Hybrids are not proficient in either gait. In the crossbreeding it is usually the result of the whitetail buck breeding with the female of the other species because the whitetail buck, today, is more aggressive in breeding than the other species' bucks. According to Dr. Valerius Geist, DNA has proven that the white-tailed deer is the progenitor of both the black-tailed and the mule deer, showing up as fossils of four million years ago in the un-glaciated eastern half of the United States. About a million years later, the whitetail reached the West Coast where it evolved into the black-tailed deer and the two became spatially isolated.

In tracing relationships through DNA, researchers have found that the mitochondria nucleic acid is most important because it is carried only through the female lineage. This is how researchers have been able to trace the evolution of all humans back to the prehominid "Lucy."

The large size of this Texas buck confirms that it is a descendant of one of the large northern subspecies imported into the state.

Biologists have found that the mitochondria of the mule deer is almost identical to that of the whitetail and have postulated that mule deer are the result of blacktail bucks breeding with whitetail does when their ranges again overlapped. For years it was believed that the blacktail evolved from the mule deer, but science has proved the reverse to be true.

However, the greatest crossing of subspecies was done deliberately, by man. That is, in order to replenish deer populations, almost exterminated by the late 1800s, breeding stock was transferred from one state to another, regardless of the subspecies. Such interstate transfers continued until the recent epidemic of chronic wasting disease (CWD) discouraged the practice.

Naturally, owing to the influence of hunting groups, which wanted the largest deer possible, almost all of the transfers involved northern deer being imported to southern states. However, the importation of larger deer was only successful if there was no remnant native population and if both bucks and does were released.

The release of just a few large bucks did not increase the size of local deer because in just four generations the genes of the big bucks became so diluted with those of resident deer as to be negligible.

As a result of so many transfers, the exact subspecies of deer in a given region becomes a moot question and truly doesn't matter. The deer you have in your region are the deer you have. What is needed is improved management of deer and their habitat.

Chapter 2

Whitetail Sizes and Weights

Size

I am always amused when an excited hunter describes the "monster" buck he just saw as "this big," holding his arm out level with his chest. An antlered animal whose back would be that height would have to be an elk, because the backs of most whitetail bucks—referred to as their shoulder height—would come only to the hunter's belt, or roughly forty inches from the ground.

The information I am about to give refers to average-size whitetails, found over most of our continent, not to the diminutive Key deer of Florida or the Coues deer of southern Arizona and New Mexico. The average whitetail buck will measure thirty-six to forty inches high at the shoulder, with a huge buck standing as tall as forty-two inches, although I have never seen a buck that big. And from nose tip to tail tip, the average buck will measure sixty-eight inches to seventy-eight inches.

Ernest Thompson Seton (1860–1946), one of the greatest naturalists, was—through his works—as much a mentor as I ever had. Seton documented the longest-bodied buck for which I can find records. He reported that Henry Ordway killed a giant buck near Mud Lake in New York's Adirondack Mountains in 1890. It was scale weighed before dressing at 388 pounds. The deer had been bled and so had probably lost at least twelve pounds of body weight. Its live weight was thus justifiably estimated to be

This large adult whitetail doe, shown with my wife, Uschi, measures just thirty one inches high at what's known as the shoulder, *in other words at spine height.*

four hundred pounds. Even more remarkable were that deer's measurements. Its overall length from nose tip to tail tip was 115 inches, its shoulder height was fifty-one inches, and his neck circumference behind the ears was thirty-seven inches. I have found no measurements anywhere for other whitetail bucks that come close to this record. The buck had nine tines on one antler beam, ten on the other. The longest tine was thirteen inches in length. The Boone and Crockett Club, the official keeper of big-game records, had been formed three years earlier, in 1887. But unfortunately, the antlers were never measured by a club official scorer. More unfortunately, no one knows what happened to the head.

Body Weights

Okay, now that we have talked about the record for size, here are some records for weight. There are far too many records of whitetail deer weighing in the four hundred pound class to list more than a few here, in ascending order.

1962 Dean Coffman shot a buck near Blencoe, Iowa, with a scale weight of 440 pounds.

1972 Boyd George shot a buck in Worth County, Georgia, with a scale weight of 443 pounds.

1955 Horace Hinkley shot a buck near Bingham, Maine, with a scale weight of 480 pounds.

1941 Arnold Peter shot a buck in Iron County, Wisconsin, with a scale weight of 481 pounds.

1924 Robert Hogue shot a buck in Sawyer County, Wisconsin, with a scale weight of 491 pounds.

The record is still held jointly by the following two bucks, killed in Minnesota:

1926 Carl Lenander Jr., shot a buck near Tofte, with a scale weight of 511 pounds.

1981 George Himango shot a buck on the Fond du Lac Indian Reservation, with a scale weight of 511 pounds.

The heaviest bucks are usually found in the farming areas of the heartland states of Ohio, Indiana, Illinois, Iowa, Missouri, Minnesota, Wisconsin, Michigan, and the provinces of Saskatchewan and Alberta, because of their good soils, moderate climate, and abundant and nutritious farm crops. Mature bucks taken from those farmlands will average two hundred pounds to three hundred pounds. Mature bucks, taken from the forested areas of New York, Pennsylvania, New Jersey, Vermont, New Hampshire, and Michigan's Upper Peninsula, tend to weigh only one hundred and fifty pounds to two hundred pounds. Maine produces many big bucks, despite the fact that it does not have much good farmland. What it does have is dense forest, which is difficult to hunt and allows the bucks to grow older.

I am stressing the weights of "mature" bucks. A whitetail buck does not become a true adult until he is about four years old, even though he is capable of breeding at one and a half years—just like some immature twelve-year-old boys. During his first four years, the bulk of the ingested nutrition supports the buck's body growth. After four years, skeletal growth stops, allowing more of the nutrition to be diverted to antler growth and body weight. No matter how well a buck has fared

This mature whitetail buck weighs more than 250 pounds and measures about forty inches high at the shoulder.

in his second and third year, he will fare better from his fourth year on, provided he has access to nutritious food, until he passes his prime at about age nine. The added weight can easily be seen as the mature buck's belly hangs lower and the entire deer takes on a more blocky build.

For many years, up to 86 percent of the deer shot and tagged in my home state of New Jersey were one and a half years old and averaged 125 pounds to 150 pounds. They just hadn't had time to achieve either the body weight or antler growth needed to make them trophy deer. Today, bigger-bodied and larger-antlered deer are being recorded from most sections of North America, and this trend is likely to continue because more hunters and states are interested in "trophy deer management," which requires laws that prohibit the shooting of small bucks and encourages the planting of foods that deer favor.

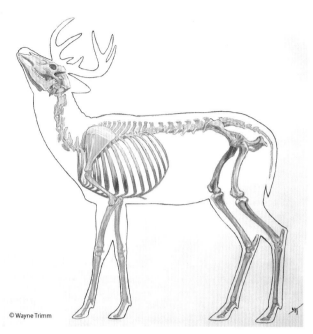

Deer skeleton.

© Wayne Trimm

Deer vital organs.

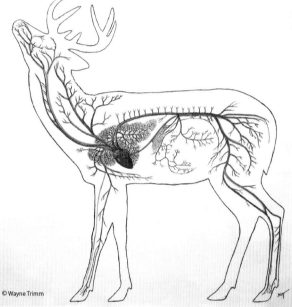

© Wayne Trimm

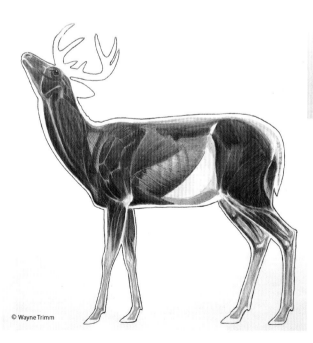

© Wayne Trimm

Deer muscles.

Deer Habitat

Development of the land is usually thought to be the end for most types of wildlife, and in many cases it is. However, the whitetail is one of the most adaptable of all creatures. Not only can it survive in the midst of most development, it can also thrive there.

One of the most adaptive of all creatures, whitetails thrive even in urban and suburban environments.

In my home area, the township has passed an ordinance making building lots ten acres minimum. Prior to that ordinance, a building lot needed to be only three acres. My home region has always been rural, and its fallow fields and woodland won't likely be built upon. Home to large numbers of deer, New Jersey allows deer to be hunted only with shotgun, muzzle-loading rifle, and bow. The current state law forbids firearm discharge within four hundred feet of a dwelling. Owing to the three-acre minimum ordinance, we have miles of road frontage that cannot be hunted because the houses are less than eight hundred feet apart. Because hunting is forbidden there, for the first time, deer populations are growing to full potential in numbers, and in body and antler size.

Male/Female Size Differences

The term "dimorphism" is used to describe either of two traits within a species: (1) different colors between males and females or (2) considerable difference in body size between the sexes, as in the case of whitetails. There is very little body size difference in monogamous animals, such as the wolf, coyote, and fox. However, for animals that form harems, there is a great difference in size between females and the males, which are competing constantly for the breeding favors of many females. The greatest male/female size disparity I know of is with elephant seals. The males are as much as six times larger. It used to be that, as a general rule of thumb, a whitetail doe was one-third smaller than the bucks. Now, as more bucks are allowed to become older, their weight often doubles that of the does. The greatest weight record for a doe that I know of is 176 pounds. It should be noted that does reach maturity and full skeletal growth when they are two years old, and that also helps explain the difference in body size between does and mature bucks, which need four years to reach full growth.

Deer Weights

Deer should be dressed, eviscerated, and gutted as soon as possible after being shot to prevent the continued growth of the bacteria in the paunch and intestines, which will spoil the meat. This makes the deer lighter to drag out but rules out accurate weight estimation later.

Most estimations of a deer's weight grow in direct proportion to the time, distance, and difficulty of getting the deer back to the hunter's car or truck. In addition, accurate "live" body weights of deer are hard to verify because it is often difficult to get the entire deer out of an area to weigh it. With the advent of all-terrain vehicles, the job has become easier for some hunters, but the majority of hunters don't have access to them or are forbidden by law from using them on the state lands being hunted.

Field Dressing: Two Methods

There are two different methods of dressing out a deer. For either method, I do this first step to eviscerate a deer. With my knife, I cut all around the deer's anus so it can be pulled through the pelvic arch when I remove the intestines from the inside.

Method 1: Then I roll it onto its back and, with the deer's head behind me, straddle its rib cage with my legs, to keep it in that position. This will cause the deer's internal organs to settle against its back and help avoid cutting into any of the organs when opening the skin on the belly. To avoid cutting any organs, I always pull the belly skin up as far as it will go and make a first, small incision at the end of the rib cage where the ribs meet the sternum. I then insert two fingers into that slit and cut the deer's belly skin between my fingers as I move my blade toward the pelvic arch. When field dressing a deer, remove all internal organs behind the diaphragm.

Method 2: The more common method is to "hog dress" the deer. In this case, the windpipe and esophagus are severed where they enter the rib cage. Then, the heart, lungs, liver, paunch, intestines, kidneys, bladder, and anus are removed. This results in most of the blood being removed, too. If you don't intend to mount the head, open the rib cage, which makes it much easier to cut the windpipe and esophagus and remove the heart and lungs. If you plan to have your deer shoulder mounted, DO NOT open the rib cage because doing so will spoil the skin of the chest and neck.

Step 1: To eviscerate a deer, what hunter's refer to as "gutting," I first cut the anus loose from the surrounding tissue.

Step 2: I then roll the deer on its back and pull up the belly skin so that my knife does not puncture the innards as I make an incision from the sternum (where the ribs join at top) down to the pelvis.

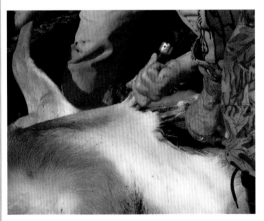

Step 3: Caution–DO NOT cut up through the rib cage, as I am about to demonstrate, if you plan to have your buck shoulder mounted by a taxidermist.

Step 4: After severing the windpipe and diaphragm, and then loosening the kidneys and pulling the loosened anus in, I roll out all of the innards. This entire job should take no more than about seven minutes. Here, my friend Manny Barone is holding his buck while I eviscerate it.

Calculating Live Weight

I have used two methods for calculating the live weight of deer, both methods based on the deer being hog-dressed as explained in the accompanying sidebar.

There is a definite correlation between the circumference around a mammal's chest (known as heart girth) and the animal's body weight. The mathematical formula was first developed by agricultural colleges and has long been standard in calculating the weight of domestic cattle. Based on extensive records of heart girth and the weight of dead deer before they were dressed, a similar formula is now used to estimate live weights of deer that have been dressed.

I currently use a measuring tape made especially for this purpose by Trail Sign Products Co. of Germantown, Wisconsin. By measuring the circumference of the deer's chest, directly behind its front legs, you can calculate its live weight and its hog-dressed weight.

Some additional numbers of interest: One-fifth of a deer's weight is blood and entrails. Fortunately, many states maintain check stations where all deer must be registered and weighed. Divide the scale weight of your hog-dressed deer by four and then add the two numbers to get a close approximation of the deer's live weight. Or, you can simply multiply the scale weight by 1.25 to come up with the same total.

After taking measurements, my "adopted son" Rod Parsons will use them to calculate the weight of his buck, based on a formula.

Weights and Heart Girth

| | HOG-DRESSED WEIGHT | | | | LIVE WEIGHT | | | |
| Heart girth | Fawns | | Adults | | Fawns | | Adults | |
in. (cm)	lbs.	(kg)	lbs.	(kg)	lbs.	(kg)	lbs.	(kg)
20 (50.8)	27	(12.2)			36	(16.3)		
21 (53.3)	30	(13.6)			40	(18.1)		
22 (55.9)	33	(15.0)			44	(20.0)		
23 (58.4)	37	(16.8)			48	(21.8)		
24 (61.0)	40	(18.1)			52	(23.6)		
25 (63.5)	43	(19.5)			57	(25.8)		
26 (66.0)	46	(20.9)	46	(20.9)	61	(27.7)	60	(27.2)
27 (68.6)	50	(22.7)	52	(23.6)	65	(29.5)	68	(30.8)
28 (71.1)	53	(24.0)	58	(26.3)	69	(31.3)	75	(34.0)
29 (73.7)	56	(25.4)	64	(29.0)	73	(33.1)	83	(37.6)
30 (76.2)	59	(26.8)	70	(31.8)	77	(34.9)	90	(40.8)
31 (78.7)	63	(28.6)	76	(34.5)	81	(36.7)	98	(44.5)
32 (81.3)	66	(29.9)	82	(37.2)	85	(38.6)	106	(48.1)
33 (83.8)	69	(31.3)	88	(39.9)	89	(40.4)	113	(51.3)
34 (86.4)	73	(33.1)	94	(42.6)	93	(42.2)	121	(54.9)
35 (88.9)			101	(45.8)			128	(58.1)
36 (91.4)			107	(48.5)			136	(61.7)
37 (94.0)			113	(51.3)			144	(65.3)
38 (96.5)			119	(54.0)			151	(68.5)
39 (99.1)			125	(56.7)			159	(72.1)
40 (101.6)			131	(59.2)			166	(75.3)
41 (104.1)			137	(62.1)			174	(78.9)
42 (106.7)			143	(64.9)			182	(82.6)
43 (109.2)			149	(67.6)			190	(86.2)
44 (111.8)			155	(70.3)			197	(89.4)
45 (114.3)			161	(73.0)			205	(93.0)

Credit: Charles Smart, Robert Giles Jr., and David Gwynn of the Division of Forestry and Wildlife Resources at Virginia Polytechnic Institute and State University at Blacksburg.

For example, if your deer's dressed-out weight is 160 pounds, divide that by four, which comes to forty pounds. Add the forty pounds to the 160 pounds and you have a total estimated live body weight of two hundred pounds.

Heart, Lung, and Bone Weights

I weighed a buck in the 140-pound class and found that the heart weighed two pounds. This is twice the weight of a heart of a human, having the same body weight. The larger heart allows the deer to pump the blood and oxygen needed by its body to meet the demands of the exertion it expends. Under normal conditions, an adult doe that is peacefully lying down has an average heart rate of thirty-seven beats per minute. When chewing its cud, the energy increases and the heart rate goes up to about forty-one beats per minute. A deer standing quietly has a heart rate of approximately forty-five beats per minute. While foraging, taking a few steps, taking a few mouthfuls of food, its heart rate increases to fifty beats per minute. According to the walking speed, its heart rate may range between sixty to seventy-eight beats per minute. A doe, running to catch up with other deer, has a heart rate of 104 beats per minute. When that same doe is frightened and forced to run hard, her heart rate will increase to speed up oxygen

Blowing up deflated deer lungs to show their original size and shape.

delivery to the muscles to a rate of 138 to 160 beats per minute. The highest recorded heart rate for an adult deer was 210 beats per minute.

The lungs of the 140-pound buck I just mentioned weighed three pounds. Deer normally take twenty-five to thirty-five breaths per minute when relaxed. Their breath rate may triple after they have been running hard. The liver, which is the heaviest organ in the body, weighs five pounds. A deer has no gall on its liver because bile goes directly into the intestines to break down fat globules. The bones of a deer weigh about one-tenth its total weight—about fourteen pounds of my 140-pound deer.

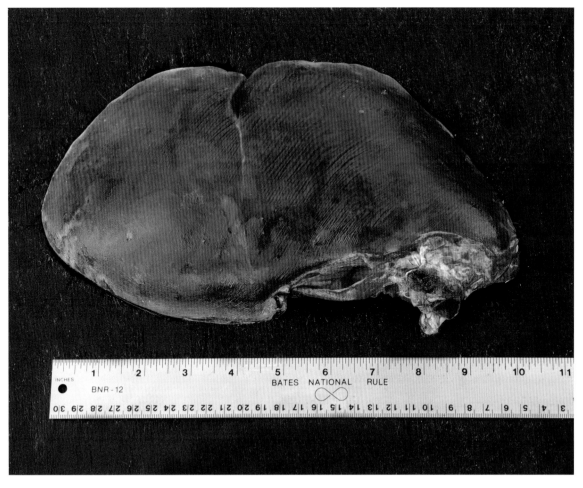

The deer's liver is its largest organ and weighs about five pounds.

Chapter 3

Physiology

Feeding, Digestion, and Blood

All deer are classified as "ruminants" because they have a four-chambered stomach, the largest portion being the "rumen." Deer are a prey species, and their four-chambered stomach provides them, and all other ruminants, with a marvelous survival adaptation.

The rumen is a storage compartment, allowing the deer to gather and swallow a large amount of food quickly and then retire to a secluded place where it can regurgitate and re-chew the food in relative safety, and at leisure. While the deer is feeding, it is at a disadvantage because each intended mouthful of food distracts it momentarily from its constant vigil for danger.

In its search for food, the deer uses its sense of smell more than any of its other senses, which means it is not constantly checking the air currents for potential

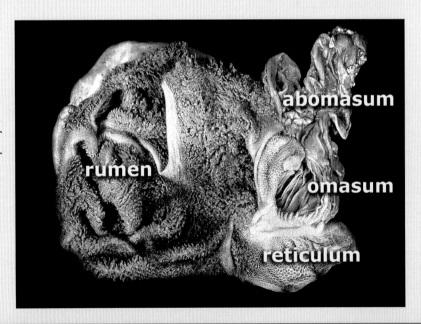

Here are the four chambers of the ruminant stomach.

predators as it ordinarily would. The noise produced with each bite of food is carried via the jawbones to the auditory canal and thus can prevent the deer from hearing a predator. *Unceasing vigilance is the price paid to survive predators.*

Food Requirements

On average, a deer needs to eat about eight pounds of vegetation, per one hundred pounds of body weight, per day. A 150-pound deer needs to eat twelve pounds of food in a twenty-four hour period over most of the year. Deer usually consume their daily rations during five feeding periods. These feeding periods usually vary in length because they involve different food types and quantities. Thus, a deer may be able to satisfy its hunger in feeding periods as short as eighteen minutes or upwards of two hours. Much of the food a deer eats is of low nutritional value, so large quantities must be consumed to ensure adequate caloric intake. For this reason, the rumen, or storage compartment of the stomach, holds far more food than the deer eats in one day and is never empty except in winter, when that deer may be starving.

Over the years, various researchers have figured that a human and a deer of equal weight would require approximately the same number of calories in a twenty-four hour period. A person or a buck weighing 175 pounds would need two thousand to 2,400 calories per day with normal activity. Of those calories, 65 percent are used for daily body maintenance, growth, and heat production, 5 percent are lost in urine, another 5 percent are lost as passed methane gas, and the remaining 25 percent are excreted in feces.

Naturally, the more active a creature, the more calories it needs. Researchers have calculated that football players and running deer may burn up to 900 calories per hour. Michael Phelps, the famed Olympic swimmer, often swims at high speed for 2 hours while practicing and consumes between eight thousand and ten thousand calories a day. Calorie consumption like that can only be gotten from food or metabolized from the body itself. That is why a buck, whose food intake is restricted during the rutting season, will lose up to 25 percent of his weight in that month. This is also why the hard working members of Lewis and Clark's expedition each ate about ten pounds of meat per day.

The Digestive System

The four sections of a deer's stomach are the "rumen," the "reticulum," the "omasum," and the "abomasum." The food initially enters the rumen, which can hold eight to nine quarts, or sixteen to eighteen pounds.

A bezoar is a stone-like impaction of hair, occasionally found in the deer's stomach. In olden days it was believed to have magical qualities. This particular stone is approximately three inches in length.

The rumen has the combined function of storing unchewed food and acting as a fermentation vat. It contains about 80 percent of the entire contents of the stomach. The rumen is lined with small, spaghetti-like "papillae," about

Credit: Willi Boepple.

two millimeters in diameter and varying in length from three-eights to one-half inch. There are over one thousand of these papillae per square inch of the rumen, and their purpose is to provide a large expanse of absorption surface in a restricted space. These papillae lengthen when highly nutritious food is available in spring and shorten when the deer go on a restricted diet in early winter. About 40 percent of the nutrition a deer gets is absorbed through these papillae. Minimal digestion starts to take place in the deer's mouth with the saliva, but the organisms, acids, and the heat of the stomach really do the main job.

There is a symbiotic relationship between the deer and the billions upon billions of microorganisms that live in its stomach. The deer provides the food that the protozoa feed upon, which, in turn, produce the short-chain fatty acids (ascetic, proprionic, valeric, and butyric) that provide the energy that a deer needs to live. The microorganisms themselves are also processed as food.

The chewing of a cud, or "bolus," is an "autonomic" function much like the beating of its heart or breathing. A deer can be standing, lying down, or even be fast asleep, yet it will continue regurgitating, chewing, and re-swallowing its cud. The main difference is that the deer cannot temporarily stop the beating of its heart, but it can hold its breath and stop or start the cud-chewing process.

The cud is a mass of partially chewed material about the size of a small lemon. It is regurgitated up into the deer's mouth and re-chewed in a rotary motion of the deer's lower jaw. The ridges on a deer's premolar and molar teeth pulverize the vegetative material, so there is more surface area exposed on each fragment that can easily be consumed by the microorganisms in the rumen. On average, a deer chews each cud forty to forty-five times before reswallowing the material. Very fibrous browse may be re-chewed again until it is fine enough and passed on to the reticulum.

The reticulum's lining looks like a honeycomb, with hexagonal ridges about three-eights of an inch apart. Each ridge is about one-sixteenth of an inch high. The reticulum holds about 5 percent of the multi-chambered stomach's foodstuff, roughly the size of a softball.

There is a lapse of fourteen to eighteen hours from the time a deer eats the plant material, regurgitates the cud, chews and re-swallows it, and passes it through the reticulum. The food then goes into the omasum, where intensive digestion and absorption takes place. The omasum holds 7 to 8 percent of the stomach's contents. Its lining has forty concentric laminae, or flaps, of varying heights, from one-eighth to one and one-eighth inches high.

The last stomach compartment, the abomasum, has a very smooth, slippery lining with about a dozen elongated folds and holds 7 to 8 percent of the food. From the jumbled mass of recognizable vegetation in the rumen, the food becomes finer, more liquefied, and less identifiable as it passes through the four compartments. Entering the rumen as a coarse mass, it passes through the abomasum as a liquid slurry.

The deer has about sixty-five feet of intestines. Of that, the small intestine is about forty-nine feet in length and two-fifths of an inch in diameter. In addition to the acids and enzymes in the food, bile from the liver helps to break down and absorb the remaining long-chain fatty acids and the fat-soluble vitamins. Most of the nutrition the deer gets from its food is absorbed into its blood stream in the small intestine.

The large intestine is about sixteen feet long and about five-eighth of an inch in diameter. Here, most of remaining water is absorbed, leaving an impacted mass of undigested particles that is passed as excrement.

Reading Sign

My experiences fur trapping as a kid started me on the road to becoming the naturalist I am today. To be a successful trapper, I had to know as much as possible about all types of wildlife. And I had to be able to "read sign," such as tracks, feces, hair, food particles, dens, scratchings, and figure out which creature had made them and

Deer feces throughout the year.
Upper left: Diet in spring includes succulent berries, grasses, and fruit.
Upper right: In late summer, deer feed on drier vegetation.
Lower left: In fall, this deer has been feeding on farm crops. Note corn particles.
Lower right: In winter, pellets show feeding on browse.

when. To get the greatest enjoyment in the outdoors, hunters and nature lovers alike need to be able to read sign.

Although the size of feces reflects the size of the deer, various foods cause changes in the appearance and consistency of deer feces. When deer are feeding on grasses, forbs, or fruits, their feces will often be a soft, unformed mass. Whereas the feces of deer feeding on corn, soybeans, or acorns will be more firm, perhaps segmented with bits of the undigested grain or nutmeat still noticeable. Feces in pellet form tell you that a deer has been feeding primarily upon browse, that is, leaves and tips of twigs. Feces of all shapes are usually dark brown when voided and bleach to a light brown in about two weeks, even without rain. Rain, according to its intensity, softens the feces and causes them to lose shape. By looking at the feces, you should have some idea what the deer is eating, and if you know the plants in your area, you might know where the deer has been feeding.

Estimating Local Deer Populations

During the winter months, deer will void feces about twelve times in a twenty-four hour period because food intake is limited. During the rest of the year, deer will void feces about thirty-six times a day, or once every forty-five minutes. I realize that may seem like an inordinate amount of defecation, but it bears mute testimony to the bulk of low-quality food that a deer needs to process in order to get the nutrition it needs.

Counting feces (taking pellet counts) is a useful tool for the estimation of deer density. The counts should be done in November in the North, after the leaves are down or after a fresh snow so that you have the day count needed to give you a time basis. You need to know the size of the area in which the counts are made. Then walking a transect across the property, count all of the pellets in one hundred by one hundred square feet blocks. Ten such blocks will give you 1/10 of a square mile, or sixty-four acres. If on snow, divide the number of pellets by twelve; if on fresh leaf fall, divide by twenty-four. If the snow fell three days ago, divide your snow number by three and the resulting figure should give you an estimation of the number of deer you have to the square mile.

For example, if you count 100 heaps of pellets per block, averaging 1,000 heaps per ten blocks and divide that by twelve you get eighty-three, which you divide by three days, giving you twenty-seven deer to the square mile. The deer population exceeds the ideal carrying capacity of the land, which is about twenty deer to the square mile.

Environmentalists are greatly concerned about the tremendous amount of methane gas passed by cattle, horses, and other herbivores due to the vegetation that they eat. It may be due to my loss of hearing, and I work in close proximity to deer almost daily, but I have never heard a deer fart.

Blood

Deer, as all mammals, are "homeothermic," meaning they are warm blooded. Deer have a body temperature of about 102 degrees Fahrenheit. Blood is circulated through the body by the heart in about twenty-seven seconds. A human weighing about 175 pounds has about ten fluid pints of blood. A buck in the same weight class has about the same amount. Bucks have approximately 8 percent more blood than does of the same body weight. A deer, or

This is a bright red drop of arterial blood from a wounded deer.

a person, must lose about three pints of blood for any wound to be fatal. Contrary to common thinking, it is not the loss of blood itself that kills a deer; rather, it is the loss of oxygen to the brain, carried by blood, that causes all of its body systems to shut down—a nuance, though the result is the same.

Contrary to common opinion, deer are not frightened by the odor of blood, because they do not associate blood with danger or death as we humans do. I have observed that blood stimulates a deer's curiosity about it, enticing the deer to sniff it and even lick it. If the deer are not being driven by hunters, they will most always inspect the carcass of a deer that has just been killed and smell the blood. Bucks have been seen trying to mount a dead doe.

Tracking Wounded Deer

Deer shot in the vertebrae, neck, or spine will usually drop in their tracks with little blood loss, so they don't need to be tracked. However, because the vertebrae is too narrow a target to hit easily, I suggest that hunters try for the heart/lung area, which is always fatal. A deer's heart is located about two inches behind its elbow and four inches above the bottom of its rib cage.

The lungs are around and above the heart for about twelve inches with the liver lying directly to the rear, thus presenting a target of about twelve by fourteen inches. A shot in any of these three major organs is almost always fatal, but the deer will usually dash off.

Hunters, in tracking a wounded deer, can often tell by the color of the blood where they hit the deer. Blood from the chest area is a light frothy pink. Blood from the abdominal cavity is a greenish-red. Blood from an arterial wound is bright red, while venous blood is darker in color.

There is much debate about how soon to follow a deer after wounding it. Some hunters claim that a deer should not be followed for at least twenty minutes or longer to give the deer time to "stiffen up." Deer don't stiffen up until after they die and then the leg joints will lose flexibility in about one hour. A dead deer's eyes do take on a green cast in about twenty minutes.

I recommend following a wounded deer almost immediately, but slowly, because deer that are not pushed have a tendency to lie down and that will often allow the blood to coagulate, clot, and stop bleeding entirely. It is true that a deer that is followed may go farther before dropping, but when it goes down it will probably stay there, because it will have lost so much blood.

As mentioned, it takes a loss of three pints of blood for a deer to die of blood loss. But depending on the severity and placement of the wound, a deer may go a long distance before it loses that much blood. The deer will go even farther if it was running on adrenaline before it was shot. Deer have been known to go two hundred yards after being shot in the heart.

Using a Coleman gas lantern will aid in tracking wounded deer at night because the blood spots will often reflect in the light. I have read of flashlights that have special lenses that also cause the blood to reflect.

Some states, New York and Maryland notably, have volunteer organizations that employ tracking dogs to help hunters recover wounded deer. The dogs are kept on a leash and follow the blood and scent trail. This has been a very successful program and should be offered in more states. My home state of New Jersey has started a dog-tracking program.

It is imperative that every effort be made to find a wounded deer. I am sorry to say that I lost the largest-antlered buck I ever shot because of a cloudburst that washed out every vestige of tracks and blood. I even enlisted the help of an entire scout troop that was in my camp at the time but to no avail.

Hair and Hair Color

The white-tailed and the black-tailed deer have tails with white undersurfaces, but only the white-tailed deer has the ability to flare the hair out widely. A mule deer's tail is pendant shaped and white all around with a black tip. The whitetail is the only one of the three deer able to raise its tail so high that it sometimes arcs forward over the animal's back. From this conspicuous display, the whitetail got its name.

However, the name also leads to the mistaken notion that this deer always displays the undersurface of its tail when it runs off. But quite often, it doesn't.

White-tailed does almost always fully raise their tails, flare them widely, and wag them from side to side when they run off, because they are usually followed by their fawns. At night especially, the bouncing white tail serves like a beacon the fawns follow. Many of the hairs on the tail are four inches to five inches in length, allowing the tail to flare as wide as eleven inches. Many times the deer will not raise its tail but just flare it widely so that the white under hairs are visible. This sign of alarm is as readily noted by other deer as is the raised tail. Under ordinary conditions, as many as 40 percent of the white-tailed bucks run with their tails clamped down tightly, never raising them.

Almost all bucks will run off with their tails clamped down when they are trying to be inconspicuous. Any hunter who is trying to stalk a deer should remember

that a deer almost always wags its tail before raising its head. The wagging tail is your clue to stop moving because as the head comes up the deer will look around for danger. However, if a deer is suspicious of danger, it may pretend to feed, and then raise its head without the tail wagging.

Whitetail does usually run with the white underside of their tails showing and the tail flopping loosely from side to side.

The pronghorn antelope is often called the "heliographer" (as in mirror signaling) because it can signal danger over long distances by reflecting light off the raised rosette of its white rump hair. The whitetail creates a similar display by reversing its long rump hair and by raising and flaring its tail. Sunlight reflecting off this large area of white hair is visible farther than the animal itself.

The flared tail of this button buck will alert other deer to potential danger.

The black-tailed deer was so named because the hair on its upper tail surface is black. The upper tail surface of a white-tailed deer is usually brown but may have 25 to 75 percent black hairs, or even entirely black hairs. This coloration is a genetic characteristic and is quite prevalent in some areas. It is not the result of crossbreeding between the two species because, except for a few regions, their ranges do not overlap.

This is a good place to bring up the topic of what I call "visual genetics." We hear so much today of genes being tracked down through the testing of some part of the creature's body—be it hair, saliva, or just a swab of mucus. Such tests allow the tracking of genes through many previous generations. What I am talking about is being able to see the definite relationship from one generation to another by outstanding characteristics. If the dominant whitetail buck in the area has the top of his tail covered with black hair, you will soon see that characteristic showing up in the deer he sired. Or, if he has white on top of his tail, it will show up in his offspring.

Reflecting genetically inherited traits, here are four examples of the upper tail surface of whitetail deer. Left to right: (1) Normal coloration found on most deer. (2) Lower third of tail is black. (3) Two-thirds of surface is black. (4) Tail top is all black.

The black ring of hair around a deer's muzzle, the amount of white around the eyes, the size and shape of its throat patch, the amount of white showing on its hooves, the amount of white hair and the placement of it showing on a deer's brisket, the shape and conformation of the antlers, and tail length are all examples of visual genetics.

Annual Coats

The whitetail, blacktail, and mule deer grow two annual coats of hair, while other members of the deer family (elk, caribou, and moose) grow only one. This is because the deer had southern origins, whereas the other three have evolved in the colder climes.

In both the summer and winter coats, the hair on the whitetail is of different lengths on different parts of its body, with the longest being its white belly hair. White hair is always longer on any animal, even where it adjoins dark hair. I discovered this

Hairs in a fawn's white spots are longer than surrounding hair, making the spots protrude. In most mammals, white hair is longer than dark hair.

as a kid, while clipping the hair from our black-and-white cows to make them easier to clean prior to milking. The difference in the white hair length is most readily seen on newborn fawns. The white spots of their camouflage coats stick up like little round brushes with the hair being twice as long as their reddish base coat.

White hair reflects the sun's warming rays away from the body, while black hair absorbs the sun's rays. The animal is kept equally warm during the daytime, because the white hair provides warmth through its greater depth of insulation, while the black hair provides heat absorption. Deer and many other creatures have what is known as counter shading. That is, they are light colored on the ventral, or belly area, and darker on the dorsal, or top side. The darker, upper coloration usually provides camouflage, while the white belly hair is thought to prevent the deer's shadow from being readily seen.

The summer coat of the whitetail is a bright russet-red, which has high reflectance and bounces away the sun's rays, thereby allowing the animal to stay cooler. The actual summer color depends upon where the whitetails live; those of the desert areas are

A whitetail's summer coat is a bright russet red.

lighter in color than the deer of the woodlands, an evolutionary trait in the desert, where the sun's heat is more intense. The guard hairs are short, about three-fourths of an inch, solid and thin. There are about 5,200 guard hairs to the square inch on the animal's back. The deer's winter coat of hair starts to be shed in April and gives the animal a moth-eaten appearance. Small birds soon gather most of the shed hair to line their nests.

Glands at the base of each hair follicle secrete a sebum that acts as water and insect repellent for the hair. In the summer, there is very little hair on the deer's ears and on the bridge of the nose.

There, the minimal hair allows the ears to act as thermoregulators, as blood flowing through them cools down before reentering the body. Because southern deer are exposed to more heat than northern deer, they are lighter in color, as mentioned, and have larger ears. The Coues desert whitetails have the largest ears of all, in proportion to their body size.

Biting flies concentrate on the bridge of the deer's nose because it is practically hairless.

The lack of sebum in those two hairless areas allows flies and other biting insects to concentrate there.

Bucks start to lose their summer coats about the middle of August. But does do not change their coats for another month, because they need another month to recover their prime physical condition, owing to the debilitating effects of nursing their fawns.

A deer's winter coat has about 2,600 hairs to the square inch, but it takes almost three months, beginning in August, to reach its full hair length. Three months is appropriate, because a deer would otherwise become overheated if the hair grew too fast while the weather was still warm. When full grown, the winter hair is two to three inches long, kinky, hollow, and brittle, the hollowness providing excellent insulation. However, this brittle hollowness is the reason tanned deer hides with winter hair should not be used as rugs.

The hollow winter hair of the deer's coat provides excellent insulation, preventing loss of body heat, while also keeping the snow from melting.

The winter coat of deer can range in color from dark brown to deep shades of gray. The coat becomes progressively lighter throughout the winter as the color is bleached by exposure to the sun. Beneath the guard hair is a dense woolly undercoat of hair about three-fourths of an inch long. Although the guard hairs of the winter coat start to grow in mid-August, the wooly undercoat does not begin to grow until the temperature drops to about forty degrees Fahrenheit. In cold weather, the deer cause their hair to stand on end, because that increases the depth of insulation. A great example of the insulation efficiency of a deer's winter coat can be seen during a snowstorm that covers bedded deer with snow. The snow will not melt on the hair because almost no body heat is being lost.

A well-fed, adult deer can withstand almost any subzero temperature, provided there is no wind. Deer are forced to seek shelter in the winter to prevent the wind from blowing between their hairs, which causes loss of body heat and increases their caloric expenditure at a time when they can least afford it. In the winter, deer usually shake their bodies vigorously after they get up, which fluffs up hair that may have compacted while they were bedded, thereby reestablishing its full depth of insulation.

They usually shake their body first and then rapidly rotate their head back and forth.

Ordinarily, most of the hair on a deer's body lies somewhat like shingles on a rooftop, pointing toward the tail or down the legs to facilitate the runoff of rain. The exception is a ridge of hair in front of the deer's brisket that points forward. I have never been able to ascertain the reason for this.

Head and Neck Hair

Deer have eyelashes on just their upper eyelids. They also have sparse

Deer have eyelashes on just their upper lids.

long hairs encircling their eyes, whereas humans have mere eyebrows. Most mammals have three or four rows of whiskers lying parallel above their mouths; deer have three rows of whiskers that completely encircle their mouths. Beneath the center of their jaws, they have half a dozen or so exceptionally long hairs about six inches long.

Chin whiskers tell deer exactly how far from the ground their lips are when feeding.

Those long hairs tell the deer how close its head is to the ground when feeding on a dark night. All of the long hairs are extended sensory nerves that warn the deer of projecting branches that could injure its eyes and face.

Some deer have a ridge of stiff hairs on the top of their necks, forming a mane extending from the back of their head to their shoulders. Unlike a horse's mane, which grows constantly, a deer's mane grows to only about one inch long. Manes in deer are a fairly uncommon genetic characteristic, but they are not rare. A real rarity, however, is for a deer not to have any guard hair but just an extra-long woolly undercoat; my references record only two instances of this.

Whitetails have a band of white hair behind their muzzles, and another encircling their eyes, and a large patch of white hair on their throat, directly below their chin, known as a "bib." Some deer have a black band surrounding their muzzle, behind their nostrils, another variable genetic characteristic. These white patches vary widely in size and are a genetic characteristic.

Coat Color

White-hair mutations on deer are quite common and are often mistaken for albinism. Albinism is a genetic condition in which the animal produces no pigmentation, resulting in pure white hair and pink eyes. The pink seen in the eyes is not pigmentation

A true albino has pure white hair, pink eyes, and gray hooves.

but is the blood of the animal passing through the blood vessels in the eye; this would ordinarily be obscured by the eye color. If a deer has even a spot of brown, no matter how small, the animal is considered a piebald mutation and not an albino. Many piebald deer also exhibit hunched backs, bowed legs, and short, rounded noses. Some states have laws, protecting the mutations from being hunted. But this policy is misguided because the mutation is genetic and this crippling complex of genes should be eliminated from the gene pool.

There is a race of white deer in New York State's former Seneca Army Depot that are not albinos, because they have brown eyes. Unfortunately, the army base was closed and developers are dividing the land. Without the depot's fenced protection confining these deer, the future of this unique deer herd is in jeopardy.

Melanism in deer, resulting in nearly black animals, is extremely rare but does occur. This is caused by an overproduction of melanin. While I was lecturing on deer in Hammond, Indiana, in 1983, a taxidermist showed me a photograph of a totally black, melanistic buck he had mounted. This was the first time I had ever seen this aberration. Also, I have just received a letter from a man named Bill Banks, who reported seeing

This white deer is neither an albino nor a mutant. It has all white hair but has brown eyes.

Credit: Len Rue Jr. / Len Rue Enterprises.

a totally melanistic doe in South Jersey in mid-October, also in 1983. I was emailed a photo of a melanistic buck killed in Michigan during the 2006 season. That eight-point buck was totally black except for the white undersurface of its tail. Even its hooves were jet black. Brendon Pearson of Lewiston, Idaho, shot a six-point totally melanistic buck in November 2008. Dr. John Baccus, of Texas State University, an authority on melanism, calculates that only one thousandth of 1 percent of deer are melanistic.

Hooves

Taxonomists place the Deer Family in the order *artiodactyla,* meaning even-toed, because they have four toes, which incidentally correspond to digits on the human hand—the forefinger, middle finger, ring finger, and pinky; the equivalent of the human thumb has been lost over the ages. The tips of a deer's toes are encased in a wall of protein called "keratin," the same substance as our fingernails. Like our fingernails, deer hooves grow an average

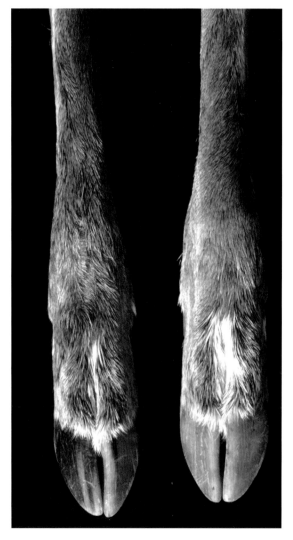

Abnormally colored hooves.

of about one eight of an inch per week. Whereas we cut our fingernails to keep them from growing too long, deer wear off the tips of their hooves through contact with the ground when they walk. Hooves are usually black in color but occasionally some will lack pigment and will be light colored.

Two vs. Four Toes

We humans walk on the flat portion of our entire foot, which is known as "plantigrade." The dog walks up on its toes; this is called "digitigrade." A deer walks on just the tips of its toenails, which is "unguligrade." The deer's digits corresponding to our middle and

If a deer does not walk on its hooves properly, due to ankle deformity or injury, they will not wear down normally and may grow into "ski-hooves."

ring fingers are its main weight-bearing hooves, while the digits corresponding to our forefinger and pinky are called dew claws, which on a whitetail are behind the main hooves and are raised up about 1 1/2" above the ground. They do not make contact with the ground or show in the deer's tracks unless the deer is walking in mud or deep snow.

Deer walking on rocky soil wear their hooves down faster than those living in swamps. Occasionally, through some accident, a deer is not able to walk on its hoof, pushing its weight toward the hoof tip as is normal. When a deer does not walk on its hoof normally, the weight is shifted to the fleshy heel of the hoof, allowing the tip to lift upward slightly. Without the normal wear on the tip, the hoof continues to grow, producing what are often referred to as "ski-hooves."

I have such a hoof in my collection. Its tip is four and a half inches longer than normal. Such hooves greatly reduce the deer's ability get a good "grip" on the ground.

The two hoof tips ordinarily point slightly toward each other but spread apart when the deer runs at high speed or is jumping. The hard, outer wall of the hoof gives a good grip on soil of any type. The center of the hoof has a fleshy protrusion known as the "frog" that gives a good grip on slippery rocks. The frog retracts slightly in the winter and does not make contact when the deer walks on ice or an oiled blacktop road. Thus, the hard outer wall is the only surface that makes contact on such surfaces, which may cause the deer to slip and fall. If the hind legs are pulled out of their socket or the front leg ligaments are torn during a fall, the deer won't be able to get up.

I am often asked why deer venture out onto ice-covered ponds, lakes, and rivers if such places are so treacherous for them. There are times when it is much easier for the deer to walk on the ice than in the snow because there is little snow on the ice. Many times deer are chased out on the ice by predators and deer assume they will find safety of water when chased, only to find that it is frozen over. Also, standing on ice puts additional browse within a deer's reach that is not available when the edges of the ponds and lakes are not frozen. Then, too, I honestly believe deer go out on the ice for the same reason most kids do—because they can. Curiosity has to be a big part of it and deer are curious creatures.

On January 6, 2007, a most interesting rescue took place of a deer that had fallen on the smooth ice of Lake Thunderbird in Oklahoma. The deer's legs were undamaged but it couldn't get up on its feet. The ice was judged too thin to allow a person to go out on the ice. So, a genius of a helicopter pilot, Mason Dunn, flying for News 9, brought his chopper down close to the ice and blew the deer safely to shore using the downdraft of the huge rotor blades!

Extra Hooves

Although it is extremely rare, as with humans, extra digits have been found on occasion. In 1994, Ike Branthwaite sent me a photo of a deer shot in New Jersey that had a small fifth hoof growing backward between the two main hooves. In November 1984, Gary Beeland shot a six-point buck in Scott County, Mississippi, that had a third functional hoof on its left hind foot. In December 2006, Rick Lisko of Fond Du Lac, Wisconsin, hit a hermaphrodite deer with his truck that had seven feet. A three-inch set of hooves were growing out of the deer's normal front feet. A six-legged fawn found in Rome, Georgia, was operated on by veterinarian Dan Pate in 2008. The vet removed the two inner hind legs from the fawn's second pelvis. At last report, the fawn was doing fine on its regular four legs.

A deer track measuring about four inches in length will have been made by a buck weighing at least 250 pounds.

Reading Hoof Sign

The front leg hooves of the whitetail are larger than the hind hooves because they support more of the deer's weight. One recently killed whitetail buck whose hooves I measured had a live weight of 151 pounds. One of its front hooves measured three and one quarter inches in length and two inches in width. The hind hoof measured two and three quarter inches in overall length by one and three fourth inches in width. Any track measuring about four inches in length has to be made by a buck weighing well over 250 pounds. The tips of an adult buck's tracks are usually more blunt than those of a doe because of his greater body weight, and this shows in his tracks.

A whitetail deer's normal walking stride—the distance measured from toe tip to toe tip—is eighteen to nineteen inches. At this walking pace, the track of a deer's hind foot nearly superimposes the track made by its corresponding front foot. A doe's hind

A deer trots at a speed of four to six miles per hour.

hoof usually steps slightly beyond the front foot track. But a buck's hind hoof, because of his longer body, usually lands on the rear portion of the track made by his front hoof.

Deer usually walk while feeding.

When walking steadily, they move a little faster than a man would walk, moving about three and a half to four miles per hour. When trotting, they travel six to ten miles per hour, according to the urgency they feel. Ordinarily, whitetails run at speeds of twenty to twenty-five miles per hour, but they have been clocked running ahead of vehicles at up to forty-two miles per hour for short distances. I personally have seen whitetails jump over 9 1/2-foot high fences. The longest horizontal jump that I have measured was over twenty-six feet. C.W. Severinghaus measured the tracks of a deer running down a slight grade. The deer had to leap over a 7 1/2-foot windfall, and it still cleared twenty-nine feet horizontally.

When bounding, a whitetail pushes its body forward and up with tremendous force from its hind legs.

It then flexes and fully extends its body.

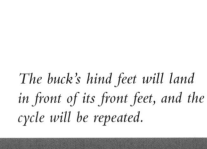

The buck's hind feet will land in front of its front feet, and the cycle will be repeated.

The deer's best protection is the willingness to remain motionless.

When deer are startled, they dash off as though they were late for an appointment in the next county. Yet they'll maintain headlong flight only long enough for them to feel they've reached protective cover.

Unless a predator pursues them, deer usually stop once they get in cover and watch to see if they are being followed. A deer will not run when it can walk and will not walk away from danger if it believes it can escape detection by remaining motionless. By the same token, a deer moving from its bedding area to a feeding area will carefully scan the open area for a considerable amount of time before stepping out to feed.

Deer moving from place to place will almost always follow a trail that was established and used by generations of deer. In hilly country, the trail usually ascends by the gentlest slope and avoids obstacles. Many of our modern highways follow long-gone

Deer prefer using a trail where possible. Trails are usually clear of obstructions and always on the easiest grade. Deer tend to use familiar trails daily.

bison trails for the same reason. Using familiar trails allows the deer to concentrate on escaping danger when necessary.

We need to be cautious when trying to estimate the size and weight of a deer by looking at its tracks in the snow. If the tracks are made in a fresh damp, snow, they will be accurate. But dry, powdery snow does not register size accurately, because that snow does not compact. If a track has any glazing, it is an old track and is larger than the original track, having been melted by the sun before freezing again. In a snow depth of one inch or less, a buck will leave drag marks in the tracks, whereas a doe will not because she lifts her feet higher.

Deer tracks can also cause significant amounts of erosion. In hilly country, where the deer are overpopulated, the hooves push into the well-used trails, cutting the soil apart, allowing it to be washed away by heavy rain. In such cases, what started out as a deer trail often ends up as a gully.

External Glands: Vital Communication

In a deer's world, scent is the major means of communication and is often key to survival. Odors given off by a deer's own glands stimulate responses in other deer ranging from fear to rage, lust to tenderness, curiosity to revulsion. These odors may

A deer's most important scent glands are pinpointed in the photo.

be intentionally deposited on branches and the soil as messages that inspire close-up sniffing by other deer, or they may be airborne throughout a deer's environment, as described in the following sections.

Forehead Scent Glands

The deer's most important glands are its forehead scent glands, located above its eyes to behind its ears. Thomas Atkeson and Larry Marchinton discovered the suderiferous glands on deer in 1992. These are located just beneath the forehead skin. In their extended study, Atkeson and Marchinton showed that bucks and does both had these glands but that the bucks were more richly endowed with them. Research also showed that these glands were basically quiescent during most of the year but became much enlarged during the rutting season, along with a great increase in secretions. I first photographed a buck rubbing these glands on a weed stalk in 1972 and was sure that the deer was depositing scent, but I had no way of proving it. I have since seen bucks rub their forehead scent on twigs, branches, and saplings at all times of the year—but gently, except during the rutting season, when they rub much more vigorously.

For years, I felt that the most important glands were the tarsals, on the lower leg, because they were large, conspicuous, and heavily used by deer to distribute scent. However, years of close observation have persuaded me to change my view. Deer make frequent, almost constant, use of their forehead scent glands.

Everyone has noticed dogs urinating on nearly every fire hydrant, every car tire, every fence post that they pass. These dogs aren't incontinent; instead, they are marking what they consider to be the bounds of their territory. As every animal's scent is as individualistic as its DNA, the urine tells other dogs whose urine it is, what the sex and health of the dog is, what it has eaten lately and how long ago it was deposited. The dog is, in effect, putting up NO TRESPASSING signs.

Deer do not establish a territory the way dogs and wolves do. I define *territory* as "a parcel of land that is claimed by an individual, or a family group, and from which all other members of the same species are excluded." The one exception is the birthing territory that a doe lays claim to when her fawn is born; then she will drive other deer away. During the rutting season, a buck marks almost every projecting twig with his forehead scent gland.

He is not claiming a territory; instead, he is in effect handing out "business cards." His markings tell every other deer which buck passed by, when, and his status. A deer usually knows the status of every other deer it encounters. If it doesn't, that will soon be taught.

1. *White-tailed doe rubbing her preorbital gland.*

2. *White-tailed doe depositing forehead scent.*

3. *Then licking the scent off.*

Although does also have forehead scent glands, I have seen only four does rub their foreheads against a sapling, and they did so using very little pressure. However, I photographed a doe rubbing her forehead scent glands on a bedded buck's antlers during the rutting season. All does are very interested in the rubs made by the dominant bucks, and I have seen them smell and lick buck rubs, as well as the licking sticks. I also photographed a four-month button buck rubbing his forehead scent gland on a sapling. Button bucks are very interested in a mature buck's forehead scent glands and his antlers.

Tree Rubs

When rubbing a small two- to four-inch sapling, a buck will rub it between his antlers directly on the forehead glands. On larger trees, the buck usually has trouble making contact with the bark with his forehead glands because his antlers get in the way. He

Only big bucks rub big trees.

then has to rub the tree with the gland directly below the antlers. In rubbing small branches and finger-sized saplings, the buck will rub against the gland directly behind the antlers, in front of the ears. Even though I can't prove it, I believe this to be the site of the greatest scent production because the deer prefer to rub with that spot more than any other. I'm always puzzled that, despite the frequency of the rubbing and the tremendous pressure that is applied, I have not seen hair worn off in the process.

Tearduct Glands

The "preorbitals," also known as the "lachrymal" or the "tearduct" glands, are located within the rolled fold of skin at the forward corner of the deer's eye. This gland is less used in regular identification marking but is heavily used when the buck is making a "scrape,"

Bucks can evert their preorbital scent gland when they want to release more scent.

To deposit scent from their preorbital glands, bucks rub them against branches.

defined a few paragraphs below. The bucks always give the impression of enjoying such rubbing as a very sensual stimulation.

Although the whitetail cannot open this gland as much as elk do, they can open it enough to give off scent directly into the air without making actual contact with a branch.

Nose Glands

A deer's nose is kept wet by underlying glands, which allow more scent molecules to become trapped there. To increase this moisture and ensure such trapping of scent molecules, the deer frequently licks its nose with its tongue. Under hormonal influence during the rutting season, the deer's nose is much moister from those subsurface glands. There are also interior glands that cause the deer's nose to drip, much like a runny nose in humans. Also, with smelling rubs, overhead branches, and scrapes, a buck deposits some of his nasal scent on everything his nose touches.

Salivary Glands

The salivary glands in the mouth are very important to deer. Their primary functions are to moisten food so it can be swallowed and to aid in digestion. The glands produce two different types of fluid: a heavy mucus, which is occasionally seen drooling from the mouth in long strings, and a "serous," or watery, type that deer drip copiously during the rutting season. The saliva is ammonia-based and individualistic.

One of the most important uses of this scent is in helping the doe imprint her fawns to her as soon as they are born. The doe spends hours licking the fawns to remove every vestige of blood and amniotic fluid from their birthing. At the same time, she is covering the fawns with her saliva so that the fawns recognize her instantly.

In making a scrape, a buck, after hooking the overhead branch and depositing both forehead and preorbital scent on it, will chew and crush the tip of the branch, with a result that it will hold more saliva.

The "parotid" is the largest of the salivary glands, and its duct empties its watery excretion from the roof of the deer's mouth. Under the influence of the male sex hormone testosterone, this gland drips almost continuously.

The more dominant the buck, the more excited he becomes, the more liquid drips from the roof of his mouth. Occasionally, the saliva mixes with mucus saliva, probably from the buccal glands, allowing it to form strings. As all animals are individuals and vary in what they do, different bucks drool different amounts of saliva. I have videotaped some dominant bucks drooling long strings of saliva. Using an eyedropper to simulate the amount of drooling that I documented, I've concluded that some bucks drool more than a pint of saliva a day, literally painting their home range with their individual odor.

Bucks drool copiously during the rutting season, painting everything with their saliva scent.

Foreskin Glands

The "preputial" glands are found in the foreskin of the deer's penis sheath. They apparently play a very small role, if any, in the marking activities of the deer. There is no doubt that scent from these glands is inadvertently deposited each time the buck urinates, but I have never seen it deposited deliberately.

Tarsal Glands

The deer's tarsal (ankle or hock) glands, located on the inside of the tarsus joint, are very important in communication. Both bucks and does have tarsal glands.

This young buck is greatly excited and has flared his tarsal glands, allowing more scent to become air-borne.

However, under hormonal stimulation, both sexes use them more during the rutting season.

The tarsal glands have subcutaneous "sebaceous" glands that exude an oily secretion through the skin, via ducts alongside of the hair follicles. Although individualistic pheromones are given off in the oil, the primary odor of this gland is caused by the bacterial action of the urine that is trapped in the fatty residue on the tarsal hairs. "Erector pili" muscles along the side of the hair sheath allow the hairs to contract so that they tightly close and resemble the bristles on a brush used to apply shoe polish. The closed hair minimizes the odor given off by this gland. When the deer is alarmed or aggressive, the erector pili muscles cause the tarsal hairs to flare widely, like a rosette, maximizing the scent dispersal because more surface area is exposed.

The combined odor of the pheromones and the urine on the tarsal glands gives dominant bucks their strong odor during the rutting season. The more dominant the buck, the more frequently he rubs, and the darker the hair is stained. I have seen dominant bucks whose tarsal hairs were stained almost jet black and had a wide band of black-stained hair running from the gland down to their hooves.

On several occasions I have seen beta-ranked bucks' hind feet acquire the dark urine streaks in just two days after having beaten the dominant bucks in a fight. On achieving dominance themselves, they urinated on their tarsals much more frequently than they had done. Previously, the presence of the dominant bucks had caused their brains to produce corticoids that suppressed their libido. Attaining dominance, they set to work eliminating every sign of the ex-dominant bucks by placing their urine on top of every urine spot the other bucks had made.

No matter how much I learn about deer behavior, I often encounter actions that puzzle me and for which I can't find an answer. I wonder, for example, why both bucks and does urinate on their tarsal glands and then, while it is still dripping, lick the urine off. Deer often lick the urine off each other's tarsal glands, and when two strange bucks first encounter each other, they often sniff each other's tarsals.

I have repeatedly videotaped fawns, just one week old, urinating on their tarsals and energetically rubbing these glands together. I have not seen fawns lick the urine off their tarsals but have seen the does lick the fawn's tarsal after the fawn urinated.

When urinating, deer usually just spread their hind legs apart and hunch their backs slightly. Does

The more dominant the buck, the darker the stain running from his tarsal glands down his hind feet.

usually squat closer to the earth than the bucks do. None of the whitetails squat as low as the mule deer. In rub-urination, bucks and does balance themselves on their front feet and bring their hind feet forward until they are directly behind their forefeet. This places the tarsal glands directly beneath the doe's vulva and the buck's penis sheath, so the urine is dribbled onto the gland. All the while, the hind legs move in an up-and-down motion rubbing the two glands together.

Deer cannot urinate while they are bedded; they must arise to do so and usually urinate immediately after arising and stretching. Ordinarily, the urine is a light yellow in color. As with humans, the longer the urine is retained in the bladder, the darker the color, because the kidneys have had more time to filter impurities out of the bloodstream. Deer are most reluctant to get up in the middle of a snowstorm and, as they remain bedded for extended periods of time, their urine will be a much darker color when they do get up and urinate.

White-tailed doe rub-urinating on her tarsal glands.

Starving deer utilize their stored body fat first when they are on greatly reduced food intake, and they catabolize their own muscle mass. When they do this, their urine is a dark orange in color. During the winter months when the deer feed heavily upon the deep-purple berries of the cedar and juniper, their urine often takes on a bluish coloration.

Tarsal Taint and Tarsal Lure

Old-timers used to tell me that I should be sure to remove the buck's tarsal glands as soon as I shot him to prevent the glands from imparting a "gamey" taste to the meat. When I became a successful hunter and did all of my own butchering, I soon realized that there was not a smidgen of truth in this folklore. If the hunter, while butchering, is sloppy and gets the scent from the tarsal glands on his hands and then touches the meat, he—the hunter, not the gland—will transfer the scent and bacteria. I always remove the deer's foot above the ankle, including the tarsal gland, before I begin skinning the deer, so I never have a contamination problem. If the tarsal gland has not tainted the meat while the deer was alive, it sure is not going to taint the meat after the animal is dead.

After field dressing a deer, you can remove the tarsals by cutting off about a four-square-inch piece of hide. The skin and glands can be placed in your freezer in an airtight plastic bag and used the following hunting season as an attractant. Hang them around your tree stand, and at the end of the day, put them back in the plastic bag and refreeze. Besides attracting deer, they provide a good cover scent.

Metatarsal Glands

On the outside of a whitetail's hind foot, about midway between the heel and the hoof tips, is the metatarsal gland.

Over thousands of years of evolution, I believe this gland has been atrophying because of disuse. The gland is a ridge of dry, cornified gray scales, surrounded by a tuft of short white hairs. Some authorities suggest that the metatarsal emits a garlicky odor, but I have never been able to detect any odor or moisture. I have never seen deer use their metatarsal glands or pay any attention to them; they are just there. The only use I have found is that its size distinguishes whitetails from blacktails and mule deer. The tarsal gland of the whitetail deer is a one-inch slit; that of the blacktail is a 3-inch crescent while that of the mule deer is a five-inch "S" shape.

Interdigital Glands

Located between the two center toes on each of a deer's four feet is the "interdigital" gland.

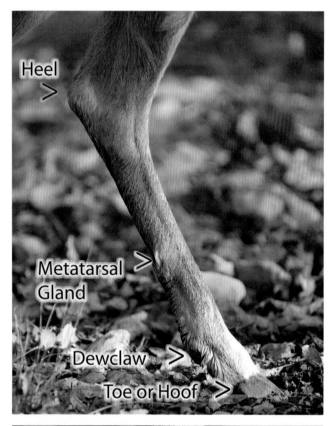

Heel >

Metatarsal Gland >

Dewclaw >

Toe or Hoof >

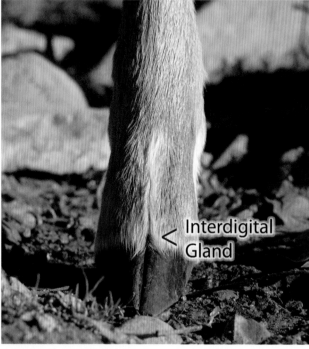

< Interdigital Gland

The metatarsal is a small gland, one inch in length, on the outside of the deer's hind foot.

This gland is often overlooked because the opening to the gland is concealed by long, stiff hairs. Those hairs help to "paint" the secretions from this gland on the vegetation that the deer walks through. If you run a cotton swab between a deer's main hooves an inch or more up into the interdigital gland, the swab will come out coated with a grayish secretion the consistency and odor of human earwax. This scent is used by the deer in tracking one another.

A number of years ago, I observed just how important the interdigital gland is to deer. I was watching a dominant buck tending an estrus doe on a small island of high ground, surrounded by a wet mucky area. Whenever one of the inferior "satellite" bucks tried to get near the doe, the dominant buck would chase him about fifty to sixty feet. This required that the dominant buck wade through the mud. When both bucks were back on dry ground, they would lick the mud from between their toes on all four feet.

The interdigital gland is located about two inches up, between the two center toes on all four feet.

After walking through mud, which may clog the interdigital gland, deer lick it clean so that its scent can be released.

Then I realized if the bucks were that eager to keep those scent glands open, those interdigitals had to be more important than researchers had acknowledged.

Chapter 4

The Five Senses

Formerly, when I was asked in my lectures which of the deer's five senses was the most important, I unequivocally championed the sense of smell. Now I qualify that by saying that would be true only when conditions are favorable. What caused me to qualify my statement?

Hearing

It is true that deer can detect danger for a longer distance using their sense of smell, but only if the wind is blowing that scent toward them. If the wind is blowing away from them, the deer cannot smell danger even if it is close. In view of that reassessment, I now say that, under most conditions, the deer's hearing is its most important sense, because even if the wind is not favorable, there is the chance that the deer will hear something. In addition, there are times when a deer simply isn't using its other senses but is always using its hearing. A deer can be in a deep sleep, but its ears never stop moving, winnowing its surroundings for the slightest sound of danger. What is more remarkable is that even while a deer is sleeping, its brain is analyzing and filtering out sounds that don't represent danger. A deer's brain remembers a huge file of nonthreatening sounds, such as tree limbs rubbing gently against one another; dried leaves and nuts falling; mice, voles, and shrews scampering in the forest duff. Even the noisy sound of a squirrel scurrying in nearby leaves will not cause the deer to awaken. Yet the distant footfall of a human, a twig snapping, or hard-surfaced clothing scraping against brush will waken that deer in an instant. That's why wool and fleeces are better materials for hunting clothing. Their soft-napped surfaces aren't nearly as noisy as denim, canvas, and Gore-Tex.

A deer's sense of hearing may be its most important one. It's large ears help funnel the slightest sound to auditory nerves.

A deer can turn its ears to the rear to listen behind. It also pivots its ears rearward so they don't impair vision in that direction.

When we humans want to hear something better, we often cup a hand behind our ear so that more sound waves are directed into the auditory canal. The deer's large ears do that same thing, but they do it better.

The average whitetail's ear is about seven inches in length and about four and a half inches in width, giving it approximately twenty-four square inches of receptive surface. Deer have a further advantage over humans because their ears are movable and can pivot in all directions. Much of the time a deer will have one ear turned forward and the other pivoted to the rear so it can listen for sounds in each direction. They also pivot their ears backward so they don't block their vision when they want to see to the rear.

We have to turn our head to hear best from a given direction. But we can usually sense the direction when the sound enters equally in both ears, guiding our eyes toward the source.

Mr. Andrews, my high school principal, liked to ask such theoretical questions as, "If a tree fell in the forest and no one were there to hear it, would it make noise when it fell?" Of course it would, because the crash would create sound waves. Noise, or sound, waves are created whether or not creatures hear them. Hearing becomes involved only if some creature's auditory nerves are stimulated.

Sound is a form of energy that reaches the ear as cyclic vibrations. With low-pitched sounds, the waves are fairly shallow and wide spaced. High-pitched sounds compress the width of the wave, forcing them into high peaks, or frequencies. The adult human ear can hear in the range of forty to sixteen thousand cycles per second. Deer have a greater hearing range. I can attest to the fact that they can hear frequencies higher than thirty thousand cycles. As a wildlife photographer, I occasionally use a "silent" dog whistle to get some creature's attention. The human ear cannot hear this very high-pitched whistle, which was calibrated by machine, but dogs and deer respond to it readily.

Despite the difference in the size of the external ears of humans and deer, the auditory canal opening is the same in both: about one-third inch. The sound waves entering the auditory canal are compressed and directed to the "tympanic membrane," or eardrum, causing the membrane to vibrate. These vibrations activate the three tiny bones of the inner ear, which in turn amplify the incoming sound as much as ninety times. These vibrations also cause the thousands of tiny hairs in the "endolymph" fluid to be stimulated, allowing them to turn a mechanical motion into an electrical impulse that activates the auditory nerve. The nerve impulses are then transmitted to the temporal lobe of the brain, which deciphers what is being heard.

The volume of sound is measured in decibels. Here again, deer have the advantage. They do not wear iPods, use jackhammers, or stand close to jet engines, all of which gradually destroy the tiny hairs that make hearing possible. Most of the current generation of young people will suffer tremendous hearing loss as they age because of the destruction they've done to their ears by playing music at high volume.

Deer become extremely nervous during periods of high wind, when the crashing of branches drowns out other sounds. Many hunters have noticed that deer leave the area, when a flock of wild turkeys comes feeding through the woods. It's not that the deer are afraid of the turkeys; instead, the deer may sense that the turkeys' constant scratching in the leaves would mask sounds of potential danger.

I have found that a gunshot does not represent danger to deer. It will alert the deer, but if there is only a single shot the deer may not be able to ascertain the direction of the shot any better than we humans do. Deer can even become habituated to gunshots; in fact, they can get used to almost all types of noise that does not represent danger to them. On many army bases, deer are not hunted because of the military facility. Such deer often feed on artillery practice ranges, where even the constant booming of the big

Fog will hold all types of scents close to the ground where deer will more easily detect it.

guns does not disturb them because it's not a threat. Everyone has seen deer feeding alongside highways, with huge tractor-trailers roaring by, yet if no vehicle stops, the deer don't even look up.

I have also noticed that sound often stimulates the deer's "bump of curiosity." The old saying that "curiosity killed the cat" can also be the undoing of a deer. Curiosity is a sign of intelligence, and deer are intelligent creatures. I know that deer do dumb things at times, but at times, so do humans. Sometimes when a deer hears a sound and can't confirm the source by scent, it decides to check it out. The deer will either circle around to get the wind in its favor or advance very cautiously, directly toward the sound. At such times, a deer is as fully alert as it will ever be. It walks stiff-legged in the direction of the sound, with its head bobbing up and down or side to side and both ears swept forward. A deer may snort in the attempt to startle the unknown something into betraying its location. But such curiosity may get it into trouble.

Scent

At what distance can a deer detect danger by scent? How can a person eliminate human odor? For answers, let's go back to basics.

Almost all odors in the natural world are of organic composition and are released as molecules of gas. For gases to be smelled, and there are some odorless gases, they must be mixed with or dissolved in liquid. Many variables affect a deer's ability to smell, such as barometric pressure, humidity, temperature, rain, snow, and wind direction and velocity. Ideal scenting conditions exist at sixty to seventy degrees Fahrenheit, with a humidity of 60 to 70 percent. High temperatures will waft scent aloft; low temperatures keep the scent molecules close to the ground, but they make it harder for creatures to smell the scents because low temperatures dry out the lining of their nostrils. Rain and snow drive scent molecules to the earth and dilute them. And wind disperses them—the stronger the wind, the faster and farther they are dispersed.

I recall a very graphic example of my scent diffusing outward. I had a permanent photographic blind set up on Helen Whittemore's estate. Helen had fed the deer every day for years and my blind had been in place for years, built right into her fence. The deer were accustomed to feeding in safety, and my blind was a part of their environment.

That day, I was in the blind and the scenting conditions for the deer were ideal; there was not a breath of a breeze. My scent diffused outward from the blind in a circle, and although the deer couldn't see me, it was if a barrier was physically pushing the deer backward as my scent moved outward, and they refused to cross that scent barrier. This explains why a hunter's stand can be fantastic one day and useless at another. If the hunter goes into his tree stand on a fabulous October afternoon when the air is crisp, the sun warm, and the sky cobalt blue, his chances for success are high. The sun, warming the earth, will create thermals, lifting his scent almost directly upward so no matter what direction a deer approaches the area from, it is not likely to detect the hunter's scent. If, early the next morning, the hunter goes back to the same stand, while the ground is shrouded with light fog, his chances of being successful are almost nil. That's because his scent is dropping to the ground and rolling outward toward the deer.

How far can a deer detect a scent? Under those ideal conditions of sixty to seventy degrees Fahrenheit and 60 to 70 percent humidity I just described, if the scent is pushed along by a moderate breeze, I am sure a deer can detect human scent at half a mile if not farther.

Can you eliminate human scent? NO. Wearing charcoal-impregnated clothing will help because the charcoal will filter out body odor caused by bacterial action on our sweat glands. Keeping your hunting or photography clothes in a clean plastic bag with cedar branches when not in use will help, because it will prevent their absorbing human or other household odors. Using cover scents, such as fox or deer urine, will help, because they can mask human odor. Using chlorophyll tablets to cleanse your breath does not help, because goats eat lots of grass filled with chlorophyll, and I can verify that chlorophyll doesn't mask a goat's breath or odor. Your breath is going to be your undoing every time because as long as you are alive you have to breathe, and every time you exhale you are pouring out body odor. If you stop breathing, you will smell even worse in a very short time.

I want to bring up an aspect of human odor on which I do not have an answer but will state my views. I have read articles, corroborated by very successful deer hunters who urinate from their tree stands when they need to empty their bladders. They claim that deer are attracted to urine no matter what the source. Some professional hunters have written that they've used regular household ammonia as a deer attractant, with results as good as using the deer's own urine. All I can say is that all of those methods contradict everything I have experienced and learned over a lifetime of studying, observing, trapping, hunting, and photographing wildlife. I stick by my statement, "The scent of man, in any form, means danger to deer, under most circumstances."

Especially in no-hunting areas, deer have learned that human scent does not necessarily mean danger.

Deer continually lick their nose because the moisture helps trap scent molecules.

It is true that urban and suburban deer are not as alarmed by the odor of man as their ancestors were, because they are exposed to human scent in "safe areas" where man does not represent danger. Where deer are hunted, the odor of humans still means danger.

I have run numerous experiments testing the efficacy of household ammonia and have gotten absolutely no response from the deer. It is not the ammonia in deer urine that attracts other deer; the attractants are the other components in deer urine. When I was at the peak of my fox-trapping career as a young man, I had a captive fox, as did most of the other top trappers, in order to collect its urine. We would leave the collected urine uncovered so that the ammonia would dissipate.

I know several dairy farmers who have collected, and successfully used, urine from their cows in estrus as an attractant for whitetail bucks. It wasn't the ammonia that attracted the bucks; it was the pheromones in the cow's urine.

In hopes of rerouting deer to my stand, I sometimes urinated on a trail that I did not want the deer to use, basically saying "deer detour." If you are going to urinate on the ground around your stand, why bother to do any of the things that increase your chances of success? Why use a cover scent; why put your stand downwind of where you hope the deer will come; why keep your clothing and body as scent free as possible; why use the wisdom employed by hunters forever? The Indians would stand in smudge fires of sweet grass or evergreen boughs to help overcome their body odor. They always took advantage of the wind direction to make sure the deer were not aware of their presence. I bet they didn't urinate in the spot they were standing while waiting for a deer, and I advise you not to do it either.

The sense of smell is the response to "chemoreception" by the limbic system, found on the base of cerebrum, the front portion of the brain. The olfactory bulb then transmits an electrical impulse directly to the brain stem where the odor is classified. This area of the brain also controls appetite, digestion, and emotions, linking the sense of smell closely to all three.

The "rhinarium," the hairless skin covering on the front of the deer's nostrils, is moist from subcutaneous glands, but the deer increases the amount of moisture by frequent licking with its tongue. The moose and caribou, being northern animals, have hair covering their rhinarium to protect it from freezing. The deer's long muzzle also aids in the collecting of scent molecules because its extra length has a greater "epithelial" surface for the scent molecules to adhere to.

We know that the deer's sense of smell is far superior to that of a human and may not be as good as that of the average dog. A human can detect skunk odor, "mercaptar" even when it is dissolved to one to twenty-five hundred thousand part of one milligram. On a foggy night, you can walk a quarter mile through an unpleasant fog of skunk scent, even though the skunk released only a few drops of its musk. Most of us can identify hundreds of odors, while the trained noses of professional "perfumers" can identify thousands. It is claimed that dogs can detect odors one hundred million times better than we humans can. Unfortunately, we don't know what deer can smell because they do not lend themselves to testing. Deer just aren't as interested in pleasing humans as dogs are.

I find it very interesting, and puzzling, that a mother deer cannot recognize the voice of her own fawn. A doe will respond to the distress call of any fawn but will not allow any fawn to nurse, until she has first proven to herself that it is her own by smelling it.

Deer live in a world rich with scents that we humans can't even imagine.

Vision

There is nothing that moves within a deer's range of vision that deer do not detect. Yet, if a person stands motionless, detection is unlikely. However, unless you blend into your surroundings, the deer may become suspicious, even if it does not recognize you as a human. Deer are so thoroughly familiar with everything in their home range that any unfamiliar object is cause for suspicion. In an effort to blend in with my outdoor surroundings, I always wear camouflage clothing, which might not always blend with my background, but it does break up my human outline.

The deer has a much larger eye than we humans. And its elongated pupil helps give wide-angle viewing.

We humans have eyes in the front of our heads, as do most predators, which provides us with binocular vision and greater acuity of sight—both factors helping us gauge distances. We have a range of vision between 170 to 180 degrees of a circle—roughly a half circle. Deer have eyes on the sides of their heads, as do most prey species, and their eyes protrude beyond the skull, which allows them to see almost a full circle around themselves, roughly 310 degrees, except for a small wedge behind the skull of about fifty degrees.

The human eye has a round pupil that is of different color, primarily according to race. The deer has a brown rectangular pupil that enhances its wide-angle view of its world. I have seen photographs of a local deer that had blue eye pigment instead of the normal brown—the so-called watch-eye that is fairly common in horses. The blue or white pigment does not seem to affect the horse's vision. This is a genetic condition, and all of the Catahoula hounds, the state dog of Louisiana, have the watch-eye. The condition is also quite common in husky dogs.

Deer have much larger eyes than humans do, and this adaptation enables them to move about after dark. The larger eye allows more transmittal of light. In addition, deer see better in the dark because they do not have the yellow filter in the lens of their eyes that humans have. Because humans are basically "diurnal" creatures (sleeping at night), the yellow filter helps to shield our eyes from the sun's harmful ultraviolet rays. By contrast, deer are "crepuscular," moving about primarily at dawn, dusk, or at night. Not having the yellow filter allows deer to see in the cold or blue range

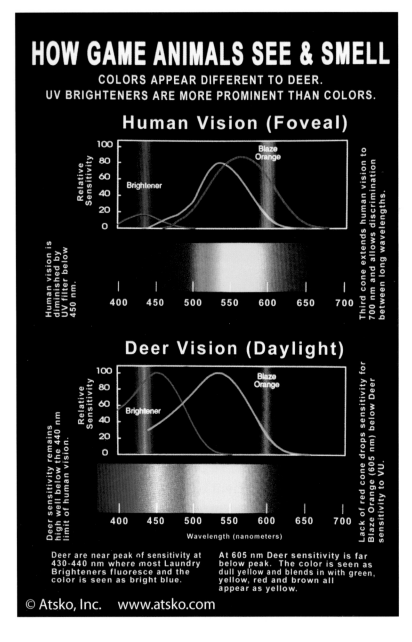

HOW GAME ANIMALS SEE & SMELL

COLORS APPEAR DIFFERENT TO DEER.
UV BRIGHTENERS ARE MORE PROMINENT THAN COLORS.

Human Vision (Foveal)

Relative Sensitivity

100
80
60
40
20
0

Brightener

Blaze Orange

400   450   500   550   600   650   700

Human vision is diminished by UV filter below 450 nm.

Third cone extends human vision to 700 nm and allows discrimination between long wavelengths.

Deer Vision (Daylight)

Relative Sensitivity

100
80
60
40
20
0

Brightener

Blaze Orange

400   450   500   550   600   650   700

Wavelength (nanometers)

Deer sensitivity remains high well below the 440 nm limit of human vision.

Lack of red cone drops sensitivity for Blaze Orange (605 nm) below Deer sensitivity to VU.

Deer are near peak of sensitivity at 430-440 nm where most Laundry Brighteners fluoresce and the color is seen as bright blue.

At 605 nm Deer sensitivity is far below peak. The color is seen as dull yellow and blends in with green, yellow, red and brown all appear as yellow.

© Atsko, Inc.   www.atsko.com

of the light spectrum, which is a tremendous advantage in low-light situations.

As to color vision, it was long thought that deer and most mammals except primates see everything in shades of gray. That seemed to partially explain why there are no brightly colored mammals. We now know that deer have "dichromatic vision" and can see through the violet, blue, green, and yellow region of the light spectrum. They cannot see color in the orange and red range as we humans do. This is why the blaze-orange color that hunters are required to wear in most states has been so effective. The use of blaze orange has dramatically reduced hunting accidents but has not reduced hunting success because the deer don't see that color; they see it as a shade of light yellow. Wherever legal to do so, I recommend that hunters wear blaze-orange camo to break up what would otherwise be a large, blaze-orange block of light yellow.

The eye works along the same basic principle as a camera. The cornea acts as filter to protect the lens, much as I use a skylight filter on my camera lens. The lens allows for the transmission of light. But, whereas the pupil of our eye opens or closes

A deer's eyes reflect light shined on them because they have a mirrored surface at the rear of the retina called the "tapetum lucidum."

according to the intensity of the light, that of the deer does not. The lens focuses the image seen on the retina at the back of the eye, which is comparable to the film in the back of a camera. The retina, the photoreceptive surface at the back of the eye, is composed of rods and cones. Sharpness of vision and sensitivity to color depend on the cone cells. The rod cells are used primarily for night vision, and deer have more rods, while we humans have more cones. We do have a circle of rod cells that we can use at night if we do not look directly at what we want to see, but rather look slightly off to the side of it. Behind the deer's rod cells—as in many animals, but not primates, including humans—is a reflective layer known as the "tapetum lucidum," which reflects the light back through the rods, doubling the amount of light that the optic nerves receive. This produces the "eye shine" that deer show when a light is directed in their eyes at night.

Under the cover of darkness, deer will often bed in the open area they are feeding in, something they would not do during daylight hours. Many times when driving into these open fields at night to census the deer, I would see dozens of eyes reflecting my headlight like scattered diamonds. Scientists have calculated that deer can see at least one thousand times better than humans in low-light situations. The optic nerves receive the image and generate the neural impulses that send the image to the occipital lobes of the brain where the images from the two optic nerves are coordinated into one.

Grooming and Bonding

The bonding, done through touch, is as important to deer and other creatures as it is to humans. From the moment of birth, the doe spends hours licking the amniotic fluids from her fawns, cleansing their bodies but also creating the bond that will unite

A doe licks her fawn's anal region while it nurses, and this stimulates its bowels. She consumes the waste as it's voided.

them until they become adults and even beyond. Fawns at a very young age will reciprocate by licking their mother in what is known as "mutual grooming." This no longer serves a cleansing function; rather, it reinforces recognition and reassurance, important in the relationship. Each time the doe returns to nurse her fawns, she will lick their anal region, while they nurse, to stimulate their bowels. She then consumes both feces and urine that is voided. This helps protect the fawns by eliminating the potential odor of their waste. After the nursing is completed, the grooming continues until the fawns wander off to seek a place of concealment.

Deer live in a matriarchal society, and the female fawns may stay in their mother's family group until they are two and a half to three and a half years old, and mutual grooming continues to knit the family together. At dispersal time, one and a half years of age, young bucks leave their mothers to form juvenile bachelor groups or join a group of adult bucks. Mutual grooming also bonds these male groups together, which are rent by the increasing competitiveness of bucks, young and old, as the rutting season begins. In the bachelor groups, all bucks mutual-groom one another, but the subordinate bucks usually initiate the grooming. Grooming may be done to all parts of the body but is most often concentrated on the head and neck areas where deer can't groom themselves. Frequently, the grooming concentrates in licking each other's forehead scent glands.

Touch

Quite often when a doe and her fawns lie down they will bed close enough so their bodies touch.

Touch is also very important during the breeding season and is engaged in much more by the sexually experienced adult bucks than by the yearlings. Even at the peak of a doe's estrus period, she will usually run off a short distance before allowing the buck to breed her again. To shorten the distance involved in chasing, the experienced, older buck will rub his body against the doe; he will groom her head, neck, and body and lick her vulva.

There are times when the doe will not only reciprocate but actually initiates sexual grooming. Young bucks that haven't learned the proper courtship proceedings chase does all over the place before they can get them to stand. The chaos created in a herd from which all of the adult bucks have been removed is one of the big drawbacks to the emphasis by state game departments on trophy buck management. Does that have been run ragged during the rutting season by inexperienced young bucks may have a hard time surviving a severe winter.

Bucks and does mutually groom each other during courtship, which is a form of foreplay.

Tactile sensations are also important when deer stomp a front hoof to signal that they detect something that might prove dangerous. Such a message is often received by deer that can't even see the sender. They feel hoof-stomp vibrations through the earth.

Taste

I often think that taste should be considered in combination with smell. Have you ever noticed that you can't really taste many things until you exhale the odor past the scent receptors in your nose, which are ten thousand times more discerning than your taste buds? We know that deer are usually able to distinguish between poisonous and nonpoisonous plants, but we don't know if they do so by taste or smell.

I recently learned from Dr. James Kroll that some of the deer in the hill country of Texas eat a plant that effectively emasculates the bucks. The toxins in the plant cause the buck's testicles to shrink to the size of marbles and the resulting lack of testosterone prevents the full antler cycle from occurring. We don't know if the same plant prevents the does from becoming pregnant. And we don't know which plant is the culprit and why the deer don't avoid eating it.

Deer love to eat both mushrooms and lichens.

In September, the woodlands in my area produce untold numbers of the deadly amanita mushroom, yet the deer never eat them.

Deer also discriminate among the acorns they eat, always eating the white

Deer eat many kinds of lichen, which are high in protein.

oak acorns first, because they have the least amount of the bitter tannic acid. Deer will eat the chestnut oak acorn only when they have to, because of its comparatively high tannic-acid content. Research lists over seven hundred different plants that the deer will eat in my area of northeastern United States, but circumstances and season often determine *when* they eat many of those plants. In some areas, the deer will eat daylilies; but they seldom do near my home in New Jersey. A list of deer foods for Massachusetts includes spicebush, but in New Jersey I have seen it eaten by deer on only three occasions, and only when all other foods were in short supply. In the fall of 2004, when the acorn crop was very poor, deer ate spicebush even though the volatile aromatic oil in the plant inhibits the bacterial fermentation in the deer's rumen.

Chapter 5

Age and Aging

Antlers and Deer Age

Over the years, I have tried to work out a system for aging deer by measuring the convex spicule base of the antlers with micrometers. Using antlers from known-age deer, I found that most antler bases grew about one-eight inch in diameter per year. My findings led me to believe that the mass of the antlers depended on the amount of nutritious food the buck ate that particular year but that the base grew larger regardless. Now, with more years of experience and a larger collection of antlers from older deer, I have found that is not true. I have found that not only does the antler mass regress with age after the buck reaches an age of eight or nine years but so does the pedicle surface area. The pedicle also appears to become shorter with age because the buck's skull thickens and grows up around the pedicle as he grows older.

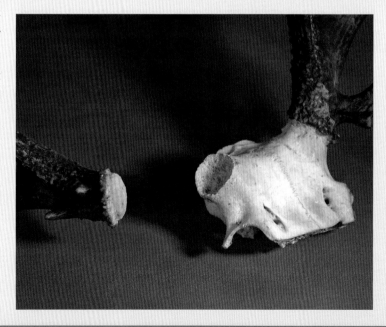

The convex base of the deer's antler fits into the concave cup of the pedicle.

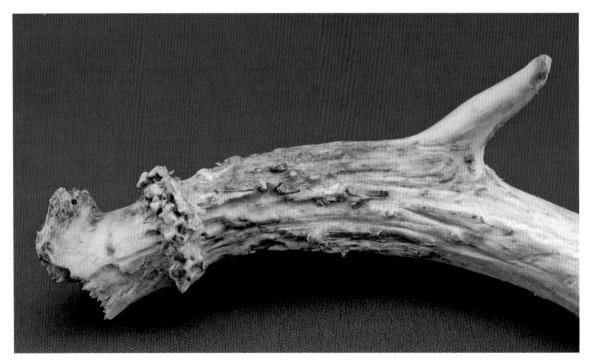

New research shows that the bacterium Trueperella pyogenes *can cause an infection beneath the skull at the base of the pedicle, allowing it to break off as shown, causing death.*

Ordinarily, when an antler is cast, the burr makes a clean break; but that is not always the case. I have several antlers in my collection that, when cast, a piece of the pedicle stayed attached and broke off, too. In most cases, the piece adhering to the antler is just a flake from the outside of the pedicle. As shown above, the largest piece of pedicle remaining on an antler that I have, measures one inch in length and has actually broken off part of the skull plate. My good friend Larry Kleintop has a cast antler with a strip of pedicle and skull plate attached that is one and a half inch in length. I do not know if losing a small piece of the pedicle causes the buck to grow a nontypical antler the following year, although I strongly suspect that it would.

Many states and provinces require that all harvested deer be taken to check stations where they are weighed and aged. Important data is attained from such information. Whereas some game agencies age deer by checking the wear on their teeth, others age them by measuring the diameter of the antler one inch above the burr. Under most circumstances, the diameter measurement will give a good guesstimate of the buck's age. Yet in a drought year, or a year following a severe winter, the antlers will be undersized and thus the deer is more likely to be underaged.

Almost everyone is fascinated with a buck's antlers because they are looking at a natural, one-of-a-kind work of art. We stand in awe as we look at the displays of the hundreds of heads at sports shows and buckaramas and realize that those antlers all grew in about five months and would have fallen off four months later—and that another set would grow the following year.

Teeth and Deer Age

Almost everyone is familiar with the saying "Don't look a gift horse in the mouth." Basically that means if someone gives you a gift, be appreciative and don't try to examine it for flaws while in the presence of the giver. That is, a horse's age could be told by the wear on its teeth. If the horse were old, its teeth would be worn out, and it could not properly process the food it ate or do the work wanted of it, making the horse of little value.

Basing aging on tooth wear and replacement, C. W. Severinghaus and Jack Tanck of the New York Game Department created the system in 1949 that became the standard method of aging deer. Burton L. Dahlberg and Ralph C. Guettinger of Wisconsin refined the method in 1956. Jack Tanck made additional modifications in 1966. Over the years, Jack Tanck was kind enough to verify the ages of a number of deer that I had calculated using his methods. Just before his death, Tanck shipped me the original set of jawbones that he used in lecturing and demonstrating his aging methods. His was the set that was the model for all of the artificial sets used for aging deer today. I have his personal calipers on my desk as I write this.

Dentition and Tooth Growth

Like a human, an adult deer has thirty-two teeth. But a deer has no upper teeth in the front of its mouth; the space is instead filled with a hard-surfaced pad of gristle. Unlike a rodent, whose upper and lower incisor teeth neatly clip off twig tips, a deer tears the twigs using its lower incisors to hold the twig against the hard pad. This helps to identify the creature that ate the twig. If a twig is neatly clipped off, a rodent or a rabbit ate it. If a twig is broken off, showing fibrous strands, a deer ate it. The deer's upper jaw has six premolars and six molars, three of each on each side. The lower jaw has eight incisors, two of which are modified canines, six premolars and six molars, a total of twenty teeth—ten on each side. I have several jawbones of deer that have only two premolars instead of the usual three, and I know of other oddities.

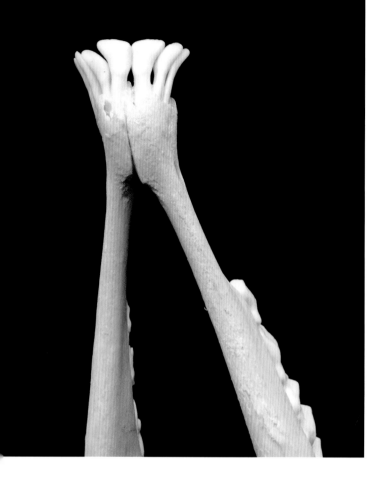

Fawns are born with eight incisor (pincer) teeth in the front of their lower jaw, as well as six premolars on each side, top and bottom.

The canine teeth of deer are not the meat-piercing canines of the dog family or the stubby ones that we humans have. They are considered the deer's incisor teeth because that's basically what they are. Occasionally, white-tailed deer will have tiny, rudimentary canine teeth, where as foreign deer species, such as the primitive water, musk, and tufted deer, have long curving canines that they use in fighting. These canine teeth are only found in the upper jaw at the front of the gap that deer have between their incisors and their premolars, which is known as the "diastema." So far as I know, no one has found opposing canines in any deer's lower jaw.

C.W. Severinghaus found only twenty-three upper canine teeth in eighteen thousand whitetail deer he examined, or 0.1 percent. The farther south one goes, the more canine teeth are found in deer. In Florida, Charles M. Loveless and Richard F. Harlow found four canine teeth in ninety-five deer, for 4.2 percent. At the Wilder Wildlife Refuge in Texas, 162 whitetail skulls disclosed forty-nine canine teeth in twenty-nine of the skulls. Some of the skulls had only one canine tooth, some had both. Twenty-six of the teeth were rudimentary and did not protrude through the gums and so were discovered only by scraping the gums. Among females, 18 percent had the upper canines, while 17 percent of the males had them. And the percentages rise the farther south the deer are found. The only explanation that I can give for that phenomena is that whitetail deer originated in the tropics, and this may be some sort of a holdover.

Elk are famous for having well-developed maxillary canine teeth, and thousands of elk have been killed for these teeth. In museums, I have seen beautiful dresses of Indian women that were decorated with hundreds of elk canine teeth.

Whitetail fawns are born with eight incisor teeth in the front of their lower jaws that are exposed. They also have six premolars, three to a side, top and bottom. These teeth are lightly covered with tissue that tears away in a day or so. All of these teeth are the so-called baby or milk teeth that will be replaced, just as ours are. The two central incisors are larger than the others and are referred to as "pincer" teeth. Between the fifth and sixth months, the milk pincers are lost and are replaced by permanent pincers that are much larger and very noticeable. Between the tenth and eleventh month, the other incisor teeth are lost and replaced by permanent incisors. Using incisors as an indicator of age is accurate up until the time that the fawn becomes a yearling.

At birth the six premolars have sharp ridges. These teeth are soft and wear rapidly. The first premolar has a single cusp, or peak, the second premolar has two, the third has three. When the deer is six months old, the first molars are fully erupted. By the ninth month, the second molars are usually fully erupted. At twelve months, the third molars are usually partially erupted. When first erupted, these teeth are deeply ridged and have sharp points. The inside and highest ridge of the tooth is known as the "lingual crest." The outside and lower ridge is called the "buccal crest." The first and second molars are bicuspid (two pointed), while the third is tricuspid.

From a distance, a young deer can be distinguished from an adult by looking at its face; a young deer's face will be much shorter than an adult's until its jaw has lengthened to accommodate its molars. This is true with most baby animals and gives them the "cute" look that they gradually outgrow as they begin to look more like their parents. During their first winter, seven- to nine-month-old fawns, because of their short jaws and long winter hair, have round, fuzzy heads.

Bud Disbrow, a very dear friend of mine, shot a six point buck in Maine that his guide said was six and a half years old. Using a jaw wrench, I cranked the deer's jaws apart so I could check its teeth. Bud was surprised when I told him that his buck was not six and a half years old but exactly seventeen months of age. Incredulous, he asked how I knew that. By the time a deer is eighteen months old, its milk premolars are worn down and ready to be replaced. I showed Bud how the third premolar had already raised up so that you could actually see the space between the tooth that was ready to be lost and the new tooth that would replace it. It is easy to tell whether or not you are looking at the milk tooth or the permanent tooth. The deciduous third premolar has a tricuspid cap, while the permanent tooth has a bicuspid crown. After the replacement of the teeth has been completed at one and a half years, aging becomes more difficult in the field.

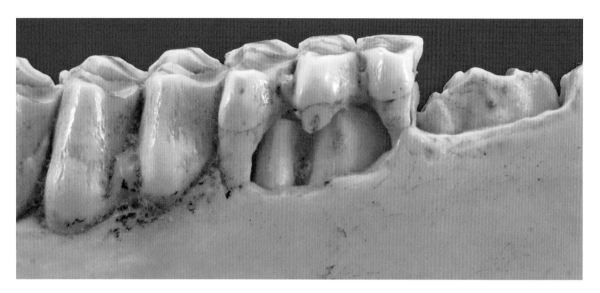

At seventeen months of age, a deer loses its three-cusped third premolar, which is then replaced by a two-cusped premolar.

How to Age Deer by Their Teeth

Tooth-wear estimation is really very simple. But you will need calipers, or at least a millimeter rule to make your measurements.

As mentioned, a deer has three premolars and three molars for a total of six teeth in a row, top and bottom, on both sides of its mouth. The main wear is always on the

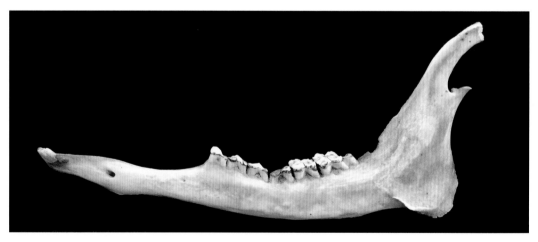

Note the extreme wear on the third premolar and first molar caused by this deer's cutting large twigs with these two teeth.

third premolar and the first molar—the two teeth in the middle of each row.

The reason for this is that when a twig is too large to be nipped off with its incisor teeth, the deer cuts it off using those two teeth. When a deer is one and a half years old, about ten millimeters of tooth shows above the gum line, and it wears down about one millimeter per year. Measure from the gum line to the top of the buccal crest.

How many millimeters are left between the gum and the top edge of the tooth? If you measure eight millimeters of

Deer can be roughly aged by using calipers, which show how much the teeth have been worn down by usage.

tooth, your deer is three and a half years old, because there were ten millimeters when the deer was one and a half, and this tooth is showing two years of wear. This method is not as accurate as the sectioning of a tooth because of the variables that enter into the equation. For example, the teeth of the deer in South Jersey always wear down faster than do the teeth of the deer in my own northeastern part of the state, and this is for two reasons. First, we have a lot more limestone in the soil, so our deer have harder teeth that are more resistant to wear. Second, the soil in South Jersey is sandy and the constant wind coats vegetation with particles of silica. Eating the gritty vegetation causes the deer's teeth to wear down faster. Also, some deer, like some humans, are born having harder teeth than their siblings, and that tends to be genetic. Captive deer, having access to commercially ground feeds, don't experience the tooth wear that wild deer do because they don't have to chew their food as much.

Laboratory Aging of Deer Teeth

The most accurate way of aging a deer is to pull one of the incisor teeth, slice it vertically, stain it, and look at the section under a microscope. Most people are familiar with telling the age of a tree by counting the annual growth rings. Many of us have learned to tell the age of a fish by counting the rings on its scales. The age of all horned animals, such as sheep and goats, can also be told by counting the dark winter rings. The winter rings are more pronounced because there is little or no growth in the winter, so the winter rings are very tightly laid down together and appear darker. The same thing shows up inside a deer's tooth, the rings of "annuli," or "cementeum," show up darker. But such testing can only be done in a laboratory.

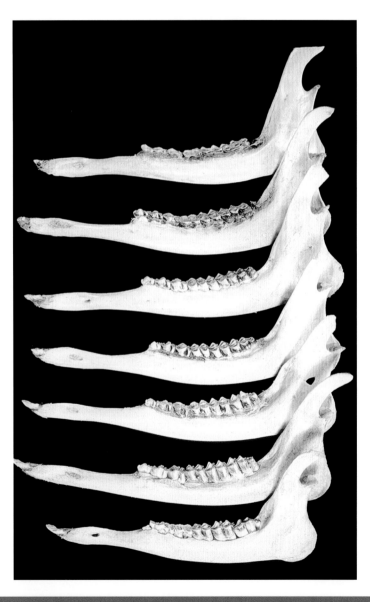

How Long Can Deer Live?

Tooth wear largely determines how long a deer can live, because when its teeth are worn out, the deer can't process its food and will starve to death. The potential life expectancy of the white-tailed deer is reckoned to be twelve years because that is about how long its teeth last under normal conditions.

There are many records of captive deer, eating soft commercial feeds, living to be nineteen to twenty years old and even older. Also interesting: Does do not have a menopause; they are capable of bearing young so

From bottom to top, the age of these deer jawbones are one and a half, two and a half, three and a half, five and a half, seven and a half, nine and a half, and eleven and a half years.

long as they can maintain a decent body weight. There is no such thing as a barren doe because of her age; a doe is only barren if she is not getting enough food.

Few wild bucks ever live twelve years. Because of exceedingly heavy hunting pressure, 80 to 86 percent of all bucks in New Jersey are killed when they were one and a half years old. States that set aside trophy buck areas have bucks that reach four to five years of age. Yet even under the most ideal conditions, most bucks do not live beyond their prime of eight to nine years. The dominant bucks do most of the breeding, and with constant tending of does in heat and driving off suitors, the stress may cause more weight to be lost than they can regain before severe weather.

The oldest doe I ever raised was given to me by Joe Taylor, and he was not sure whether she was two or three when he gave her to me. That doe reached seventeen or eighteen years. She had a single fawn the last year of her life. The oldest doe that Joe ever had was one that he called "Mommy." Mommy gave birth to a single fawn when she was a year old and to twins every year thereafter until she was seventeen, when she reverted to bearing a singleton. But she lost that fawn due to a prolonged cold, rainy spring. At eighteen she gave birth to a single fawn and adopted a wild fawn. She nursed and raised both fawns that year. Mommy was one of the few does that would allow

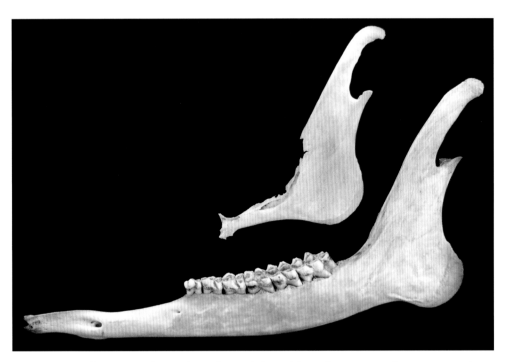

Comparison between whitetail jawbones. Top: old jawbone, worn by osteoporosis. Bottom: healthy, normal jawbone.

any fawn to nurse her. In her nineteenth year, she gave birth to a single fawn that she raised. When Mommy was twenty, she was barren for the first time, and her advanced age showed in her gauntness and in her stiff walk. She died in December 1980, having lived twenty years and seven months. I desperately wanted Mommy's jawbone for my collection, but it collapsed completely when Joe tried to remove it because of osteoporosis.

My good friend Charlie Alsheimer, one of the country's top deer photographers, wrote about a captive buck that had been raised by Ben Lingle in Clearfield County, Pennsylvania. The buck lived twenty years and ten months. What was even more remarkable was that the buck raised his biggest set of antlers when he was fifteen years old. In the wild, the largest set of antlers normally occurs from the fifth to the ninth year, but the Lingle buck had been fed soft, commercial, high-protein feed.

The 1984 issue of *Alabama Conservation Magazine* reported that a doe that had been tagged and stocked as a juvenile in 1960 was shot in 1981, making her twenty-one years old—the oldest wild deer on record. The magazine also reported that another adult doe tagged in 1961 was shot in 1983. Because she was already an adult when she was tagged, she had to be at least twenty years old. Both of those does had spent their entire lifetimes in the areas in which they been released. It makes you wonder how they got through so many hunting seasons without being shot and how much longer they might have lived. Could they have lived as long up in the North, if they had had to contend with severe winters? We will never know, but what we do know is that they lived longer in the wild than any other whitetails on record.

Harold and Sally Kriesche had a doe on their Michigan Deer Ranch that lived to be twenty four years and seven months old, possibly making her the oldest whitetail deer that ever lived. She was born in June 1977 and died in January 2002. She produced thirty eight fawns during her lifetime including twins in 2001.

Chapter 6

Predators, Parasites, Pathogens, and Accidents

Predators

For prey species, constant vigilance is the price paid for continued life. Being herbivores, deer convert vegetation to the meat that larger carnivores need to survive. As a prey species, deer are seldom completely at ease and never entirely relax their vigilance. Their ears never stop moving, even while they are asleep. And, while awake, they constantly test the breeze for the scent of possible danger. Deer usually move into the wind while feeding. This lets them move toward new scents and forces any predator stalking them to move to keep up, thereby increasing the chance that the deer will see or hear it.

When deer lie down, they usually face their back trail, so they can watch for danger while their noses check for danger that might be upwind of them. When two deer bed down, and deer are seldom solitary, they usually lie down facing different directions to better watch for danger. Deer are safest while bedded, because they can then make full use of their keen senses. Deer spend 60 to 70 percent of every twenty-four hours bedded. It is almost impossible to spot a bedded deer until it twitches an ear, moves its head so that an antler reflects light, or moves its tail.

Where possible, a cougar will kill and feed on a deer about every five days.

Cougars are the most efficient predators of deer. Researchers have determined that a single cougar will kill about one deer per week, year-round. Fortunately for the whitetails, cougars are absent from most of their range. Where their ranges overlap with that of the gray wolf, deer make up the bulk of the wolf's diet, especially in the winter. A full-grown wolf can eat twenty pounds of meat at a time. And feeding a pack requires lots of deer. Lynx, bobcat, and occasionally even a fisher—a big member of the weasel family—will take down a deer that is floundering in deep snow. Black bears and grizzlies kill every young fawn they encounter, although they seldom are able to catch an adult deer.

A friend of mine using a bow took a big, mature buck that had a droopy ear. When the taxidermist caped it out he discovered a black bear claw imbedded in the ear cartilage. From the position of the claw, he surmised that the buck had charged the bear and the bear had hit the buck from the front, over the antlers. There was no way of telling if the buck killed the bear, but he did carry a souvenir.

For years, one of the top deer predators, especially in the northern part of the deer's range, was the domestic dog—particularly packs of wild strays, often mixed with free-ranging pets. Biologists have proven that dogs in the South are not a major factor in deer predation, but then the southern deer are not exposed to the rigors of the severe northern winter weather. Even in the North, the dogs may not actually kill the deer, but by forcing them to run, they cause the death of many deer, because they make the deer expend non-replaceable calories. Well-fed house pets often chase deer in response to their latent canine instincts, just as many cats don't eat the creatures they kill.

The coyote, particularly the new subspecies of the eastern coyote, is undoubtedly the major predator of the white-tailed deer today. The western coyote averages only thirty to thirty-five pounds, while the new eastern coyote averages forty-five to fifty pounds, approaching the weight of smaller Labrador retrievers. Some male coyotes reach sixty pounds. The eastern coyote's greater weight resulted when western coyotes bred with the wolves in the Algonquin Park area of Ontario, Canada, and then migrated east. The latest DNA testing has proven that the Algonquin wolves are identical to the endangered southern red wolves and are not gray wolves as was previously believed. The research biologists claim that DNA proves that coyotes have never bred with the much-larger gray wolves, which invariably try to eradicate coyotes from their territories. Also, because of their wolf genes, the eastern coyotes come in color shades from a light sandy tan to jet black.

At the Wilder Wildlife Refuge in Texas, research has shown that coyotes take up to 70 percent of the fawn crop in some years. A study done by John Kilgo, in 2008, conducted in South Carolina, proved that 80 percent of the fawn mortality was caused by coyotes. Bob Avery, whose family ran a hunting lodge in New York's Adirondack Mountains for many years, told me that they had noticed a tremendous decline in the deer population after coyotes became common. Professor Robert Chambers, studying the coyotes there for thirty years, found that deer made up 80 to 90 percent of the coyote's winter diet. Fawns made up 50 percent of the coyote's diet in the spring and summer. Dr. Karl Miller, of the University of Georgia, in relation to coyote predation, has stated, "It's something we must take more seriously in whitetail management going forward."

In the year 2000, a pack of five coyotes decimated one of my research herds in northwestern New Jersey. The fact that my deer were enclosed in thirty-four acres made it much easier for the coyotes to kill them. Those coyotes killed my entire fawn crop and twelve out of the fifteen adults, including bucks whose antlers scored in the Boone and Crocket 150 to 160 class. We found coyote scat laced with deer hair everywhere.

Foxes are not predators of deer and the deer are well aware of that fact. In all of the literature, I have come across just one incident in Pennsylvania where a red fox attacked a new born fawn—but the fox did not manage to kill it. It might have killed the fawn if the person had not intervened. This attack may have been a case of mistaken identification by the fox.

A number of years ago a friend called me to ask if I wanted to photograph a great horned owl that had been attacked by a doe. The fellow had been spreading manure on his field when he saw the owl dive down from a tree into the high grass along the edge of the field. He heard a fawn bleat loudly and a doe ran out of the brush row and beat at the owl with her front feet. He then saw a fawn get up in the high grass and be lead away by the doe. When he investigated, he found the owl had suffered a broken wing. I took a few photos and delivered the owl to a local rehab center where it was treated and eventually released back to the wild. I am firmly convinced that when the owl attacked the fawn, it did so thinking that it was attacking a rabbit, because most of the fawn's body was hidden by the high grass. A great horned owl would not attack anything as large as a fawn, and I think that is what happened with the fox.

I have often found new born fawn hooves lying about the entrance to red fox dens. While it would be easy to jump to the conclusion that the fox had killed the fawn, I believe that the fawn had died or had been killed by something else and the fox had scavenged the remains.

I know that deer do not fear foxes. I have read many accounts of deer and red foxes playing together by chasing each other around—and it was definitely in the spirit of play. Once, I was photographing deer from one of my blinds when they all stopped feeding and instantly turned to look in one direction, their tails flared, hock and rump hair erected, fully alert. My first thought was that either a dog or coyote was coming. Looking in the same direction as the deer, I discovered that a red fox was trotting closer to the deer but at an angle around them. The entire herd immediately trotted toward the fox and followed it as it smelled around for food or perhaps for other fox sign. The deer continued to follow the fox until they all went over a hill, out of sight.

Once those deer realized that it was a fox, they were consumed with curiosity. The smallest dog, such as a terrier, would have panicked the deer, and they would have dashed away as soon they knew it was a dog, but they didn't flee from the fox. The deer are so accustomed to foxes, seeing them and smelling them all the time without being threatened, that they accept them readily. Foxes, marking their territories, urinate on every projecting grass clump, rock, or snag, like dogs peeing on fire hydrants. Because of that trait I recommend that hunters use fox urine as a cover scent while they are hunting.

Deer have no fear of foxes because they are not a threat to them.

Parasites

White-tailed deer are plagued, as are most creatures, with internal and external parasites. Most of the internal parasites are seldom noticed by the average hunter and are beyond the scope of this book and my knowledge. For more information, on internal parasites, read *Diseases and Parasites of the White-Tailed Deer* by William Davidson, Frank Haynes, Victor Nettles, and Forest Kellogg, or *Field Manual of Wildlife Diseases in the Southeastern United States* by William Davidson and Victor Nettles. When I have an urgent medical question about deer I call the Southeastern Cooperative Wildlife Disease Study, College of Veterinary Medicine at the University of Georgia: (706) 542-1741.

Internal Parasites

Here, I will briefly mention some of the internal parasites that hunters notice.

Liver flukes are trematodes (*Fascioloides magna*) that infest the deer's liver and look like white grubs. They seldom seriously affect the deer and, because they are easily seen, being about one inch or more in length, hunters can discard the liver. It is perfectly safe to eat the rest of the meat.

Hunters eviscerating their deer may encounter lungworms in the deer's windpipe or lungs. Lungworms (*Dictyocaulus vivaparus*) are long, threadlike worms common in most deer and livestock. Heavy infestations occur when the deer become overabundant. Then lack of forage and the lungworms cause the deer to lose weight, and in severe cases may cause death. The lungworms do not affect the meat.

Deer are also host to meningeal worms (*Paralaphostrongylus tenuis*), which seldom affect the deer because deer have built up immunity to them. Infected deer, in expanding their range, often infect moose, elk, and caribou, which—until they build up immunity—often proves fatal. As the parasites invade the animal's brain, they cause loss of motor control. Affected animals can no longer walk or even stand. Only by building up its own immunity has the moose been able to make a comeback, after being devastated in the northeastern states. These parasites do not affect humans.

Occasionally deer are seen with a condition known as "lumpy jaw." This condition is usually found in older deer and is evident as food impaction in the lower jaw. When this occurs the arterial worm (*Elaeophora schneideri*) usually infects the animal's jawbone and can cause tooth loss and disintegration of the jawbone. The latter can prevent eating, causing death. There are no health problems related to this condition for humans.

External Parasites

Not only are the whitetail's external parasites more obvious but many of them affect humans as well.

Nasal bots are the larval form of the *Cephenemyia* flies. They cause no problems for humans but much discomfort to the deer. Most people have seen deer kicking vigorously at their nose and sneezing loudly as they try to discharge the larvae that have been developing in their nasal passageway.

Later, the larvae drop to the ground and burrow there, where they spend the winter and emerge in the spring as adult flies that lay their eggs on the nose of the deer and begin the cycle anew.

Countless numbers of flies and mosquitoes make life hell for deer and humans during the warmer months. They are often a major annoyance but most are seldom a health problem. The deer's major protection is a sebum that comes out of the hair shafts and repels both insects and rain. If you have ever petted a deer, you will have noticed sebum residue on your hands. As someone who lives with deer, I find it more than an inconvenience when I sometimes get an allergic reaction to that sebum, causing my eyelids to itch. Because deer have practically no hair on their ears and the bridge of their nose in the summer, they have no sebum in those areas, and that's where the insects concentrate. Deer often seek out ridges, to take advantage of any breeze that blows, in order to keep insect activity to a minimum. In the North Country, deer will also feed and stand in water as a refuge from insects.

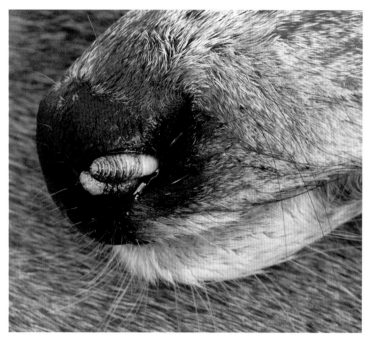

Nasal bot larvae leaving a deer's body as it loses heat after death.

Prior to 1958, the screwworm (*Callitroga americana*) took a devastating toll on the deer across the southern half of the United States. The screwworm fly laid its eggs in cuts and wounds in livestock and deer. In Texas, the screwworm wiped out an estimated 80 percent of the annual fawn crop. The US Department of Agriculture eliminated the screwworm to protect livestock but the deer were also a major beneficiary. For example, in Florida, the deer herd increased 60 percent after the screwworm eradication program for livestock went into effect.

Deer are host to many different kinds of ticks. For years the Lone Star tick (*Amblyomma americanum*) caused a fawn mortality rate of up to 30 percent. When stockmen started treating their livestock to control the ticks, it curtailed their devastation of deer, too. Kevin Kelly shot a doe near Halifax, Pennsylvania, that had, he estimated, at least a thousand ticks on just its head.

He removed fourteen ticks from just one square inch of the deer's ear. Despite that infestation the deer was fat and in good overall condition. I had never heard of a northern deer carrying such a load of ticks.

Today, the tick we hear the most about is commonly called the deer tick ("Ixodes dammini"), a creature that is the size of the period at the end of this sentence before it becomes engorged with blood. The deer tick is not a problem for the deer, but it is

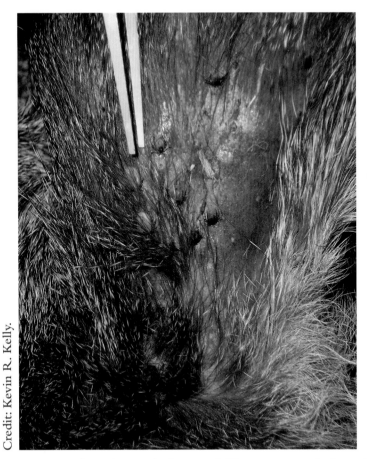

Credit: Kevin R. Kelly.

This photo of the inside of a deer's ear, taken by Kevin R. Kelly, shows the heaviest infestation of ticks on a deer that I have ever seen.

for humans because it transmits the bacterium *Borrelia burgdorferi* from deer to humans, which causes Lyme disease. Other tick-borne bacterium also cause serious illnesses, such as ehrlichiosis, and can be terribly debilitating. In many areas, the deer population has been drastically reduced to control these disabling diseases in humans. Yet many small rodents and many species of birds are also host to the tick, even though deer get most of the blame. Because I constantly work with deer, I saturate my pants and socks with Perma-kill, a tetramethrin solution that kills all biting insects upon contact.

Pathogens

Deer sometimes exhibit benign tumors known as "papillomas," "fibromas," and "lipomas."

These are caused by viral infection. They cannot be transmitted to humans or livestock and seldom injure deer. These tumors are hard, warty growths on the skin, ranging from one to a dozen or more, and varying in size from a marble to a softball. They are spread by biting insects but are not highly contagious. The growths usually freeze off in winter and do not normally occur again to the same deer. Hunters should have no concern if a deer they harvest has these growths because they are removed with the skin and do not affect the meat.

Hemorrhagic disease is fatal to deer but not to humans. There are two types of the epizootic hemorrhagic disease and five types known by the joint term of "blue

The hard, dark fibroma tumors seen on this deer are caused by a viral infection.

Credit: Bill Phillips.

tongue virus." The symptoms and results of all seven viruses are the same. The deer become lethargic, feverish, and often display swelling in the head, neck, and tongue. They seek out water to relieve their fever, and as a result their bodies are frequently found near water. In some forms, the disease can kill the deer within seventy-two hours; in other cases, the deer may live for weeks. Ulceration of the tongue is a commonly seen sign, whereas necropsy reveals the seeping of body fluids through the organs. This disease usually is seen only in late summer and is spread by biting midges. As soon as the first hard frost occurs, the spread of the disease stops. Unfortunately, in some areas of the United States the disease appears every year and is basically the result of global warming and the overpopulation of deer. The disease was particularly devastating in 2011. A friend of mine lost eighty-seven of his deer out of a herd of a little over one hundred. Because these were registered breeding deer, the financial loss was substantial.

Global warming is an acknowledged fact. I have personally witnessed many of the changes that it has wrought in just my lifetime. I have seen many species of birds and animals greatly expand their ranges northward and that can only happen with a moderating climate. I have witnessed the disappearance of the glaciers in Glacier National Park in Montana and the recession of many in Alaska. I can't prove that the warming is due to the burning of fossil fuels, sunspot activity, periodic cyclical patterns, or El Niño ocean currents, etc. But I do know that the moderating winters are allowing more deer to survive in the North while taking a greater toll on the deer in the South.

Fewer deer are dying of starvation in the North, while more are dying of the epizootic hemorrhagic disease (EHD) in the South. The extreme summer heat in the South, mid-eastern, and upper midwestern states in 2007 had the deer concentrating along the rivers and lakes where the warm water made ideal conditions for the biting midges that spread the disease. The year 2007 saw one of the heaviest outbreaks of EHD ever documented, with confirmed cases in 812 counties in thirty-one states. Frost kills the midges but the delayed cold weather of that year allowed the disease to be spread for a much longer than usual time, killing more than sixty five thousand deer.

The disease was first discovered and identified in New Jersey in 1955. In 1975, we were hit hard again, and the greatest number of deaths occurred on the farm adjoining my property. The land was part of a five-farm hunting club. There, it was not unusual to see about one hundred deer feeding in a single field. The club always took a large number of bucks but allowed no does to be killed, with the result that we had far too many deer in the area. The disease alleviated that problem and, I'm thankful to say, it has not recurred in our area, nor has that deer herd ever again gotten out of control.

People often talk about the "good old days." For whitetails, today *is* "the good old days" because their population is again as high as it was before Columbus landed.

However, chronic wasting disease (CWD) could send the whitetail population crashing down. CWD belongs to a group of diseases known as transmissible spongiform encephalophies (TSE). It was first discovered in a Colorado research facility in 1967, but it had already spread from there after some of the deer were released before the symptoms of the disease were evident. With this disease, proteins known as "prions" affect the deer's brain making it porous like a sponge, from whence comes its name, which causes the infected animal to lose weight, stagger, and then collapse. There is no cure for CWD, and it is always fatal. The disease is spread primarily through the saliva of infected animals. Deer are constantly grooming themselves and each other, which is only one of the reasons CWD has spread rapidly. It has been transmitted primarily through the transportation of infected game-farm animals, which is the reason most states have now prohibited interstate shipment of those animals. Alas, CWD has also been found in elk, deer, and moose and—at this writing—has spread to twenty-one states and two provinces.

CWD is similar to mad cow disease and Creutzfeldt-Jakob disease in humans. Although there have been no direct links of CWD infecting humans, authorities say that the meat of known infected animals should not be eaten.

There are a number of other pathogens that infect deer, but most of them are less communicable and less deadly.

Accidents

Deer, like every other creature including humans, are subject to a wide variety of accidents. In dashing through the woods, they sometimes impale themselves upon broken tree trunks, known as snags. Also, wire fences take a heavy toll on deer. I have seen deer break their jaws and their necks upon running into woven-wire and cyclone fences. I have photographed deer that got their feet tangled in fences they were jumping and died there. In my collection, I have a deer skull with antlers entangled in twenty pounds of single-strand wire, which created a cable that imprisoned the deer until it died. Recently, a deer was shown on TV that crashed through the front door of a Target department store and went out the back door. That was newsworthy but is actually quite a common occurrence.

This deer died when its foot became entangled in a fence it tried to jump.

One of this buck's antlers got caught in the crotch of a tree during rubbing. The buck then struggled so forcefully to break free that leverage from that antler broke the buck's skull plate, which pierced his brain, killing him.

Deer often break through the thin ice of ponds. A few years ago, Pennsylvania experienced a severe ice storm and reported that many deer fell down the ice-covered slopes. Deer frequently slip on smooth, wet macadam roads and ice-covered lakes, dislocating their legs, which doom them to a slow death if they are not dispatched. As deputy warden, I have shot a number of such deer that had fallen on the ice on the Delaware River and were later scavenged by bald eagles. A friend of mine found two bucks killed by lightning that hit the wire fence they had been feeding near. I once took video of a dead buck with his antlers caught in the crotch of the tree he was rubbing. In his frantic efforts to get loose, he broke his skull plate, which penetrated his brain, saving him from a lingering death.

I could probably write a book on all the bizarre accidents in which deer have been involved because the lists goes on and on. Deer are killed by planes, trains, and automobiles, but far more deer are killed in collisions with motor vehicles than by all other types of accidents combined.

According to the Insurance Information Institute, there are now more than five hundred thousand deer/vehicle collisions nationally each year. In some states, this represents an increase of more than 100 percent in the decade from 1990 to 2000. Pennsylvania has more than forty eight thousand deer killed by motor vehicles each year. That's more than four

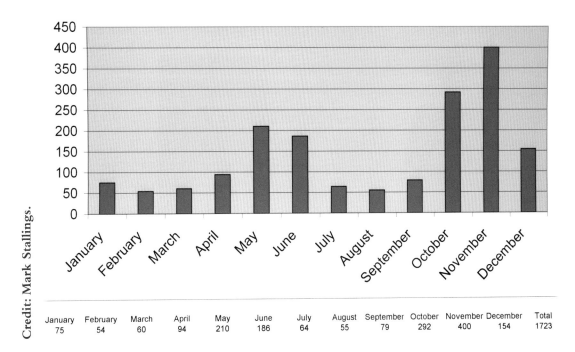

10-Year Deer Accident Study by Month

January	February	March	April	May	June	July	August	September	October	November	December	Total
75	54	60	94	210	186	64	55	79	292	400	154	1723

Ten-year study of the number of deer-related automobile accidents per month. Compiled by a major interstate trucking company.

times the number of deer living in the state of Massachusetts. Pennsylvania estimates that one out of every thirty-two deer in the state will be killed by a vehicle. In 2006, Pennsylvania had an estimated deer herd of 1,600,000, so a figure of about fifty thousand deer killed on the road proves it correct. The greatest number of deer are killed during the rutting season with a smaller peak occurring during the birthing season. This is because during the rut, the deer are most active, and during the birthing season, the young deer are driven away by their mothers and the resulting lack of maternal guidance to which they are accustomed.

All of those vehicular accidents result in more than $1 billion in total damages or more, at roughly $2,000 per accident. A far greater cost is to the more than two hundred thousand people who are injured and the more than two hundred killed each year in such accidents. I have had the misfortune to kill twelve deer with a car over the years but fortunately was never injured myself. One friend of mine had a deer crash through the windshield onto her lap, totaling her car and sending her to the hospital.

Deer and man interact through other accidents. As our deer population has exploded, more does give birth to their young in hayfields instead of in the

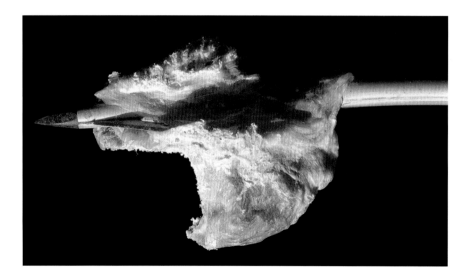

This arrow point is encased in cartilage. It was taken from a deer that had been wounded several years earlier.

overcrowded woodlands. As a result, farmers are more likely to injure or kill fawns with their mowing machines. Many deer survive wounds gotten in battle or through hunting. Bucks often are blinded in one eye or have the muscles severed in an ear as a result of fighting.

I have a hunting arrowhead that I removed from a deer that was killed by a car. The deer had been shot from a tree stand and the arrow became embedded in the deer's loin, missing the spine. The arrow shaft had been broken off and, over the years, the head was encased in a hard, fibrous lump of cartilage.

My friend Manny Barone found the skeleton of a buck that had been shot in the femur bone with an arrow. The arrow had not killed the buck and even had new bone growing over the point.

All wild creatures have a tremendous tenacity of life.

Bone has grown around this arrowhead, which became lodged in the deer's femur after a nonfatal wounding.

Chapter 7

Antlers

I've fought a losing battle, trying to persuade people to refer to the prized growths on a buck's head as antlers instead of horns. Antlers and horns are very different.

Tusks and Antlers

Of the fifty-one species of deer throughout the world, the most primitive species—eastern Asia's musk deer and Chinese water deer—do not have antlers.

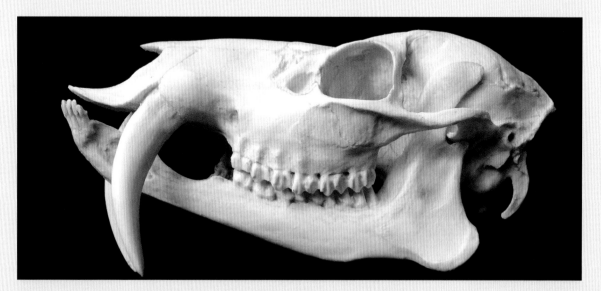

The Chinese water deer is a living example of an earlier evolutionary stage in which deer had long canine teeth, instead of antlers which they do use for fighting.

Scientists suggest that all of the earliest deer had long, curving upper canine teeth, descending as Dracula-like tusks. It appears that tusked deer that also had antlers survived better than deer without antlers, leading to gradual worldwide proliferation of deer species with antlers. The Asian deer, the muntjac, and the tufted deer have little antlers and small canine tusks that are presumably vestiges of that early step in deer evolution.

It is interesting to speculate why deer evolution rewarded antlers over canine tusks. After all, the long canines have the advantage of being permanent, allowing them to be used year-round for defense against predators as well as any aggression among herd members. By contrast, a buck's antlers are suitable for defense and dominance battles only a few months each year before being shed in winter, at a time when they would otherwise be the most useful for defense against predators.

So what evolutionary advantage did these briefly available antlers confer? Large antlers are mainly for show. They serve two purposes in what Charles Darwin called "sexual selection." First, they are a sign of fitness to which females are attracted. But antlers are costly to produce in both time and energy, requiring a tremendous expenditure of calories and nutrients. Second, large antlers intimidate lesser bucks during the breeding season, assuring the dominant buck has more breeding opportunities and more offspring with his good genes. Every buck has a sense of self-awareness and knows the size of his own antlers, and immediately knows how they compare in size to those of any other buck. Smaller-antlered bucks almost always defer to larger-antlered rivals.

Ironically, large antlers often shorten a buck's lifespan—this aside from his appeal to hunters. A big buck is usually satisfied with intimidating lesser bucks but will fight if his rival remains undeterred. This fighting can lead to injury and usually depletes fat reserves that the buck may not be able to replace before the onset of winter, when survival in northern climes depends on fat reserves.

Horns vs. Antlers

Antlers are a deciduous appendage grown and lost each year. With the exception of caribou, antlered females in the deer family are highly abnormal. Whitetail does have antlers only if they have a preponderance of the male sex hormone testosterone, which occurs only in about one of every three thousand does.

Horns grow on goats, sheep, cattle, bison, and antelope. Unlike antlers, horns are never shed but grow continuously throughout the animal's life, becoming larger each

A Dall's sheep ram has true horns that grow throughout the animal's lifetime and are never cast. Deer antlers are deciduous, falling off each winter.

year. In the case of cattle, bison, and goats, each ring on the base of the horn represents annual growth. On sheep, annual rings occur throughout the length of the horn as new keratin is added.

North America's pronghorn is the only animal in the world that sheds the outer portion of its horn, called the "casque," each autumn. The bony core remains and a new outer covering grows over it. Uniquely, too, the pronghorn's horn has a branching prong.

If horns are broken in a fight or as the result of a fall, or if they are sawed off by humans, they do not grow back. Horns have a porous core and a hard, strong outer surface composed of keratin, the same material as our fingernails. Horns are nourished by internal blood vessels and grow from the inside out, as growth is added at the base. Among horned animals, both males and females usually have horns.

Antlers are true bone, but do not have marrow because they are nourished mainly by the blood vessels in the skin that covers them while they are growing. Antlers are

The pronghorn is the only animal in the world that has branched horns: the prong.

composed mainly of calcium and phosphorous, plus traces of a few other minerals. Because antlers grow so fast, as much as a quarter inch per day, these minerals are not absorbed from the buck's diet; instead, they must be drawn directly from his skeleton, causing temporary osteoporosis. After the antlers are fully grown, the skeletal loss is replenished from the foods the buck eats—one of the reasons large-antlered bucks are more common in regions with calcium-rich limestone soils.

Though bone and some organs can repair themselves in most creatures, including humans, members of the deer family (Cervidae) are the only mammals in the world capable of completely regenerating a body part: their antlers. Scientists are studying this phenomenon for clues that could help reverse osteoporosis in humans.

The large antlers of this mature white-tailed buck are truly his "crowning glory."

The Greek philosopher Aristotle (384–322 BC) observed in his *Nicomachean Ethics* that "If stags be mutilated (castrated), when, by reason of their age, they have as yet no horns, they never grow horns at all; if they be mutilated when they have horns, the horns remain unchanged in size, and the animal does not lose them." Of course, like many hunters, he was not referring to horns but to antlers, and maybe that's where the antler-vs.-horn confusion started. Thus, two thousand years before the word "testosterone" was coined, the effects of that hormone were known and being studied.

Gender and Antler Growth

The gender of a creature may be determined at conception, but gender is not evident until the blastosphere is fairly well developed as an embryo. During the first stages of development, the blastosphere is of neuter gender known as the indifferent stage. Then, under hormonal influence, the wolffian and mullerian ducts begin to form at about six to seven weeks in deer, and in humans at about ten weeks. These ducts will later become the sex organs of the fetus. At birth, a little buck can easily be identified by his external genitalia, the scrotum and penis sheath, and a little doe will have a vulva. At birth, both genders exhibit small whorls of hair on their forehead at the site where the little buck will later develop his antler pedicles, but the hair tufts on the baby buck will be darker. In the birth of male/female twins, the little buck will usually be a bit larger and slightly heavier than his doe sibling, although the difference may not be easily noticeable.

During a buck fawn's third month, his developing testes, under the stimulation of his endocrine glands, produce testosterone. This stimulates growth of his antler pedicles on the periosteum tissue of his frontal skull plates. These pedicles are prominently visible when the buck is four months old. The periosteum is an antlerogenic layer of tissue, found on the frontal skull plate of all deer but only causes the growth of the pedicle, the antler base, under the stimulation of testosterone. Drs. Hartwig and Schrudde, of Germany, and Dr. Richard Goss, of Brown University in Rhode Island discovered this fact and experimented by excising the tissue from the skull, and then reattaching it on other parts of the deer's body. They found that a pedicle would grow wherever they attached the periosteum. The resulting antlers were only rudimentary nubs, but they did grow on the buck's leg, hip, and ears. The fact that these little stubs were true antlers was proven as they were in complete synchronization in the growing, hardening, peeling of velvet, and casting of the antlers with normal deer. That is, their antler growth was in perfect response to "photoperiodism," the gradually changing daylight hours throughout each year, as addressed in the next section.

At five to six months of age, a little buck's pedicles are about three quarters of an inch in length and they noticeably push up the skin. For most buck fawns that is as far as the development goes for its first year, and we refer to them as button bucks. However, if a buck fawn has had access to exceptionally nutritious food, either in captivity or on the rich-soil states of America's heartland, he may progress to having little antlers that will grow velvet, harden, peel, and be cast. If the six- to seven-month-old buck does produce little antlers that peel, he would be capable of breeding, even though he is not physically mature. In the wild, the precocious little buck would not be large enough to copulate with a mature doe and would also be deterred by the dominant buck.

It was Hellenette Silver, a biologist working for the New Hampshire Fish and Game Division, who discovered in 1964 that precocious bucks were sexually mature.

The little peeled antlers on this seven-month buck show that his testosterone level is high enough for him to be sexually mature.

For her research, Silver had penned fawns of both sexes together. The following summer, when the fawns were yearlings, several of the little does gave birth to fawns. No adult buck had been admitted to the pen, and she suspected rightly that one of the little nubbin-antlered bucks was the sire. Further research by Silver and others proved that early sexual maturation could be stimulated through diet.

Photoperiodism

"Photoperiodism" determines the flowering times of plants; the migration and breeding of birds; the hibernation and breeding of reptiles and amphibians; the hibernation, migration, and breeding of mammals; and more. Because of artificial light, we humans are less affected by photoperiodism. In deer, it is photoperiodism and latitude—not phases of the moon and not the weather—that determine the precise time for the antler cycle, the rutting season, and the birth of young. All species breed so their young are born at the optimal time for survival.

Photoperiodism is the mechanism setting the internal "circannual clock" that governs the growth and behaviors of almost all living organisms, including humans. Most organisms have precise life cycles that respond to the changing amount of daylight in a twenty-four hour period. The response variations are minimal at the equator where the period of daylight and dark is evenly divided and the temperature remains constant. The farther north or south a creature lives from the equator, the more critical the response because of the time factors tied to the weather, the so-called window of opportunity.

The farther north a species is found, the more synchronization of the birthing period occurs because the growing season is so short. In response to photoperiodism, the plants produce the growth needed to replicate themselves, which coincidentally provides the fodder the herbivores need to provide milk for their young. However, synchronization is an adaptation that is also found near the equator. It's a survival factor that allows more young to survive. Also, being born at the same time as others of their species helps outnumber their predator's needs.

After winter solstice on December 21, when daylight hours are the shortest, the amount of daylight in a twenty-four hour period gradually lengthens by one to three minutes per day. The retina of a deer's eye acts as a photoelectric cell, gathering light and transmitting electrical impulses created by that light to the "pineal gland." The pineal is a pea-size gland located in the center of the brain directly beneath the "thalamus" and is often referred to as "the third eye." This pineal gland is responsible for changing the electrical impulse from the retina of the eye to a chemical compound that travels to the "hypothalamus," which is the control center for the body's endocrine system. With the decreasing amount of daylight in autumn, the pineal triggers the hypothalamus to send a chemical signal to the attached pituitary gland, which increases the production of the hormone "melatonin." The pituitary gland also produces the "luteinizing" hormone that controls the production of testosterone. During the longer nights of winter, when the production of melatonin is highest, the melatonin suppresses the production of the luteinizing hormone so that little or no testosterone is produced. With the ever-increasing amount of daylight after December 21, the melatonin is suppressed by the end of March and the luteinizing hormone allows enough testosterone to be produced to start the growth of the buck's new antlers. Neural signals are sent when the message must be acted upon instantaneously, whereas chemical signals (hormones) are used when longer time periods are involved.

I saw a buck at Penn State's deer research lab that had its pineal gland surgically removed—a pinealectomy. The buck produced antlers but was about four months out of sync with the regular season, proving the control that this gland has on annual growth factors and behaviors. Other deer have been subjected to periods of extended or shortened cycles of artificial lighting conditions, with the antlers responding to the amount of light received by the pineal gland. The more light the bucks were exposed to, the sooner their antlers started to grow and the sooner they changed from their winter coats and vice versa.

Triggered by the growth hormone, and released by the endocrine system, bone salts are deposited on the antler pedicle by a network of blood vessels beneath the skin.

The skin covering an antler's pedicle is the start of the velvet that will nourish the growth of the new antler.

Under normal conditions, it takes about six weeks for new skin to grow over the pedicle after the antlers have been cast.

Velvet

The term "velvet" applies to the skin that nourishes the growth of antlers because it looks and feels like velvet fabric.

Velvet is a modification of the deer's regular skin, having an outer layer of coarse collagen fibers and an inner layer of finer fibers. Supplied with blood from the buck's superficial temporal arteries, the antler buds start to swell, as the eleven to thirteen arteries in the growing antlers begin to deposit the minerals known as "bone salts" on the top of the pedicles. In addition, there are eleven to thirteen veins returning the blood to the body. These twenty-two to twenty-six blood vessels can be verified after velvet is shed because they leave permanent longitudinal lines imprinted onto the

The new skin on a growing antler is called "velvet" because it looks and feels like that material.

surface of the antler. Because of the tremendous blood flow through the velvet, the antlers are warm to the touch. Growing antlers are one of the few external appendages that have an internal temperature of about 101 degrees Fahrenheit. The antlers are also thermoregulatory because they give off heat from the coursing blood, helping to cool the buck in hot weather.

The skin at the end of each growing antler tip is known as the "apical epidermal cap." Unlike most mammalian hair, which lies horizontal to the skin, all of the velvet hairs on the antler stand on end and are about a quarter inch long. Every hair grows out of a "sebaceous gland," which produces a "sebum" that has both water- and insect- repelling properties and also gives growing antlers their shiny look. The sebum helps minimize the amount of blood that would be lost to the hordes of bloodsucking flies and mosquitoes that plague all wildlife.

The entire velvet is a maze of nerve endings originating from the trigeminal nerve; the erect hairs serve the same purpose as the deer's whiskers—as sensory receptors. To prevent damage to the soft antlers, the hairs "feel" obstructions and, via neural pathways through his nervous system, warn the buck to avoid them. Even after the velvet has been shed, the buck will retain a memory of precisely where his antler tips are, and this allows him to dash through thick brush without becoming entangled. The "memory" is also seen in the

The shredded velvet hangs in long bloody strips until the buck can rub it off.

succeeding years' antlers replicating and expanding upon the basic configuration of those preceding them.

As the velvet dries, it itches—much like our sunburned skin does when it dries. To get relief, bucks rub off their velvet. There is a varying amount of residual blood left in the velvet. On some bucks, the velvet peels off in bloody, longitudinal strips, staining the antlers bright red.

Some bucks rub off just the hair of the velvet, leaving the antlers encased in the blood-red skin, which later rubs off over time. According to the configuration of their antlers, some bucks have a hard job applying direct pressure to their velvet strips, making it almost impossible to remove them. Some of the bucks are able to rub their velvet off anywhere between ten minutes to an hour. Others have bloody strips hanging for a day or so. And those long, bloody strips drive a buck absolutely bonkers! The strips sway back and forth with the buck's every movement and touch his ears or his head, or hang in front of his eyes, blocking his vision. The buck will constantly toss his head, and the more he tosses, the more the strips touch him somewhere. He will try to catch the velvet strips with his mouth and often chews them, but seldom can he pull them loose with his mouth. Strips he can't remove in a couple of days usually dry into rawhide and may not be removed for weeks.

The velvet strips are seldom found because most bucks eat them as fast as they rub them off.

Bucks trying to remove their velvet often catch it in their mouths and attempt to chew it off.

Buck Rubs

When I was a boy, the old-timers believed that every tree rub was made by a different buck and that bucks only rubbed to remove their velvet. I can't fault them for that misinformation because, in the 1930s, there were not enough deer to be studied. I can remember being shown a patch of aspen saplings of which a dozen were rubbed. I was told that that was *the* place to hunt because at least a dozen bucks had rubbed there. But in those years, there probably weren't a dozen bucks in the entire county. Only later did I learn that a buck makes the first rub to remove velvet, and from that time on he may make a dozen rubs each night to communicate his presence.

Recently, my friend Larry Kleintop reported he lost two of his biggest bucks on his deer reserve through sepsis infections. The bucks had started to peel their velvet, the weather was warm, and the flies were bad. The flies laid their eggs under the loosened velvet, which the bucks could not remove for several days. When the maggots hatched, they caused an infection in the blood that had been nourishing the velvet surrounding the pedicle. The blood spread the infection throughout the deer's entire body, and both deer were down within a few hours. Although Larry administered antibiotics and rehydration fluids as soon as he found the bucks, he could not save them. This may not be an isolated instance. There are probably many things occurring in wild deer that we don't know about, simply because we don't witness them. I have never heard or read of bucks getting an infection in this manner, even though I have photographed many bucks with dried velvet strips hanging for weeks from their antlers.

Antler Color

Many hunters believe that a buck's antlers become darker and increasingly stained by the resins from the trees that he rubs. Not so. As soon as the velvet is peeled, the antlers become lighter due to bleaching by sunlight and the leaching of color by rain and moisture. The longer the antlers are carried, the lighter their color bleaches until they become white as bones—which is what they are. On some bucks, the velvet is almost dry and leaves the antlers stained a light brown.

Basic Requirements for Good Antlers

Large antlers result from three factors: nutritious food, increasing buck age, and good genes. The shape, or configuration, of the antlers is strictly genetic. Some bucks have very wide-spreading antlers, while the antlers of other bucks sweep upward.

Antler conformation is a genetic characteristic, with some bucks having wide growing antlers.

The tips of the main beams on some antlers arch inward, almost touching, while still others have either long, thin tines or shorter, thick tines. The dominant buck in the area passes his antler shape to his sons. And females he sires will transmit some of their father's genes to their male offspring too.

Nutritious Food

The first and most important requirement for large antlers is the availability of highly nutritious food in an unlimited amount, "ad libitum." Research has proven that the optimum protein should be at least 16 percent, no matter what food it is derived from. Access to minerals, particularly

Some bucks have antlers that grow almost straight up.

Spike antlers are usually due to a lack of high protein in the diet and are not a genetic characteristic.

calcium, is also important, and deer feeding on limestone soils grow bigger than other deer. However, research has not proven that deer do better on the 30 percent protein found in some of the commercial feeds. Excess vitamins are excreted from the body, and the same is probably true of protein the body cannot utilize. Under ordinary conditions, a buck's antlers grow larger every year as long as his teeth remain good enough to process available food.

Many people mistakenly believe that bucks have spikes their first year, four points the second, six points the third, and so on. On rare occasions, spike antlers may be a sign of a genetic deficiency; they are almost always a sign of a lack of nutritious food.

A few years ago, studies done at the Kerrville Research Station in Texas seemed to prove that genetic deficiency

On this old white-tailed buck, the antlers have regressed due to age. Here the velvet is peeling in bloody strips.

was the basis for spike antlers, but that has since been discounted. The old saying about humans, "you are what you eat," is still basically true and is just as accurate for deer.

I started my research herd with local animals given to me by Joe Taylor when he was live trapping deer on private estates in New Jersey in the late 1970s. They were not special deer that had been imported because of their genes. My bucks have consistently grown much larger than their peers the wild deer because they were fed unlimited 16 percent feed and allowed to live until they died of old age. I have never had a spike buck in my herd, and only once did I have a buck that had four points for his first set of antlers. All of my other bucks had six- and eight-point racks at one and a half years of age and most grew to be in the Boone and Crockett 160- to 170-point class as adults.

Buck Age

The second basic requirement for trophy antlers is increased buck age. As mentioned, a buck doesn't attain his full skeletal growth until he is four and a half years of age, and only after that can the nutrients not needed for daily body maintenance be fully exploited for antler growth. For years, 86 percent of New Jersey's bucks were shot when they were one and a half years old; they never had a chance to reach their full growth potential. New Jersey had no bucks that qualified for the Boone and Crockett record books because of that extremely heavy hunting pressure. Today, through better game management, some of our bucks are living longer and are becoming trophy deer. No matter how good a buck's antlers were when he was three and a half or four and a half years of age, they will be better for the next five years if he has good food. After that time, the antlers of a buck in the wild will usually regress, because his teeth begin to wear out and he can no longer efficiently process the food he eats. Old bucks' antlers may become smaller in overall size or maintain long beams, but have fewer and smaller tines. The antlers of some old bucks become extremely malformed.

The raised ridges, found on the base of a buck's antlers, known as the "pearlation," grow larger and more pronounced each year. The bark removed from saplings and trees when a buck makes a rub is actually grated off by these ridges of pearlation. A buck in captivity, having access to ground feed, may be able to prolong the size of his optimally large antlers for a much longer time.

Good Genes

Heredity, based on genes, is extremely important and is the third basic trophy requirement. Being brought up on a dairy farm, I understood the importance of an animal's genes early on, as a fact of life. We joined an artificial insemination dairy cooperative. There was no way that we could ever afford the champion bulls that the cooperative

When rubbing, bucks use the ridges of the pearlation on their antlers to grate off tree bark. Note the shredded pieces of bark embedded in between the pearlation ridges.

owned and from which the cooperative collected semen. The bulls were champions because their mothers were the highest milk-producing cows in the nation, and those bulls had the ability to pass their mother's qualities to their offspring. Just as grain farmers have always planted their best seed, livestock farmers have always bred their best animals. And today, deer farmers are doing the same in hopes of producing the biggest, best bucks.

I have always maintained that the doe's genes are as important as the buck's, if not more so. The value of the doe's genes is a reflection of her status in the hierarchy. The matriarch of each blood-related family group is the dominant doe and with that goes the privilege of having access to the best of everything, and having it first. Perhaps

Not having antlers, does fight by striking out with their forefeet. Bucks will fight with front hooves, too, after their antlers have fallen and before their new antlers have hardened in the fall.

I shouldn't use the word "privilege," because this is really a privilege earned and maintained only as long as she is physically capable of dominating. Being dominant means that she gets the best birthing territory. It also means that she is able to feed first on available food and may selfishly claim the only food when scarce, especially in winter. Being dominant also means that all of those advantages are available to her fawns, as long as she allows them to eat. In starvation times, she will take precedent over even her own fawns. Having all of their dominant mother's advantages supplied, even before birth, helps her fawns grow bigger, faster, and stronger than any of their peers. And this is an advantage they will usually maintain for the rest of their lives. Just as children of rich parents usually enjoy advantages over other children, convey an air of entitlement, and have a far easier time in life, young deer also benefit similarly from their mother's status. Fawns of dominant does have the opportunity to eat first on the best food, because their mother does.

Record Book Trophy Antlers

To describe antler parts, I'll here use terms established by the Boone and Crockett Club for measuring all whitetail trophies, as illustrated in the accompanying official score chart. The Boone and Crockett Club is the official North American registrar of trophy heads, taken by "fair chase" with either a bow or a firearm. The Pope and Young Club employs virtually the same scoring system as Boone and Crockett but records only bucks taken with a bow.

On the scoring sheet, the length of the first tine is recorded on the G-1 line, the length of the second tine is recorded on line G-2, and so on, hence the "G" designation. Ordinarily the G-2 is the longest tine on the main beam. To be listed in the Boone and Crockett record book, a set of whitetail antlers needs a minimum score of 170, meaning a total of 170 inches. To be listed in Pope and Young records, the antlers need a total of 125 inches. The discrepancy in the qualifying score is the recognition that it is harder to take a buck with a bow than with a firearm. Bucks taken with a bow can also be registered in Boone and Crockett. The number one Pope and Young head, taken by Melvin Johnson in Illinois in 1965, scored 204 4/8 points and ranks number four in the Boone and Crockett book. Milo Hansen in Saskatchewan, Canada, took the top whitetail head of all time in 1993, with a score of 213 5/8. The top non typical whitetail head was picked up in a fence row in Missouri in 1981 and has a score of 333 7/8.

As each antler grows, the brow tine (G-1) will form as an outgrowth on the main beam. In another three weeks the second tine (G-2) will start to grow even though the first tine has not reached its maximum length. The G-2 tine is usually the longest. But I have seen many bucks whose longest tine was the G-1. Three weeks later, the third tine (G-3) starts to grow, and so on. The most typical antler formation for a white-tailed buck is to have three upward projecting tines, with the end of the main beam counted as the fourth tine, though it is measured in that beam's length.

In the East, a buck having four tines on each side is referred to as an eight-pointer. Out West, that same buck would be called a four-pointer because westerners count only the tines on one side; I have not been able to find out why it is done this way. The disadvantage of the western system is that it fails to account for bucks with an unequal number of tines on each side.

250 Station Drive
Missoula, MT 59801
(406) 542-1888

BOONE AND CROCKETT CLUB®
OFFICIAL SCORING SYSTEM FOR NORTH AMERICAN BIG GAME TROPHIES

TYPICAL
WHITETAIL AND COUES' DEER

MINIMUM SCORES		
	AWARDS	ALL-TIME
whitetail	160	170
Coues'	100	110

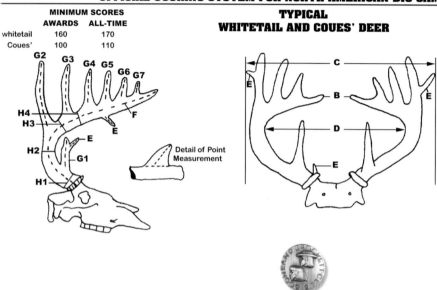

BOONE AND CROCKETT CLUB®
OFFICIAL SCORING SYSTEM FOR NORTH AMERICAN BIG GAME TROPHIES

NON-TYPICAL
WHITETAIL AND COUES' DEER

MINIMUM SCORES		
	AWARDS	ALL-TIME
whitetail	185	195
Coues'	105	120

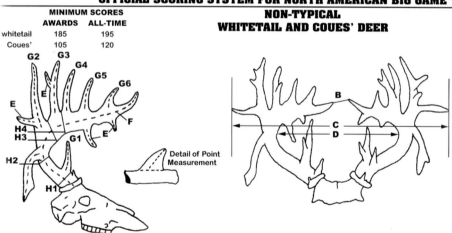

Boone and Crockett scoring sheet for whitetails.

Credit: Boone and Crockett Club.

Years ago, any antler projection that was long enough to hold a finger ring was classified as a tine, or point. Today, according to the Boone and Crockett Club, a tine must be at least one inch long and its length must exceed the length of its base. Many antlers have one, often several, small projections of varying lengths that are commonly referred to as "sticker points." If the individual projections qualify as a tine, they will be subtracted from the score of a typical head but will be added to a non typical head.

The actual density of an antler varies throughout the antler itself and also with the buck's age. Researchers have found that the hardest, densest part of the antler is the tip of the brow tine, the G-1 tine. Each succeeding tine, the G-2, G-3, etc., is less dense, with the main beam tip having the least density. One reason for this is that the buck's body supply of calcium is steadily depleted as his antlers grow. In addition, the antlers start to calcify at the base before mineralization of the beam tip is completed.

To qualify for consideration, the antlers must be intact upon the skull exactly as they grew. The skull plate must be cleaned, and antlers and plate must be allowed to dry in the air for at least sixty days. In those sixty days, the sutures in the skull plate will tighten up ever so slightly, bringing the antler tips closer together. On a young buck, because its skull is thinner than an older buck's, the antlers might move inward as much as a quarter inch. On older bucks, which have much thicker skulls, the shrinkage is less noticeable. Loose, separate antlers or antlers on a split skull are not accepted for an official score.

Sportscasters often say that you can't tell how good a player is without a scorecard. The same is true of antlers. Most sets of antlers you are likely to see mounted probably wouldn't meet the minimums for Boone and Crockett. If you are interested in big whitetail antlers, I heartily recommend that you get the Boone and Crockett Club record book at 250 Station Drive, Missoula, Montana, 59801 (www.booneandcrockettclub.com), or the Pope and Young Club record book at 15 E. 2nd St. (PO Box 548), Chatfield, Minnesota, 55923 (www.pope-young.org)

Antler Size and Growth

Hunters are like fishermen when describing the size of their catch, and I have to admit that I, too, sometimes get carried away when describing antler size. I have heard hundreds of hunters exclaim, "The buck had antlers the thickness of Coke cans!" Nothing puts claims of thickness, length, or weight into perspective better than a micrometer, a caliper, a ruler, or a scale. I have just gone through my collection of hundreds of antlers and find that the largest antler measured one inch above the burr has a diameter of 1 15/16 inches. I photographed that buck when he was in velvet, and assuming a half-inch for the velvet, his antlers would still only have measured 2.37 inches. That's nearly a Coke can diameter, which measures two and a half inches. Just for the heck of it, I measured a Canadian moose rack that I have. The antlers have a spread of fifty-six inches and a diameter of 2.4 inches at the base. So not even those moose antlers are as thick as a Coke can. The bases of many huge non typical sets of whitetail antlers do

This shows complete antler development of a buck's antlers throughout the year.
At the beginning of April, the antler base starts to swell.
Within one month, the antlers have grown three to four inches.
By June, the brow tine, or G-1, has developed.
By July, the antlers are about three-fourths developed.

By August, the antlers are almost fully grown.

In September, the antlers are full grown and the buck rubs them to remove the velvet.

In October, the antlers are in prime condition. Throughout the rutting season the buck uses his antlers for sparring and fighting.

The antlers are cast sometime between January and April, leaving a raw, bloody antler base.

get to be the size of Coke cans, but they are considered "freaks," or non typical, which I'll discuss a bit later.

Adult buck antlers start to grow around the last of March or early April, and grow at the rate of about a quarter inch per day. Younger bucks begin growing their antlers a little later, and theirs grow at a slower rate. If a growing antler is scratched and the velvet torn, the antler will bleed but not very much.

This buck's broken antler tip is dangling on a strip of velvet.

The arteries supplying this vast amount of blood to the buck's antlers have thicker walls than do the internal arteries. These thickened muscular walls allow the arteries to constrict and virtually shut off blood flow from a cut in less than a minute, which prevents hemorrhaging. Some blood is supplied and returned through the center of the antler's "spongiosa" but this flow gradually diminishes and eventually stops as the base of the antler begins to "ossify" or harden.

Because antlers are so easily damaged while in velvet, bucks in velvet restrict their activity to a bare minimum. Many hunters, trying to keep track of deer activity year-round report seeing almost no bucks during the summer months. And there are several good reasons for this. Mindful of their tender antlers, bucks in summer don't usually need to go far to fill their rumen. Also, to avoid the daytime heat, bucks don't feed until dusk or after dark, and so they just aren't often seen.

Grass grows by adding new growth at its base. Woody twigs grow by adding new material at their tips, and antlers grow much like woody twigs. As the epidermal cap is pushed upward, it lays down a mineralized cartilage that hardens into a "spongiosa," or soft bone, as the antler elongates. Blood flows through this spongy bone in both directions. Continued growth causes the base of the spongiosa to calcify completely. Eventually, most of the antler base becomes solid bone, completely shutting off the internal

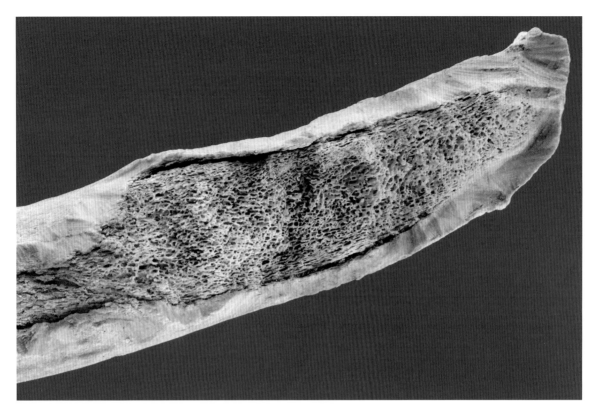

The honeycombed inner portion of an antler is known as the "spongiosa."

blood flow through the antler. The dried spongiosa has a honeycombed appearance and is filled with minute pockets of air.

The antlers of yearling bucks are almost solid bones with no spongiosa. Bucks, if they have sufficient nutritious food, usually grow larger antlers each year, and the spongy core becomes larger. Increased spongiosa means the buck can grow larger antlers without a greater corresponding drain of minerals from its bones. As the buck matures, he becomes more dominant and fights more to prove this dominance. And having more spongiosa lessens the chance that the mature buck will break his antlers.

Antlers over most of North America attain their maximum growth for that particular year by the end of July or the first week in August. Under the influence of "gonadatrophic hormones," produced by the pituitary gland, the buck's testicles enlarge, his scrotum descends from his body to keep the sperm cooler, and the level of the hormone testosterone is increased dramatically. The increased level of testosterone speeds up the calcification of the buck's antlers by causing the burr to grow outward,

shutting off the blood flow to the antlers. Antlers solidify from the base to the tips, and as they do so, the velvet begins to dry and constrict, giving them a shrink-wrapped appearance.

During the rutting season, while antlers have an outer cylinder of hardened bone with a spongy core, they can sustain a greater impact without breaking. Contrary to what might be expected, antlers become more brittle as they turn to bone just prior to being cast. And this is why more antlers are broken during the last part of the rut, even though more fighting is done in the first part. Also, in the northernmost part of the whitetail range, extreme cold makes antlers more brittle, increasing the chance they will shatter upon impact. The main reason that bucks cast their antlers and grow larger ones each year is to replace their damaged antlers.

In addition to using his antlers in fighting and to mark trees, a buck uses them to scratch itches on his body in hard-to-reach areas. He does this gently while the antlers are in velvet and roughly after the antlers have hardened.

Typical vs. Nontypical Antlers

Although antlers are officially classified as being typical or nontypical, some people prefer to describe them as symmetrical or nonsymmetrical because those terms are more descriptive. I can appreciate the mass and the odd formations of nontypical antlers but personally prefer a long-tined, mirror-image, symmetrical set of typical antlers.

Yet many hunters prefer huge non-typical antlers because of their rarity as well as for their unpredictable mass and configuration.

I videotaped a big ten-point buck in West Virginia years ago whose antlers were so evenly matched when viewed from the side that only the near antler was visible. That's what I mean by mirror image; the two antlers looked identical. That buck was the most beautiful I have ever seen, and I have seen tens of thousands over my long life.

Deer hunters (sixteen million of us annually) never seem to tire of looking at trophy buck heads. That fact has not been lost on the retailers of hunting equipment whose displays of trophy deer heads have made meccas of their stores. The greatest assembly of trophy white-tailed deer heads in the world has been collected by John L. Morris and is displayed in his Bass Pro Shops all across the country. At this writing, Mr. Morris owns the Jordan Buck, which is the number two typical head in the world. He also has sixteen of the top fifty-two heads. In addition, he also owns the number two and number three nontypical heads, as well as twenty-six out of the top fifty-five nontypical heads. Hunters should be grateful that Mr. Morris secured these heads from private collections and put them on display for the public.

While we understand a great deal about antlers, there is much that we don't know about nontypical antlers. While most nontypical antlers are the result of injury, many are genetic characteristics that can be passed on to offspring.

Testicle Injuries

If a buck is castrated before his antlers start to grow, he will never produce antlers because testicles are needed to produce the testosterone required for a complete antler cycle. If a buck is castrated while his antlers are in velvet, they will remain in velvet and continue to grow for the rest of his life. That does not mean that they will continue to grow larger for the rest of his life, because in the northern part of the country, the tips of velvet antlers will freeze off. When the tips freeze off the antlers often produce a basal mass that covers the top of the entire head, like a wig, hence the name "peruke" for such heads. In warmer parts of the US, where the tips do not freeze off, the antlers produce so many little spikes that they are referred to as "cactus" bucks. H. James Tonkin shot such a buck in Utah that had more than one hundred small points, and that head did indeed resemble the branches of cholla cactus. If a buck is castrated after his antlers have hardened and peeled, the antlers will drop off within two weeks after being deprived of his testosterone. This condition is almost identical to what occurs normally after the rut.

How, you might ask, would a buck be castrated if not cut by a human? A buck's testicles might be damaged in a fight, if a third buck hit one of the combatants from the rear. A buck could also injure his testicles while jumping a fence or bounding in brush.

Antler Injuries

Deer in my herd have broken their antlers by running into a fence, causing them to grow nontypical antlers that year, but they showed no sign of the damage thereafter. If the break occurred to the antler itself, permanent deformity seldom resulted, even though the antler might have grown in all sorts of freaky configurations that year. But if the pedicle is damaged, the antler growing from it will probably be nontypical for the rest of the buck's life.

Dr. Anthony Bubenik, a Canadian deer researcher, claims that antlers often have a "memory" in that succeeding antlers will replicate the original damage. I have a set of ten antlers in my collection, from the same buck, that broke his right antler above the burr when he was one and a half years old. That buck's second set of antlers grew with the right main beam bent upward at almost a right angle. Over the next eight years the right beam gradually straightened out; although it always showed evidence of the break, it grew less pronounced each year. Antlers definitely do have a "memory."

Memory is also in evidence when side, or sticker points, grow in the exact same antler location each year. Antler projections that grow downward from the bottom of the antler are called "drop tines," another phenomenon that is not understood or satisfactorily explained. In the early 1970s, I photographed a huge mule deer buck in Yellowstone National Park that had a long drop tine growing from each main beam. Either the antlers were responding to a memory or else the drop tine was caused by a genetic condition, because the buck had the two drop tines each year. Even if drop tines are genetic, and the buck has them in the same location in succeeding years, it does not seem to be a genetic trait that passes to his sons.

I have photographed three whitetails with drop tines—two

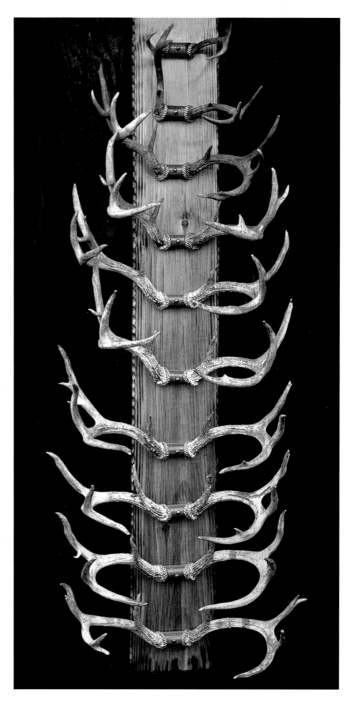

These are one buck's sets of antlers over ten years. He broke his right antler at one and a half years and subsequent antlers retained a bend for the rest of his life, proving a physiological "memory" of the accident.

of them in Texas. The drop tines were about three inches in length and matched the color of the rest of the buck's antlers. I have seen a number of mounted trophy heads with large drop tines six to eight inches in length, bulbous in shape, and dark brown or black in color. The coloration in most cases was caused by the velvet the buck could not remove and had turned into leather. On the antlers where the velvet had been removed, the dark coloration was caused by dried, dark residual blood.

In humans as well as deer, the cerebral hemisphere on each side of the brain controls the motor activities on the opposite side of the body. An injury to a buck's right leg or foot will cause a freak antler to grow on the left side of his head and vice versa.

I first photographed this "contra-lateral condition" in the 1970s. The buck had sustained an injury to his left hind foot and could stand on the hoof tip but could not walk

This buck has lost the lower part of his left hind foot, which caused the contra-lateral freak growth of his right antler.

Palmation occurs when the antler's main beam becomes greatly enlarged and flattened.

on the hoof proper. He had a normal four-tine antler on the left side of his head but an elongated, freaky spike antler on the right.

I photographed an even more severe deformity on a buck that had had his left hind foot completely severed midway between the hoof and the ankle. A mowing machine might have cut off the hoof when the buck was a fawn, and I have heard of such mishaps on a number of occasions. The buck's right antler was a normal four-point while the left was just a bumpy mass. Because half of the foot was missing, the buck limped badly while walking, but there was no sign of his loss when he ran. The intact left hind leg had grown stronger through use, and that compensated for his handicap.

Palmation, in the form of webbing between a tine and the main beam or the actual flattening either of the tines or the beams, is quite common.

The most extreme example that I have seen was on a buck shot in Texas that had a basket-like palmation of the main beams that were twelve inches across. The buck's antlers resembled those of a small moose with small tines on the edge of the palmation.

The oddest antler formation in my personal collection was given to me by my dear friend Joe Taylor. The buck had been killed by a car a few miles from my home in northwestern New Jersey. Killed in early September, its antlers still had a few shreds

This is the oddest antler set in my collection. Deformity was probably caused by the deer's antlers being struck by a vehicle during growth.

of dried velvet. That buck had evidently been hit by a car once before because something had severely smashed its antlers while they were growing, causing them to grow like an upended bunch of bananas.

The pedicle under the antler on the left-side of the photo is normal, one and a quarter inches in diameter, while the antler base is a grotesque three and a quarter inches. The seven main beams have thirteen tines that point in all directions. Except for that freak rack, the earlier collision apparently had not injured the buck seriously because he was in excellent physical condition. I couldn't predict what his rack would have looked like the following year.

I have photographed several bucks that had two main beams growing from a single antler base.

Rarely, bucks will grow two main beams from one pedicle.

I have seen several bucks that had three or more antlers growing from separate pedicles.

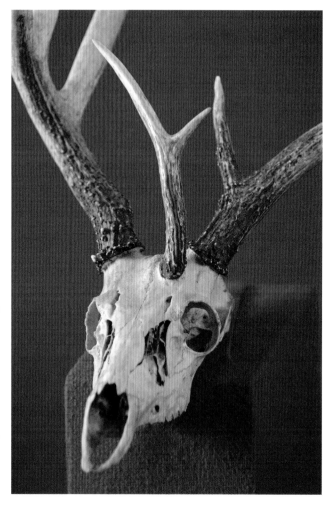

But I have photographed only one buck that actually had three antlers, although I have seen a number of racks in private collections that had multiple antlers growing from their own separate pedicles.

Multiple antlers are real oddities today, although they were evidently quite common among the forerunners of the Cervidae family thousands of years ago. It is not known if the extra antlers are the result of the periosteum being damaged while the buck was a fawn, or if he was born with multiple patches of periosteum.

All of the antler malformations I just described, with the exception of palmation, are the result of injuries that usually cause just the antlers on one side of the head to be deformed and may or may not show that injury the following year. The most spectacular non-typical heads are definitely the result of genetics because they are replicated year after year and are passed on to subsequent generations, and that is what the deer farmers are counting on.

In the wild, although it is possible, there is little chance of inbreeding among deer. Yearling bucks disperse to new home ranges an average of five miles beyond their natal home range. During the rutting season, the adult dominant bucks increase the area they normally occupy by a factor of four to five. Thus, there is a good chance they will be away when does related to them on their home range come into estrus. The bucks would gladly breed related does but cannot do so if they're not at their home range. Inbreeding has a deleterious effect on most creatures, usually producing inferior offspring. However, some deer breeders conduct controlled inbreeding, or "line breeding," to produce bucks with huge nontypical antlers by breeding nontypical bucks to their half sisters. That is, the breeders use the offspring of the same, nontypical buck, but from different does.

Both the number-one and number-two nontypical whitetail heads were from bucks that were found dead. The number one head scored 333 7/8 and had nineteen points on his right antler and twenty-five points on the left. The number-two head scored 328 2/8 and had twenty-three points on his right antler and twenty-two points on the left. We have no way of knowing what type of antlers those bucks had in previous years, and so far as I know, no cast antlers that could have come from either buck has ever surfaced. We have no way of knowing what the bucks they sired looked like, because I have never heard of any bucks that could be proved to be offspring. We do know that huge nontypical bucks being used as breeders in captivity are producing huge nontypical offspring. Another thing that I find fascinating is the generalized uniformity of the racks that most of the huge nontypical bucks produce. Yes, there is a discrepancy in the number of points that may be found on each beam, but overall the two sides are remarkably alike.

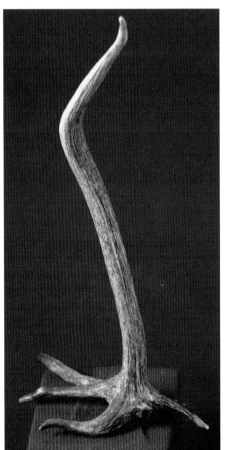

Freak Antler Growth

I had always assumed that new antlers could start to grow only after the old antlers were cast and the new skin growth was completed. But in 2002, I saw photos of two captive bucks raised by a friend of mine that had started to grow new antlers under the base of the old, retained antlers. Eventually, the new antlers forced the old antlers to cast, but the pedicle did not have to be covered for the new growth to start. The skin surrounding the pedicle base began to lay down the bone salts, starting the new antlers in response to photoperiodism. Since that time, I learned of more than a dozen other captive bucks

My good friend Gary Knepp has one antler that closely resembles a turkey's foot.

This buck's new antler grew out from under the old antler, which had been cut off but was never cast.

that had the same type of freak antler growth, and all of the antlers are nontypical in conformation because they had to grow out from under the old antler.

Although nontypical antlers often result from physical injury to the buck or to his growing antlers, nontypical antlers can surely be inherited. A buck I photographed in 2005 was from the bloodline of a buck that produced antlers that resembled his. I also surmise that inherited nontypical antlers might be fairly common because, if it has manifested itself in twelve other captive deer, how many bucks in the wild might experience such growth? Most likely, the old antler would fall off before the hunting season started and so the condition would not be seen.

Antlered Does

Antlers grow on only one of three thousand to four thousand does, and the antler types fall into three categories. The highest percentage I ever heard of was at Camp Wainwright in Alberta, Canada. At these controlled hunts, every animal was accounted for, so the figures are correct. Out of 517 does shot, eight had velvet-covered antlers for a ratio of one out of sixty-five. Each of these does had milk in her bag, proving that they had given birth to fawns. The high ratios may have been the result of inbreeding among the fenced-in animals. And, if so, this would be a genetic condition.

Roughly one in every three thousand does may have enough testosterone in her system to cause antler growth.

The male hormone testosterone and the female hormone estrogen are usually present in both genders of the vast majority of mammals. Each sex's own hormones suppress that of the other sex under normal conditions. In many human females after menopause, their production of estrogen is curtailed, their voices deepen, and facial hair becomes more evident. In deer, where a doe's estrogen levels are not as high as normal, she may produce antlers that will reach the velvet stage, even though she can breed and produce fawns.

Most of the time, the testosterone in her system, although high, is not high enough to complete the antler cycle and the antlers do not harden, nor is the velvet rubbed off. The soft antlers usually freeze off and the bases are cast. I have heard of no cases of does having the peruke effect found in castrated bucks.

In the second scenario, the doe has more testosterone than estrogen and produces larger antlers that go through the entire antler cycle. Such a doe is more male than female, and although having female sex organs, she does not go through the estrus cycle and cannot breed, nor does she use the antlers for fighting.

A reader of my columns in *Deer and Deer Hunting* wrote to tell me of a big eight-point buck he shot that had the organs of both sexes. Such a buck/doe would be a hermaphrodite; this is the rarest of the three sexual conditions and the animal would be sterile. The animal had polished antlers and was scale weighed at 196 pounds, hog dressed.

The Casting of Antlers

Many factors determine when a buck casts his antlers. When a buck's testosterone level drops, a layer of specialized cells at the base of the antlers called "osteoclasts" begin to

The "spicules" on the antler's base show where the calcium was reabsorbed.

reabsorb the calcium from the antlers. The solid mass of the antler becomes grainy until only chambered "spicules" remain.

Eventually, the weight of the antler causes the remaining spicules to break and the antler drops off at the pedicle. The calcium reabsorption occurs exceedingly fast. One day the antlers can't be knocked off and the next day they fall off. The little pinpricks that can be felt on the base of a cast antler are the remnants of the spicules.

My friend Fred Space, owner of the Space Farms Zoo and Museum in Sussex, New Jersey, had a captive whitetail that held his antlers into March and was still aggressive. When Fred had to enter the pen, he carried a steel pipe for protection. One such day, the buck charged, and Fred hit his antlers so hard that he knocked the buck to the ground. Fred thought he had killed him and planned to saw off the antlers. But before Fred returned with a saw, the buck had staggered to his feet, antlers intact. Two days later the antlers fell off, of their own accord, and the buck lost his aggressiveness.

Under ordinary conditions throughout most of the country, the rutting season occurs from the fifteenth of October through the fifteenth of December. The big bucks usually cast their antlers first because of the stress they have encountered during the breeding season. Stress signals the pituitary to produce corticoids, which causes testosterone levels to plummet, resulting in the casting of the buck's antlers in about two weeks. Injury, which also results in stress, can also cause an early casting of a buck's antlers.

Weather plays its part in the timing of antler casting. If the weather is mild, the deer can move about much more freely and thus gather more food, and well-fed deer carry their antlers longer. Conversely, a severe winter will cause the deer to yard up, where they will not only be on short rations but will also be subject to stress from the cold.

Not all bucks cast their antlers at the same time.

Despite the fact that all deer eat far less food during the winter months, my captive deer have access to all the food they can eat and usually carry their antlers until around the first of March.

However, not just captive deer can carry their antlers for longer than normal periods of time. One year, dozens of readers of my column in *Deer and Deer Hunting* magazine wrote to tell me that, due to a very mild winter, deer in Ohio, Illinois, and Indiana, carried their antlers through March and even into April. Those states have some of the best soils in the country and produce abundant farm crops, and the mild winter facilitated the deer in their search of food.

Occasionally, even genetics plays a role in the casting of antlers. For twenty-one years, I was the chief gamekeeper for the Coventry Hunt Club, the largest hunting club in New Jersey. At that time, the state had a six-day, bucks-only hunting season, starting on the first Monday in December, which usually occurred somewhere around the fifth through the seventh. Even at that early date, a number of our biggest bucks had already cast their antlers. Seeing the raw pedicles, we knew they were bucks, but we couldn't shoot them because, by New Jersey law, they had to have at least three inches of antler growth on one side. I once shot a buck and, while grabbing him by the antler to drag him out of the woods, the antler fell off in my hand. A friend of mine shot a buck, and when the buck dropped to the ground, both antlers fell off at the same time. My friend had no trouble at the check station because he had both of the antlers and the warden could see that the pedicle was raw. The earliest I have ever seen a buck cast his antlers was November 25.

There is no pain and very little bleeding associated with the casting of a buck's antlers. The skin surrounding the burr may tear slightly but I have never seen more than a few drops of blood. The same valves that shut off the blood vessels when the antlers are growing shut them off when the antlers are cast. The base of a cast antler is convex, leaving a concave pit on the top of the pedicle. The pedicle scabs over within twenty-four hours and the new skin covers the entire surface of the pedicle in about six weeks. That skin forms the basis for the new velvet in the spring.

Sheds

Today, many hunters are spending more time hunting for "sheds," the antlers cast by bucks, than they actually spend hunting for deer. Finding the cast antlers may also help the hunter to be more successful in locating a good buck the following hunting season. The cast antlers make great trophies and can be used for many purposes, such as knife handles, door pulls, and chandeliers. Even more important, the cast antlers give definite proof which bucks made it through the hunting season, how large the bucks are, and where they might be found next season. Hunting for sheds is one of the best ways of scouting for deer. I am also cognizant of the fact that bucks might not live in the same area in which they spent the winter. Yet for any hunter who lives in an area where the deer do not yard up, finding sheds indicates home range.

In all the time that I have spent hunting for sheds (and I have hundreds in my collection) I have only found four pairs that indicated that both antlers dropped off at the same time. Most of the time a buck will lose one antler and not drop the second for another hour, day, or week. It is not an easy job to find the cast antlers because a single antler does not stand out, as antlers do on a buck's head. This is especially true when

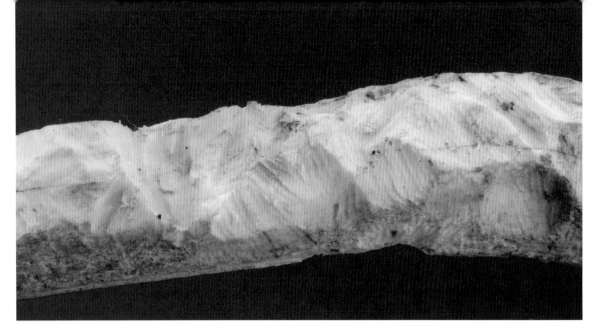

Antlers not found soon after being cast will be eaten by rodents for the calcium.

the antler lands on the curve of its beam with the tines pointing upward: a few blown leaves will soon obscure it from sight. I recently read of a farmer in Indiana who found two large antlers and wished that he hadn't. The antlers were lost to view in his hayfield and were discovered when they punctured two of his tractor tires. He thought the cost of six hundred dollars for getting the tires replaced was a little high for a pair of sheds.

There is a ready market for big-paired sheds. A friend of mine received thousands of dollars for a set in the 195-inch Boone and Crocket class. A pair of 120-inch antlers will bring eighty dollars; 150-inch is worth four hundred dollars; while 180-inch will bring around $2,500.

If you don't find antlers a short time after they are cast, they will soon be consumed by rodents and other animals desperate for the minerals.

On several occasions I have even seen deer chewing on cast antlers.

$125,000 Bucks

Getting back for just a moment to deer farming, I'd like to give you a little background on one of the most famous breeder bucks in the country. The buck's photo graced the cover of a number of outdoor magazines a few years ago.

That buck was raised in Pennsylvania and sold for forty-five thousand dollars. I believe he was sold once more before he ended up in Arkansas for a price of around $125,000. According to Dr. Harry Jacobson, a pioneer in the artificial insemination of deer, sixty-five "straws" (or vials) can be gotten from one ejaculation from a buck. A mild electric shock ejaculates the buck and the collected semen is divided into sixty-five straws. The going price for a straw from a big buck is $1,500, or $97,500 per ejaculation. I fully realize that the $97,500 is not all profit but at $1,500 per straw it doesn't take long to get the purchase price of $125,000 back—and that ain't straw. Just recently on the Internet, I saw an advertisement for the semen of some huge bucks offered for sale for four-thousand dollars per straw. Big bucks are big business!

Largest Antlers in the Deer Family

The Alaskan-Yukon moose has the largest antlers of any living member of the deer family.

The greatest spread of antlers in the Boone and Crockett record book is 80 3/8 inches. Such antlers would weigh about ninety-five pounds.

The largest antlers ever recorded were on the fossilized remains of the giant Irish elk (*Megaloceros giganteus*) that became extinct about ten thousand years ago. The greatest spread that I can find record of from this giant is thirteen feet. Although there are dozens of these heads in museums around the world I do not have the recorded weight of any, but I would estimate them to be at least two hundred pounds. It is thought the animal's antlers became so large and cumbersome that they became a handicap that it could not overcome.

Are our deer bred in captivity moving in the same direction? The cost of producing huge antlers will eventually outweigh the benefits accruing from producing them.

The Alaskan-Yukon bull moose has the largest antlers of any animal in the world today.

Chapter 8

Food and When It's Eaten

Plant Food Options

Through the process of photosynthesis, green plants use the energy from the sun to assimilate water, atmospheric carbon dioxide, and soil nutrients they need to grow, reproduce, and sustain themselves. Deer then assimilate plant nutrients for their own growth, reproduction, and sustenance.

Deer are selective feeders. Their long narrow muzzle allows them to be choosy when browsing. In roughly this order of preference, deer favor the young shoots and buds of woody plants (known as "browse"), nuts and seeds (known as "mast crops"), broad-leaved herbaceous plants (known as "forbs"), and, finally, grasses. Deer prefer to eat browse over all other food stuffs, except mast in the fall. They are known as browsers, rather than grazers.

Some years ago, deer researchers in the northeastern United States determined that deer ate almost seven hundred different plants, and I am sure if that list were reconsidered today, the number would be much higher. This is partly because new—often invasive alien—plants have naturalized and deer are eating many of them.

Browse

For firewood recently, I felled a huge black birch inside my deer research center. Even though my deer have access to unlimited food, they disregarded foods I'd provided in

Deer are primarily browse-feeding animals, preferring it to all other types of food.

order to browse off the tip of every branch they could reach. They were eating about three inches off every twig and ate nothing larger in diameter than a wooden match (three millimeters). In the wild, deer eat twigs slightly larger, and in times of starvation, deer eat twigs as thick as a wooden pencil, roughly a quarter inch in diameter. My deer ate the twigs because it is their preferred food.

Deer prefer smaller twigs because new bark is higher in protein than old bark, and there is a greater ratio of bark to wood. The nutrients lie in the bark. The older and larger the twig, the lower its percentage of protein because there is less bark relative to indigestible cellulose and lignin in the woody material.

It takes about 1,400 matchstick-size twigs to weigh a pound.

As I write this, I have just entered the house with a bunch of twigs my deer couldn't reach. Using pruning shears, I cut off the exact same size twigs that the deer had been eating. There were 1,408 twigs to the pound, and a deer needs eight pounds of food per one hundred pounds of body weight, roughly twelve pounds for an average 150-pound buck. At 1,408 twigs to the pound, it would take 16,896 twigs to feed one 150-pound buck for just one day.

Figures like that help us understand why, with an overabundance of deer, there can be no reforestation and why deer can do extensive damage to expensive shrubs and young trees in a short time. A single deer can eat every twig off three eighty-dollar yew trees in just one evening.

One of the most important components of the wild environment is known as "edge." Edge occurs wherever two different types of habitat join—where forest abuts water, where woodland abuts a field, and so on. Edge is particularly important where a woodland and field join. That is, a woodland may provide too much shade for undergrowth to flourish and sustain deer. But there's often enough sunlight at the edge to stimulate a profusion of nourishing low, brushy growth. That brush will provide food and refuge for a tremendous variety of creatures, as well as food for the deer. Brush rows growing between two cultivated fields have an almost unlimited growth of browse in the form of new seedlings and many types of berry bushes and lots of twigs. Brush rows thrive because they get sunlight on both sides. The easiest way to monitor a deer herd's population is to check for evidence of browsing in the brush rows.

Overbrowsing

I was once hired by the family that owned the Pittsburgh Paint Company to estimate the deer population on their huge property and then to make suggestions on managing it. I didn't need to census their deer herd. Driving through the property, I knew immediately it had too many deer. There was no brush growing along the edge of the woodland that joined the fields because the deer had eaten it all, creating a browse line as high as they could reach. A browse line is always an indication that the deer population has exceeded the land's carrying capacity. A browse line proclaims that there are more deer than there is food to feed them.

This browse line was created by deer overbrowsing the tree line along a field.

In whitetail country, a browse line can be recognized at a long distance. Beneath its seven-foot height, you can clearly see into the shadowed woods. From ground level to seven feet, the deer will have eaten nearly every piece of vegetation. Once the easily reached brush is eaten, deer will stand on their hind legs to reach higher. A fawn standing on its hind legs can reach to about five feet. An adult doe can reach up to about six feet—an adult buck to about seven feet, which is why the mortality of fawns is high in times of starvation; they can no longer reach food.

I have often watched deer balance on their hind legs to feed on high branches, but I have never seen them steady themselves against the trunk of a tree or attempt to climb as domestic goats do. Nor have I seen deer try to bend a sapling down with their weight as moose do.

Not only do most deer populations soon expand beyond their food source, most woody plants need ten or twenty years to grow beyond the deer's reach. Often, this growth occurs so subtly that many folks are unaware of it. I have witnessed such transitions many times in my long life.

The first game managers in this country were the Indians. They knew that deer preferred browse

This young buck is creating a browse line by feeding as high as possible.

to most other plants, and browse grew most abundantly on land that had been cleared and allowed to grow back into woodland. Prior to the arrival of Europeans, Indians were still living in a Stone Age culture. They couldn't clear large tracts of land with stone tools, so they used fire. From time to time, lightning set fire to the woodlands and burned huge tracts. Deer were attracted to these burned-over tracts within weeks after the fires, as new grasses started to sprout. Within one year, berry bushes became established, and deer love the various types of bushes and their berries. Fire also allowed broad-leaved forbs to proliferate in the bright sunshine. Within three years, "pioneer" trees such as birches, aspens, and maples sprouted in the shade provided by the berry

New growth in plant succession makes fabulous deer food.

bushes. In five to seven years the burned area was blanketed by a profusion of browse, a whitetail's idea of heaven, and deer were drawn to these areas like iron filings to a magnet. With an unlimited amount of highly nutritious food, the deer became larger and heavier. They also reached their highest breeding potential because there was low natal mortality among those well-fed fawns. The Indians, too, were drawn to these areas because to most Indians in the eastern half of North America the white-tailed deer was a major source of meat and clothing. Sometime between the 1100s and the 1300s, the Indians in the East changed from being strictly hunter-gatherer nomads to being more sedentary with the introduction of such crops as maize, beans, and squash—"the three-sister crops." Planted together in the same fields and eaten together, these three crops provided a balanced diet. Of course, the deer were drawn to these crops, too. To protect their crops, and to get meat, the Indians tried to eliminate the deer from the area around their villages. To lure deer away from their crops, the Indians managed the forests by burning, to establish new growth for the deer to browse upon. Their hunting camps were located at these managed areas, which were often several days distance from their villages.

Plant Succession

Plant succession is the natural vegetative growth progression that occurs on burned-over and clear-cut land. This succession begins with annual grasses, often overtaken by perennial forbs, and progresses to shrubs and tree seedlings that eventually become climactic forests wherever rainfall is sufficient to support such growth. In ten to fifteen years, the tree seedlings will have grown to saplings and will be beyond the deer's reach. Within twenty years, the young "bean-pole" saplings are too tall to be fed upon by deer and are producing enough shade to kill off most of the understory plants the deer could feed on. If a deer herd is large enough, their browsing may retard this process, but they cannot prevent eventual growth back to climactic forest. If oak trees are dominant, as they are in many areas in the northeastern states, they will eventually produce excellent mast crops in the form of acorns, but except for that, such forests produce little deer food. The Indians knew that and kept large areas in brush land by constantly burning off forest that had reached the climactic stage. If at all possible, deer never eat just one type of food during a single feeding. They intuitively know what nutritionists advise people to do: eat a balanced diet.

This poor deer habitat includes "bean-pole" woods of gray birch that have grown beyond a deer's reach.

The Browsing Ruminant

While feeding, deer walk along taking a bite here and a bite there and basically keep right on moving. There are evolutionary advantages in this behavior:

- Overbrowsing occurs less if deer keep moving because plants recuperate quickly from the loss of a few twigs or leaves. Every plant has its own tolerance to browsing; some can have as much as 50 percent of their vegetation removed and thrive, others much less so.
- Ordinarily, a deer feeds into the wind so the scent of any potential danger is carried to it. Predators usually stalk their prey into the wind so that their scent is not carried

to the prey species, which means they are following their prey. With every step the deer takes, it is one step farther from the stalking predator; the shorter-legged predator has to take more steps, and with every step it may betray its presence. Deer don't run when they can walk, and they walk only enough to feed and reach water, except during the breeding season. They seem to sense that they are more vulnerable to predators while moving, even more so if they are running. A running deer cannot see, hear, or smell danger as well as it can while standing or lying still.

Over most of the year, whitetails remain bedded sixty to seventy percent of the time, usually feeding five times every twenty-four hours. They feed moderately at around 2:00 a.m., heavier around dawn, lightly between 10:30 to 11:30 a.m., heaviest around sunset and lightly again between 10:00 to 11:00 p.m. While the average deer eats eight to twelve pounds of vegetation in a twenty-four hour period, it consumes only two to three pounds at one time because it is feeding five times per day. During the hunting season, if the pressure is intense, deer forego eating during the daylight hours, eating all of their food under the cover of darkness.

Movement Patterns and Feeding Schedules

There are correlations between the movement patterns of deer and humans during bedding periods. For example, we humans roll over or move twenty-eight times each night on average. This prevents our muscles from tensing up and also prevents calcium from leaching from our bones. Deer also move frequently during bedding periods and probably for the same reasons. They often arise and stretch deeply by flexing their spines both up and down before lying down again in the same spot.

They may also get up and turn around a time or two before dropping down again. Or they may get up and move just a few feet before bedding again. Deer can defecate while bedded, but need to get up to urinate. Yawning is an involuntary action done by most mammals to rid the lungs of excess carbon dioxide. Yawning occurs both before and after sleep or other periods of inactivity. Because deer spend 60 to 70 percent of their time bedded, they do a great deal of yawning and stretching.

Most hunters are aware of the deer's two main feeding periods at dawn and dusk but we don't see what takes place after dark. I, too, was not aware that the deer were so active at 2:00 a.m., until telemetry and statistics proved it.

Mark Stallings, a good friend of mine, is head of the risk management department for one of the country's largest nationwide trucking companies. He has kept track of all

When deer arise they stretch their spines by flexing both up and down.

types of collisions and accidents for years because all need to be reported to his office. Mark began compiling the data shown on the accompanying table. The table shows the time of the day when most of the accidents took place—2:00 to 3:00 a.m. That was a surprise.

When I inquired of Mark whether the timing might be skewed because more trucks travel at night, he assured me that his company's trucks moved constantly and consistently twenty-four hours a day. Another surprise was the 10:30 to 11:30 a.m. activity period—a time slot that most hunters don't bother to hunt. But I know why. Hunters are well aware of the deer's two feeding periods at dusk and dawn. They do their best to be in the woods in the morning, early enough to waylay the deer as they

10-Year Deer Accident Study-Hour

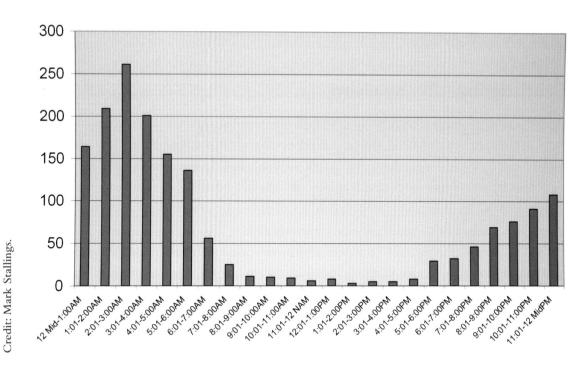

Credit: Mark Stallings.

head back from feeding to their bedding areas for the day. In October, the sun rises roughly at about 6:30 a.m., with the legal shooting time a half hour before that. Most hunters want to be in their stands by at least 5:30 a.m. to give birds and other disturbed wildlife time to quiet down before the legal hunting time. That means most hunters have to rise early enough to dress, grab a bite of breakfast, and get to their stands by 5:30 a.m. By 9:30 a.m., most hunters mistakenly assume the action is over for the morning. They have been up for five and a half hours and may be getting sleepy, want a cup of coffee, and feel the need to stretch their legs. If the weather is cool, they may be chilled from inactivity. So they walk back to their car, camper, or cabin and relax until it's time to return to their stand for the afternoon vigil. At the 10:30 a.m. period, deer usually feed in their bedding area and don't come out into the fields, so hunters may not even see them.

Long bedding times are common because, as ruminants, deer are able to eat a large amount of food in a very short time and then retire to protective cover and re-chew and digest the food in comparative safety. During the hunting season, normal feeding schedules are disrupted because deer will only feed if they feel secure. If hunting pressure is heavy, they will feed only after dark. In winter, according to the severity of the weather, a deer will be bedded for 80 to 90 percent of the time. In winter, deer will feed according to the weather conditions, rather than their more predicable schedule spring through fall.

Feeding by the Seasons

In the early spring, deer feed heavily on the emerging forbs and grasses, which are high in protein. At this time, protein is especially vital because bucks are growing their antlers and does are about to give birth or are nursing their young. Deer tend to be least active during the June and July period, mainly because the summer's heat induces lethargy in deer, as it does in humans. During this period, deer eat only enough to meet their daily body-maintenance requirements.

That all changes in mid–August as photoperiodism causes "hyperphagia" to kick in. Now, deer begin to gorge themselves to build up the fat reserves their bodies intrinsically crave before the breeding season and the winter. Fat-producing carbohydrates are needed now. Acorns are a deer's preferred food as soon as they start to drop in

Deer will often paw down through the snow to feed on grass.

September. In a good year, a stand of mature oaks will produce as many as five hundred pounds of acorns per acre. Most oaks are fifteen years old before they produce their first crop of acorns, and most need to be about thirty years old before they are mature enough to produce acorns on a regular basis. Red, black, and chestnut oaks usually produce a crop of acorns every year, although reduced rainfall makes some years less productive than others. White oaks produce more sporadically, and that is unfortunate for deer. Of all the varieties of oaks, deer prefer the acorns of the white oak because they contain the least amount of tannic acid. Although the chestnut, or basket, oak produces the largest of all acorns, its acorns are the least favored because of their high tannic-acid content. The fall of 2005 produced the heaviest crop of acorns I have ever seen over the entire northeastern states.

Deer and other mammals grow fat faster on acorns than on any other natural food. Acorns are easily gathered, crushed, and assimilated. Deer also feed heavily upon hickory nuts, although their shells are much harder than those of acorns. Deer do not eat the black walnut because the shells are too thick. Deer avidly eat American beechnuts, but the trees produce a crop only about every five years. The bucks also eat the inner bark of the trees they rub.

Most whitetails also have access to farmland corn crops, another good source of carbohydrates, as are apples. Most farmers don't mind deer feeding upon fallen apples because most farmers don't salvage dropped fruit for cider. And many farmers don't begrudge the apples that deer eat directly from the trees; what really hurts financially are the many young apple trees killed by bucks rubbing trunks with their antlers.

When I was growing up on the family farm, we

Apples are a favorite food. Deer know where every apple tree is in their area.

could not raise soybeans because deer nipped off the first two leaves as soon as they unfurled.

Conflicts with Farmers

In many parts of the country where deer populations have exploded, the amount of financial damage to agricultural crops is astronomical. A friend of mine who farms more than 2,500 acres estimates his annual loss to deer exceeds twenty thousand dollars. Deer love to feed upon the corn silk, and when they eat it, a growing ear will be stunted.

The deer also wreak havoc on my friend's alfalfa fields. Each year he applies for a farm deer-culling permit, allowing him to shoot the deer in his crop fields. His shooters donate the meat to food banks. But even harvesting seventy to eighty deer each year does not keep my friend's deer population under control. It is unfortunate that deer have to be culled in such a manner, but there are no longer enough hunters in our area to control deer numbers. And farming is a risky business at best.

Better to Be Fat

In the fall, a deer in excellent condition will have as much as 40 percent of its body weight in fat.

This fat serves the dual purpose of providing insulation against the cold and providing nourishment in times of food shortage. Through research, we know that deer in such condition can actually go sixty-five days without a mouthful of food if they are not subject to stressful situations, which burns excessive calories. Most of the fat will lie just under the skin, which I have seen as much as one-inch thick over the deer's back and hams. The intestines will be enveloped in what resembles a basketball net of fat. In the pelvic arch, fat globules will be clustered like a bunch of grapes. When a killed deer is hung outdoors to cool down over a chilly night, this fat crumbles very easily. The hardest chilled fat is found in the region of the deer's brisket. Fat will be interlaced between all of the major muscles.

During the rutting season, all deer lose weight. Does may lose up to 10 percent of their body weight because bucks chase them so much of the time. Bucks lose 20 to 25 percent of their weight because they are doing the chasing. If a severe winter sets in before the bucks can regain some of their lost fat stores—causing a total loss of one-third their pre-rut weight—they will usually die during the winter. In all deer, all body

Deer store fat beneath their skin and between their muscles. Their inner organs are enveloped in a network of fat.

growth stops around the last week of November. At that time, it is more important for the fawns to acquire more body fat than to grow larger.

Hellenette Silver first suggested that a deer's basic metabolism slowed down as a survival factor during the winter months when food was in short supply. Later research did not find evidence of a slowed metabolic rate and suggested that inactivity on the deer's part reduced appetite. I do know that from about the first of December until the latter part of February, my research deer herd prefer to eat only about 50 percent of the amount of food they eat during the rest of the year. November 2008 was especially cold, and my deer noticeably curtailed their eating on the twenty-first. If inactivity is the cause for reduced appetite, it simply means what was thought to be an adaptive condition has instead become a feeding strategy, but the result will remain the same: the deer will be able to survive on less food.

Starvation Time

When the temperature drops to twenty-two degrees Fahrenheit or the snow reaches a depth of fourteen inches, northern whitetails will head to their traditional winter yards. Well-fed adult deer can stand extreme cold but not wind, so their winter yards are usually located in low-lying white cedar or other conifer swamps, or in thick brushy cover,

Conifer trees hold most of the snow aloft on their branches.

anything to break the force of the wind. In going to a traditional yard, most deer travel five to fifteen miles, with some deer traveling up to twenty-five miles. In my part of New Jersey, deer seldom yard up, but a severe winter will force them into thick stands of red cedar or rhododendron. Not only do the conifer areas break the wind, but they create their own microclimate. Conifers usually hold aloft as much as 75 percent of all of the fallen snow, allowing deer to move about under them more freely. You may have noticed how a tree's trunk melts the snow around its base. It does this not only by absorbing the sun's rays, no matter how weak, but the tree itself also gives off a slight amount of heat. When it comes to survival, every single degree helps.

Because most deeryards are traditional, almost all of the available food has long been eaten. The deer tramp out a network of trails that allows them to move about, seeking whatever food they can reach, but what they find is of such poor nutritional value that they operate at a deficit and must fall back on their body reserves. Bucks, being larger and better able to process coarse food, often live on the periphery of the yards. Snow depths of twenty inches or more usually confine the deer to their yards until spring because travel is so difficult, and if the wind is constant, most deer will not leave their yards to look for food. The exception is farmland deer that temporarily yard up; if they have been feeding upon corn or soybeans, they will brave the elements to reach any nutritious food they know is there. I first became aware of

Here, thousands upon thousands of deer pellets and heavily browsed cedar trees show that this wintering deeryard is overused to the point of being a death trap.

this when I was chief gamekeeper for the Coventry Hunt Club. I had planted rape, a cabbage-type plant that the deer usually didn't touch until after frost. The deer had fed upon the crop heavily throughout November. The snows started in December and didn't quit for most of the winter, and we ended up getting a whopping sixty-three inches. What was also unusual was that the temperature dropped to almost zero and stayed there for three weeks. Despite the fact that the snow in December was about twenty-eight inches deep, forcing the deer to bound in order to move, they came out of the sheltering cedars to feed upon the rape every day.

By February that year, the snow was so deep that the deer could not come out to feed. Chet Kimble and Johnny Trimper had been cutting timber all fall on land leased by the club, and continued to do so even though the snow was deep. A large number of the deer had moved close to their lumbering operation to feed on the treetops of the felled trees before the snow had started to fall. As the snow piled up, they moved even closer. Each morning when the men started their chain saws, it was as if they rang a dinner bell. The deer would start to feed as soon as the trees dropped.

At that time, New Jersey still had a bucks-only season and, although we knew we had too many deer, we could not properly manage the deer herd by shooting a large number of the does. The fall of 1960 had been very poor for mast crops, so our deer went into winter in poor shape. By February, it was evident that starvation would be rampant. The deer were eating the red cedar and rhododendron in the areas where they had sought shelter and were dying with their stomachs full, because neither provides any nutrition. Although white cedar is a very nutritious food, red cedar is not. Our only recourse was to feed the deer if we hoped to save a breeding nucleus.

I am against feeding deer when other options are available, but I am all for it as a last recourse. If the deer had been in good condition, I would not have attempted to feed them because deer in winter should not be disturbed, as that requires of them a caloric expenditure at a time when those calories cannot be replaced. If deer are to be fed, they should be fed foods that they are accustomed to. Just as "feed them with an axe" is good advice, those deer were getting good food where the logging was taking place. With members of the club, I went into the cedar areas and felled many of the maples that grew there. To feed deer, I do not cut the tree off but cut it just enough to have it fall. This will make the tops available to the deer, while allowing the tree to keep growing the following year and produce more deer food. To do this, make the cut about four feet above the ground. This will cause the tree to send up numerous "sucker" shoots, which are also good deer food. Most of the deer in the valley had fed upon corn, so it was a food that they recognized. Do not attempt to feed corn to deer that have never eaten it because they will not recognize it as a food. Deer can be fed good-quality alfalfa or clover hays, but do not feed them timothy. Timothy is good horse hay, but ruminants get little or no nutrition from it.

Despite our best efforts, our losses were staggering. I found twenty-seven deer dead of starvation within a square mile of cedar copse, and I estimate that we lost at least two hundred deer on the club land.

I brought several of the starving seven-month-old fawns to my home and attempted to feed them the best browse available.

But they wouldn't eat it. Nor would they eat ground dairy feed. I tried to give them fortified milk supplements but couldn't get them to swallow it. It was then that I learned that once a deer has lost one-third of its body weight, it will die.

The feeding of starving deer should be done carefully and gradually. Researchers found that starving deer still had enough microorganisms in their rumens to process

Lethargy and gauntness are characteristics of starving deer.

Author in 1961 with one of the starving fawns he tried to save.

This is one of twenty-seven deer that starved to death in one small deeryard.

food, but the deer developed "rumenitis" (bloat) if they had access to too much food too soon.

Starving humans cannot be introduced to unlimited food either.

As a deer starves, its stored fat is metabolized from beneath the skin first, then from inside the body cavity between its muscles, and lastly from the marrow in its bones. Essential fatty acids (aceto-acetate and hydroxybutyrate) are derived from the oxidation of these body fats. Anyone who finds a deer carcass, or even its skeleton, can verify if it died of starvation by checking the fat content in the femur bone, in the ham of the hind leg. The simplest way is to prop the femur up on a rock and stomp on it with your foot. Even if the bone is old, there will be shreds of desiccated marrow inside.

The marrow in the bone of a well-fed deer is pure white, looks like suet, and is about 95 percent pure fat. As more fat is utilized, the marrow changes color and consistency. It turns yellow when the fat content is 70 to 90 percent, pink when it is below 50 percent and a bright red when it is below 10 percent. In this latter stage, it has the consistency of and resembles jellied cranberry sauce.

At the same time that the fat in the marrow is being withdrawn from the deer's bones, its muscles are also being catabolized and used for nourishment. This weakens the deer so that it finally is not able to stand. That's why a starving deer seems to be unafraid of a human; it is simply too weak to be able to escape and its brain may no longer be transmitting a danger signal.

In extremely cold weather, even if food is available, deer will seldom move before mid-morning, and all movement in the cold darkness is kept to a bare minimum. In areas where the deer do not yard up, they will seek out the eastern side near the top of any knoll or hill in order to catch the first rays of sunshine in the morning. They avoid the hollows because that's where the cold settles, and even in the coldest weather the hollow is often ten to fifteen degrees Fahrenheit colder than higher ground.

The first vegetation at the end of winter will be sprouting in the swamps and spring runs. Deer are quick to leave their yards as soon as the snowmelt is sufficient to allow them to move freely. However, a late snowstorm or a sudden drop in temperature will send them scurrying back to their yards.

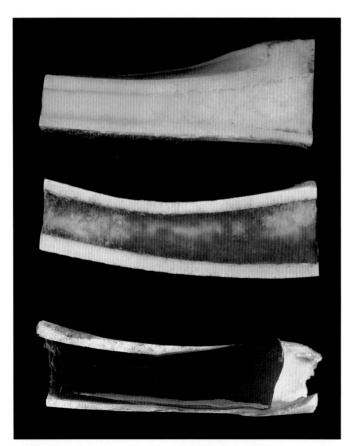

Bone marrow in healthy deer is about 95 percent fat and is pure white. As the deer starves, the fat is withdrawn and marrow color changes to pink. A deer that dies of starvation has marrow the color and consistency of cranberry sauce.

Water

Deer need water every day. In temperatures above freezing, they drink it as liquid. In freezing weather, they eat snow and lick ice.

Although deer can satisfy the need for water by eating snow or licking ice, they prefer to eat melting snow when possible for its much higher water content. In the

To get water in the winter, deer will eat snow and lick ice.

spring, much of their water intake comes from the vegetation they eat. Dew or rain-drops, clinging to the vegetation the deer eat, provide additional moisture. In the summer, deer will go to water several times a day and drink one to two gallons at a time. Unlike members of the feline and canine families, which lap water, deer drink by suction. Besides providing the water needed for their bodies, water also cools the deer down. In many areas, the deer also feed in rivers, ponds, and lakes. This has a four-fold purpose: the deer get water to drink; they cool off; they get some relief from plagues of biting, stinging insects; and they get mineral-rich vegetation to eat. Most of the rainwater runs off into the rivers, ponds, and lakes, bearing with it the minerals found in the area. The minerals settle to the bottoms of these bodies of water, and the plants growing in the water contain many more minerals than those growing on land. A filamentous alga, found floating on the surface of ponds, is a very rich source of protein for deer.

In summer, deer feed upon mineral-rich water plants.

Chapter 9

Communication

Many people mistakenly assume that deer and other wildlife are "dumb" and unable to communicate because they don't use the same type of vocalizations and communication we use. Not only don't we smell much of wildlife's communication, we don't often see it, and we usually can't hear it. We are learning more all the time, but we're simply not sensorially gifted enough to notice, let alone fully understand, deer communication. Here, I'll share what I have personally observed and have learned from published research, which is likely just the tip of the iceberg.

Most of us think of communication simply as the ability to transmit information. In their book *Animal Communication,* Drs. Hubert and Mable Frings astutely elaborated with this: "Communication is the giving off by one individual of some chemical or physical signal that, on being received by another, influences its behavior."

Today, most of us suffer from communication overload—indeed sensory overload. We are bombarded with communications from Twitter, Facebook, email, computer ads, cell phones, telephones, radios, TVs, newspapers, magazines, books, snail mail, ad infinitum. As a result, we are the most comprehensively informed peoples of all time. There are billions of cell phones in use worldwide. Watching people in malls and other social areas, I have made counts suggesting that one person in five is talking on a cell phone, most of them teenagers.

While we often subject ourselves to sensory overload, that general category of information is tiny compared with the information constantly being disseminated and processed by the white-tailed deer. "Wait a minute," you might say, "How can an animal that can't talk, read, or write do much communicating and information processing?"

The alert posture of this buck will cause the other deer to become instantly alert also.

Types of Communication

Ethologists—scientists who study animal behavior—generally group the messages that animals send under four categories: neonatal, integrative, agonistic, and sexual. Deer use both physical and chemical means to send these messages and to warn of danger, employing fifteen different methods, singly or in concert.

- *Neonatal messages* are all the forms that mother and young use to communicate between themselves.
- *Integrative messages* transmit information about danger, predators, and food. They also invite others to aggregate, congregate, play, groom, and so on. These messages are crucial for animals living in family groups or herds because the cohesion of the group depends upon each member's knowing the familial bonds, age, sex, size, and status of others.
- *Agonistic messages* convey acceptance or submission, as well as threats and challenges that lead to chasing, sparring, or fighting.
- *Sexual messages* lead to courtship and breeding, while also stirring up agonistic behaviors among bucks.

Although information can be sent, it can't be communicated without a receiver.

We humans receive messages through our visual, auditory, olfactory, tactile, and gustatory senses. Unfortunately, we have lost some acuity of these senses that enabled our ancestors to survive. This loss of acuity in some cases has resulted simply from lack of use, most obviously corrected when blind people improve their tactile sense when learning to use their fingertips to read braille print. We can also lose sensorial acuity from abuse—most evident in noise-inflicted hearing loss, chemically damaged olfactory cells, and light-inflicted eye damage.

I discussed the whitetail's five senses in chapter two. Let's now consider how those senses function in communication.

Means of Transmission

That White Tail

The whitetail's namesake, the white underside of its tail, is also its best-known means of communication. That white underside is highly useful in communicating danger to other deer. However, contrary to popular belief, bucks don't always display the white underside when alarmed.

Whitetails are quite aware of their tails as communicators. When running off alarmed, does almost always hold their tail straight up and loosely flop it from side to side. This helps the doe's fawns follow her, especially in shady woods and at night. However, when a buck dashes off, he may or may not flash the underside of his tail. I initially noted that tail flagging among alarmed bucks occurred only about

50 percent of the time. But on closer study, I realized that tail flashing vs. clamping is an individual characteristic. That is, individual bucks tend to do one or the other most of the time. On the other hand, if a buck wants to sneak off, even hurriedly, he'll clamp his tail tightly to his body, turning his rump hair inward so no white is visible. How's that for self-awareness!

Besides flagging their tail upward, alarmed whitetails also flare the white hairs of their rump patch. With tail raised and rump patch flared, a big buck's white namesake measures about eleven inches across, which is quite a large reflective surface. It's often visible more than a quarter mile away, reflecting almost as noticeably as a mirror.

In another type of tail communication, deer switch their tails almost continuously, even when they are not being pestered by flies. This integrative action helps deer remain aware of each other and each other's location, without any additional effort.

Flared tail, rump hair, and tarsal glands alert every deer to potential danger.

In fact, deer have difficulty seeing an immobile deer or person. I have often located deer I could not see until they flicked their tail or ear. On a side note, a feeding deer almost always wags its tail before raising its head.

Neonatal Communication

Communication among deer commences while the fawn is developing in the womb. The fawn first tunes in to its mother's heartbeat and then to the various grunts and bleats that she uses to communicate with other deer. I do not know if the doe deliberately "talks" to the fawns she is carrying, as human mothers talk to their fetus or play music for them. I do know that birds, especially wild turkeys, talk to their developing eggs in the same quieting calls they use after the poults hatch.

As soon as her fawns are born, the doe washes them incessantly with her tongue to remove every trace of blood and amniotic fluid from their coats.

She will eat every scrap of vegetation and even the earth that may be contaminated by those fluids. She does this instinctively, likely not aware that this helps prevent predators from smelling those fluids. In the process, she is also imprinting herself upon her fawns by covering them with the scent of her saliva and acclimating them to her scent and touch. Also, while cleaning her fawns, the mother grunts softly from time to time, the same sort of grunt she will use later to call her fawns from their place of concealment when she comes to nurse them. It seems very odd to me that a doe's fawns will always recognize her grunting, even though she seems unable to recognize her own fawn's bleating, but will respond to the bleat of any fawn. The doe is never sure if the fawn that she approaches is her own until she confirms its identity by its scent. There is a definite breakdown in communication in that instance.

I have heard does making two different sounds when they return to nurse their fawns, which they do four to six times every twenty-four hours. The most common call is a very soft, short grunt, but mothers also make a soft mewing sound. The doe knows the area where she left the fawn but does not know the precise spot, because the fawn picks its own bedding spot and may have shifted before the doe's return. When she comes back to the general area in which she left the fawn and calls, the fawn responds by getting up and approaching the doe.

For the first five days of its life, a fawn is practically odorless. During this period, dogs trained to locate fawns have a great difficulty in doing so. When the fawns are nursing they make a high-pitched murmuring sound of contentment when they are getting enough milk and a slightly higher-pitched, impatient "begging" sound when they are not getting enough. While nursing, the fawns usually make an upward kicking

While washing her newborn fawns, a doe grunts softly, which makes the fawns familiar with her voice.

motion with one of their front feet. While the fawns nurse, the doe licks their anal region, which stimulates their bowels, and the doe consumers their feces as well as urine. She also licks off any milk froth that forms on the fawn's mouth from nursing. Her grooming reduces the fawn's odor much as bathing with unscented soap reduces ours.

If, for some reason, a fawn should become lost from its mother, it will bleat loudly, and believe me, every doe within hearing will come running quickly. If the fawn is being attacked by a predator, its bleating will become longer, louder, and higher pitched according to the intensity of the situation. After a fawn reaches six weeks of age, there is a steadily decreasing response by the doe to its bleating. By then, the fawn can usually outrun most predators, and the doe does not need to be as attentive.

There is one more means of transferring information between the doe and her fawn, and that is by setting an example. When fawns are learning what vegetation to eat, they frequently taste the green stuff that hangs out of their mother's mouth.

Olfactory Communication

Deer live in a world of scent—with sensory messages and sensitivities about which we can only speculate. Deer give off scents from forehead glands, preorbital glands, and nasal glands, as well as from salivary, tarsal, metatarsal, interdigital, and preputial glands. They also give off scent through their urine and feces. With these scents, deer communicate their sex, readiness for sex, status, size, health, foods eaten, familial affiliation, and more.

Deer usually track one another by smelling the scent left on the ground from the interdigital gland between their two main toes or hooves. Apparently, this gland does not begin to function for a week or more after birth because the doe is not able to track her own fawns. Also a survival advantage, this lack of scent makes tracking by predators nearly impossible.

Once the interdigital gland begins functioning, it becomes a major means of communication. As mentioned in chapter three, I discovered that this gland is far more important to the deer than most researchers suspected. I first became aware of its importance when I noticed deer always licking and cleaning the gland after crossing a muddy area, which may have clogged the gland.

Watching deer track one another with their nose to the ground convinced me that a deer's sense of smell is not as good as a dog's. I have seen bird dogs and trail hounds follow the scent of their quarry's body odor that had settled on the vegetation they had passed. That is, the dogs did not need to follow the scent left by footprints. However, deer need to smell the actual tracks. When a buck follows the track of a doe in estrus, he keeps his head to the ground, his tail raised up, and he usually gives a soft grunt every couple of steps.

Tactile Communication

Deer express anxiety by stamping their front feet. At times this is done very softly, as though the foot was going through the motion without the deer being aware of it, but usually one front hoof strikes the ground quite forcibly. This sends a message that can be seen and heard. Its vibrations can also be felt by other deer some distance through the ground. These vibrations are very important because the deer receiving the message may not be able to see the deer sending it or the danger that prompted it. In fact,

The more dominant the buck, the more forehead scent he exudes, and the darker the forehead will be.

any deer passing that spot for the next day or so will be alerted that potential danger was detected there because some of the waxy interdigital-gland scent will remain on the vegetation. The foot stamping is accompanied by body language that also serves to alert every deer within sight. The more anxious the deer stamping its foot, the higher it will hold its head.

Forehead Scent Glands and Licking Sticks

The most common sign of deer we see are tracks. And tracks do leave interdigital scent that other deer can follow. However, the forehead scent is far more important.

The more dominant the buck, the more forehead scent he exudes, and the darker his forehead becomes.

Besides darkening the forehead, in extreme cases the secretions also darken the entire upper part of the face, down the bridge of the nose and the cheeks. When rubbing a four- to six-inch diameter tree, a buck usually rubs his forehead directly between his antlers because that is the only spot with which he can make contact. However, if he rubs a sapling of about one-inch diameter, he prefers to rub the area behind his antlers just in front of his ears, alternating one side and then the other. That area apparently is the most richly endowed with suderiferous glands.

After discovering and filming this rubbing activity, I wrote about what I called the "licking stick." A licking stick is usually a sapling, about the size of your index finger, which through frequent rubbing has been broken off about thirty inches above the ground. People seldom notice a licking stick because, although it has been debarked, there is no hoof scraping nearby or other disturbance that might attract our attention. Although we don't notice these licking sticks, all deer sure do because licking sticks pull in every deer like a magnet pulls in iron filings. Within a single hour or so, I once photographed four different bucks using the same licking stick. Still puzzling to me, bucks vigorously spend two to three minutes rubbing their forehead scent on the sticks and then spend about the same amount of time licking it off. Since my initial observations of deer using the finger-sized saplings, I have seen bucks rubbing in the same manner projecting snags, horizontal branches, vines, hanging branches, and every woody projection they pass.

In making a rub of any kind, the buck is creating a visual sign as well as an olfactory one because the white inner bark he exposes can be seen for a long distance. Bucks frequently make their rubs along the edges of woodland, fields, and such, where they will be more obvious signposts to other deer. This results in the "rub lines" that hunters are also quick to notice.

Let's analyze the messages encoded in a buck rub. First, the buck is identifying himself through the unique scents of his forehead, preorbital, nasal, salivary, and interdigital glands. He deposits these scents when he rubs the scent on the sapling, touches the rub when he smells it and also when he licks the scent off, and then again when he eats some of the inner bark that is exposed. The interdigital scent is distributed when the buck's hooves are splayed apart whenever he rubs with enough effort to lift either his front or hind legs off the ground.

When a buck walks over his home range, or past any brush, he will invariably pause to rub his forehead scent on any projecting piece of vegetation. Bucks rub vegetation

A buck first deposits scent from his forehead gland on the "licking stick."

Next, he licks it off, and no researchers seem to know why.

as frequently as city dogs urinate on fire hydrants and automobile tires. But when bucks merely rub their glands over vegetation, there is usually no visible sign. I have seen this behavior thousands of times.

Deer don't have a territory they defend, but they have a home range. A buck marking projecting branches announces his presence to every other deer: who he is, that he passed by recently, his status, and even his size. How can all that information be deducted from just one swipe of his forehead scent glands over a branch? It's easy for other deer. Every buck knows, or is soon taught, the status of every buck that he has encountered and recognizes the scent of each individual. Buck size can be gauged by the height of the branches rubbed. I have photographed a number of really big bucks standing erect on their hind legs, marking a branch too high for the average buck to reach.

While photographing in West Virginia, I watched a huge buck standing erect on his hind legs, hooking an overhead branch with his antlers. As he released the branch, he would lick it, rub it against his head, coating it with scent. That branch was definite proof that a "big" buck was in the area and for lesser bucks to "give way," which they did.

Hoof Scrapes

I consider scrapes to be the "highway billboard" of a buck's advertising program. He leaves more messages there, at one time, than by any other means. There are two kinds of scrapes: primary and secondary. I will just explain primary scrapes because, in making secondary scrapes, the buck usually skips several steps contained in the primary, and a secondary scrape may not be under an overhead branch.

A buck makes most of his primary scrapes under an overhanging branch and then visits that scrape every time he is in the area. Most scrapes are also visited by every buck that passes through. One popular misconception is that smaller bucks will not use a scrape made by a larger buck, but I have often seen them do so.

A dominant and lesser buck rubbing the same sapling at the same time.

A primary scrape is almost always under a tree where the overhead branches can be rubbed and chewed.

It's true that smaller bucks may be very cautious when they use a scrape made by a dominant buck, but then smaller bucks are always cautious in the vicinity of a dominant buck. Research has shown that the odor of the dominant buck's chemical signposts often causes brain activity in some younger bucks that produces the stress hormones corticoids, which reduces production of testosterone and thereby reduces sexual drive and activities. Many scrapes are used year after year, becoming traditional stops for all bucks in the area.

When on a scrape, the buck first hooks the overhead branch with its antlers. Then the branch is passed over both his forehead and preorbital scent glands. The rubbing of the branch over the preorbital gland is evidently sexual, sensuous, and satisfying because the buck seems to derive much pleasure from doing it. Next, the buck rubs the branch with his nose, thereby depositing nasal scent. Crushing the branch with his molars creates a brush-like tip that will hold more saliva scent than would an un-crushed twig. Starting with his right forefoot, and 85 percent of all animals are right handed, the buck paws the ground two or three times, then paws two or three times with his left forefoot. This tears up the turf and also deposits scent from the buck's interdigital glands. This pawing action is so forceful that it often throws pieces of sod fifteen to twenty feet. Stepping into the center of the area that he has just pawed, the buck balances his weight on his two front feet as he urinates over his tarsal glands while vigorously rubbing the glands against one another. Rarely, the buck will also defecate in his scrape.

Hunters aware of the importance of active scrapes place their elevated deer stands accordingly. The simplest way to determine if a scrape is being used is to rake some leaves over it with a stick. The buck doesn't need to see the bare earth to know where the scrape is because he locates by scent, and fallen leaves often blow into a scrape naturally. If you return to find an uncovered scrape, at least one buck visited after you.

Many times hunters will maintain a vigil over a scrape for a week and never see the buck that made it, nor any other buck for that matter. A dominant buck, during the rutting season, expands his range from the normal two square miles up to eight to ten square miles. The buck will invariably use his scrape when he is in the area again, but that might not be for a week because of the much greater area he is covering.

Or he may be visiting the scrape just at night. I know for a fact that some of the older, dominant bucks, in areas of high hunting pressure, don't move at all during the daylight hours, rutting season or not. That's how they survived long enough to become older, dominant bucks. When I was chief gamekeeper for the Coventry Hunt Club and ran censuses at night using a spotlight, we would see big bucks that we never saw during the daylight hours.

When I'm asked if it is possible to attract bucks to artificial scrapes, I answer resoundingly, "YES!" There are times when hunters locate a good trail crossing without a scrape and they want to add one. To the best of my knowledge, my friend Bob McGuire was the first person to make artificial scrapes. If he wasn't the first one to come up with the idea, he was the first to write the articles I encountered on the subject.

He made his most successful "fake" scrapes simply by cutting off the overhead branch from a scrape that a buck had made and tying it to an overhead branch where he wanted to attract bucks. He wore clean gloves, which he then rubbed in dirt to keep human odor to a minimum. He tied the branch at the same height as the original branch had been. Then, taking a stick, he scraped a circular depression under the branch, just as a buck would do. A liberal application of buck urine was poured in the scrape and it was finished. By using an original overhead branch, it already had a buck's forehead scent gland on it. Bob also had success with making a scrape from scratch by breaking an overhead branch and leaving it hanging, as a buck would do. In that case, he would pour the buck urine over the broken overhead branch and let it drip down into the scrape.

Most secondary scrapes are made on spots where does have urinated, which is why they are usually out in the open. The buck sniffs the wet spot and then curls his upper lip upward to help divert scent to the roof of his mouth. This lip curling, known as "flehmening," is covered in greater detail near the end of this chapter. Then he paws the spot a few times and deposits his own urine on the spot, employing rub-urination.

Both bucks and does have the tarsal glands located on the inside of their legs, the area corresponding to our ankles. Fawns actively start rub-urinating on their glands when they are a week or so old, although I don't know what message the fawns are trying to send.

The tarsal glands have subcutaneous sebaceous glands that exude a clear, oily secretion through the skin via ducts alongside the hair follicles. Erector pili muscles along the side of the hair sheath allow the hair to be contracted so that they are tightly closed and resemble the bristles on a brush used to apply shoe polish. The closed hairs minimize the odor given off by this gland. When the deer is alarmed or aggressive, the erector pili muscles cause the tarsal hairs to be widely flared like a rosette, maximizing the scent dispersal because more surface area is exposed. The secretions of the tarsal glands are basically lipids, and although they do have pheromones of their own, the basic odor is caused by the bacterial action of the urine that is trapped by the fatty residue on the long hairs.

Whitetails of both sexes engage in rub-urination throughout the year, but both sexes do it much more frequently during the rutting season; the more dominant the buck, the more frequently he does it, and the darker the hair tufts are stained. I have seen dominant bucks whose tarsal glands were stained jet black, as were streaks of dark hair on the rear of the deer's foot from the gland down to the hoof.

A secondary scrape is usually made by a buck urinating and scraping on a spot where a doe has urinated.

Deer, both bucks and does, will frequently lick the urine off their own tarsals immediately after urinating.

Lesser bucks in a fraternal group will also lick the urine off the dominant buck's tarsal glands. When two strange dogs meet, they check each other out by smelling the scent in the other's anal gland. When two strange bucks check each other out, they do so by sniffing each other's tarsal glands.

The combined odor of the pheromones and the urine on the tarsal glands gives dominant bucks their strong odor during the rutting season. Under good scenting conditions with low barometer readings and high humidity, I can smell a buck as far away as one hundred to two hundred feet, even after he's left the area. If I can do that, can you imagine how far another deer can smell him?

As a means of self-promotion and advertisement, elk spray urine on the long hairs that hang beneath their necks. Both elk and moose urinate in mud wallows and then

This buck is licking a tarsal gland after urinating on both tarsals.

roll in the goo, coating themselves liberally with the urine-soaked mud. White-tailed, black-tailed, and mule deer urinate on their tarsal glands for the same purpose.

Let's count the different ways the buck employs to get his message out by making a scrape. First, the torn-up earth is both a visual sign, as it is seen for a long distance, and an olfactory one. The odor of freshly disturbed earth is attractive to most animals and causes them to investigate the source, a fact I learned years ago when I did a lot of trapping. The distance the pawed clods of dirt had been thrown would be an indication of the buck's strength. The buck had deposited scent from his forehead, preorbital, nasal, salivary, tarsal, preputial, and interdigital glands. The scent from his preputial gland, located at the tip of his penis sheath, would have been mixed with his urine. His DNA would have told who he was and his status, while his urine and feces—if there were any—would tell of his health and his diet. Food odors can often be detected in both urine and food, as anyone knows who has eaten asparagus. Food particles can often be seen in the feces. The strength of the odor would have told how long it had been since the buck had been there. That's eighteen pieces of information that the buck used to describe himself by making one scrape. For us to confer that much information about ourselves, we would probably have to write a résumé!

Antler Rubs

As to antler rubs on saplings, the buck does not rub all around the trunk, which would girdle the sapling and kill it. On some traditional rubs, where the rubbed sapling might have a three- to four-inch girth, the sapling will continue to grow and the rubbed area will become a barkless, flattened area five to six inches in diameter where regenera-

tion failed to cover the rub. Only big bucks rub big trees. The largest tree I've seen rubbed had a diameter of about twenty inches.

Sneezing and Snorts

I was introduced to the deer vocalization in a most startling fashion. I was actually more than startled—it scared the bejeebers out of me. I was fourteen and stumbling home along our farm's back lane after spending the evening down at the summer bungalows of Manunkachunk colony. I'd been drawn there by several attractive, young "dears." This was 1940 and the war was on in Europe. Flashlights and batteries were almost impossible to buy, and I couldn't have afforded them even if

Trees rubbed repeatedly over the years often develop large flattened surfaces.

they had been available. Besides, we had no electricity on the farm at that time, and I was accustomed to stumbling around in the dark. But I had learned that even on the darkest of nights I could see the lane dimly by not looking directly at it, thus using the rods in the periphery of my eyes.

Anyway, on this darkest of nights, SUDDENLY loud sneezing shattered the stillness. NO ONE ever used our lane at night except me. Then came another sneeze. Ours was a cut-bank lane, which put me on eye level with the field on the left-hand side, the side where the sneeze had come from. From ground level, there is always a slight band of light on the horizon. On the horizon, I saw three deer that had been ALMOST as startled by me as I was by them. Because the breeze was blowing from them toward me, they couldn't tell what I was, but I could see them. To verify with their nose what their ears had warned them of, they circled downwind. And when they caught my scent, they bounded off, snorting explosively with each jump.

That was the first time I had ever heard a deer snort, and I've never forgotten it.

The deer's snort is the sound most frequently heard by humans because it is usually given to warn other deer of potential danger. There are two basic snorts that serve as a warning but elicit two different reactions because of their differing intensities. Deer give the explosive, blasting snort by holding their mouths closed, expelling air forcefully through their nasal passageway, causing the nostrils to flutter. This snort warns every deer within hearing of potential danger, but that is all it does. The other deer

immediately stop what they are doing and try to locate the cause of the alarm, but they don't run off. If they can't locate the reason for the alarm by using their senses, they watch the deer that snorted—if they can see it. The deer do not want to run before the danger has been identified and pinpointed because they don't want to run in the wrong direction. The deer that first snorted will do everything it can to positively identify what alarmed it. It will usually approach the source, either directly or by circling to get

An explosive-whistled snort sends deer flying in all directions.

When something looks suspicious, deer will often bob their heads up and down.

the wind in its favor, while continuing to snort, perhaps stamping its foot at each step, and bobbing its head up and down.

All of this body language is closely monitored by the other deer. If the snorter determines that the danger is not real, it relaxes, calming the other deer, and activities go on as before. If the snorter decides the threat is real danger, it gives a high-pitched whistling snort, made with its mouth held slightly open, and hightails away from the threat. Upon hearing this higher-pitched, whistled snort, every deer in the area explodes into action. There is no hesitancy. There is no questioning. That snort means imminent danger, and in seconds, every deer is gone.

Although snorting is done mainly to warn other deer, it also sends a message to the potential predator that the deer is aware of its presence. Because most predators depend upon surprise to catch deer, the deer's alarm snort may discourage the predator from continuing. In addition, an alerted animal is much more difficult to catch because adrenaline coursing through its system primes it for action.

In addition to the vocalizations of the does and the fawns described earlier in this chapter, bucks have a repertoire of their own. They grunt or blat in different intensities and for different lengths of time. A buck tracking a doe will do so with his head held down to smell her hoofprints and will make a short grunt of moderate volume, as if talking to himself, every few steps that he takes. A buck tending an estrous doe will make a louder, longer grunt. This is given as a warning to satellite bucks that are also interested in the doe. A buck tending a pre-estrous doe that will not stand still for him will make a long, drawn-out grunt that is actually a moan of frustration. I have recorded such moans of twenty seconds in duration. There are times when the frustrated moan is so high pitched that it sounds more like a whine.

Angry bucks will curl their lips, like a dog snarling, and hiss loudly like a broken steam pipe. This is called a "snort-wheeze."

I have documented a number of dominant bucks giving what is referred to as a "snort-wheeze." They gave the loud hissing sound as a warning to other bucks to stay away from the buck's estrus doe.

While hissing, the buck curls his upper lips, much as members of the canine families do when they are showing their canine teeth in a threat gesture. I think the lip curling is a holdover from the time when prehistoric deer actually had long canine teeth, which a few Asian deer still have today. Bull elk also engage in a lot of lip-curling but many of the bulls actually have vestigial canine teeth in their upper jaws.

While talking about elk, it is interesting to note that the more dominant the bull, the more frequently he bugles and the lower the pitch of his bugle, which results from his larger size and chest diaphragm. I have noted that dominant whitetail bucks give a deeper and raspier grunt than do the other bucks. By doing so, the "boss" is advertising his size and status to bucks and does that can't even see him. The lower frequency also allows the sound to travel much farther in a wooded area than would a grunt of higher frequency.

Agonistic, or aggressive, actions are conveyed by vocalizations and emission of scent. But because the sender and the receiver are in close proximity, body language often takes precedence. Like deer, we humans are highly attuned to the body language of others. Many times the truth of the matter is expressed more by body language than by the speaker's words.

Aggressive action by does usually takes place when a dominant animal wants to displace a lesser-ranked animal over food. A doe also becomes aggressive when she

An aggressive doe will signal her intentions by laying her ears back before she rises to strike out with her forefeet.

drives off her yearlings in the spring (as she establishes a birthing territory prior to giving birth to her new fawns) and also during the yearling dispersal time in the fall. Does usually want to be bred by the biggest buck in the area; they might instinctively know that the fawns of such bucks have the best chance of survival. During the rutting season, does will even drive off the lesser bucks. In all of these instances, the doe communicates her aggressive intentions by approaching the lesser buck by holding her head very high, with her ears back close to her head and angled as low as she can make them. This always indicates that the doe is about to rear up on her hind legs and will attempt to strike with her forefeet. Often the doe doesn't need to rear up and strike because her body language is sufficient to make other deer move out of the way. Any deer that fails to heed the warning will be hit with a resounding THUMP that can be heard for a considerable distance. That thumping blow is delivered with force, many times knocking large gobs of hair loose.

The buck on the left is approaching the dominant buck in the nose-touching appeasement gesture.

Bucks in a fraternal group where dominance has been established will approach one another, with the lesser buck showing signs of appeasement.

The submissive buck will approach the dominant buck head-on with his own head lowered. When they meet, both bucks will touch noses, and the lesser buck will again lower his head in an invitation to be groomed, an invitation that is seldom refused. As soon as the dominant buck starts the grooming process, both bucks will then mutually groom each other around the head, defusing any potential thoughts of aggression.

Meeting for the first time, dominant bucks that have not tested each other go through a ritual that has been choreographed in their DNA. Each buck knows his approximate size and the exact size of his antlers (intrinsic knowledge, self-awareness), so he knows at a glance how his rival's antlers compare. Yet it's not just body weight and antler size that count, even though they are often the main factors. Age, experience, and attitude can be equally important. The key point is that *only bucks that deem themselves equals will fight*. Lesser bucks acknowledge submission immediately by breaking

Only bucks that feel equal to one another will fight.

off eye contact and either leaving the area or by lowering their head and pretending to graze. When unsure of the other's status, bucks will often rub-urinate to release the scent of their urine in the air. Redirecting aggression, one or both bucks may rub saplings or thrash bushes to show the other just how tough each is.

When two bucks consider themselves equals, they usually dispense with such preliminaries and signify their "put-up-or-shut-up" attitude by giving each other the "hard stare." Each buck will stare directly at his opponent, and if neither backs down, each will tuck in his chin, which tilts his antlers forward into the fighting position, his ears will go back, and erector pili muscles cause all of his hair to stand on end. The erected hair maximizes perceived body size and causes him to look much darker because the light is no longer reflected off the buck's coat but is absorbed between the hairs. Simultaneously, the buck everts both his preorbital and tarsal glands, which releases scent into the air. The bucks will also make a very deep-pitched grunting as each turns sideways so that his opponent can see how big he really is. One or both of

The "hard stare" is given by the buck with his ears laid back, his hair standing on end, and his antlers projected forward in the fighting position. If you ever encounter a buck showing body language this threatening, shoot him or get up a tree.

the bucks may paw the ground with his forefoot. Then with short stiff-legged steps, each buck will sidle toward the other in a circle with his head turned slightly away from the other. When their heads are in the fighting position, the whites of their eyes show. One or both of the bucks may show extreme aggression by holding its mouth open and flicking his tongue up his nose, alternating between the nostrils. When the bucks are done communicating, in close proximity, they muster all of their strength and crash antlers. After the initial crash, the fight becomes one of brute strength as each tries to throw the other off his feet and gore him. This seldom happens because both animals are well matched. But in most cases, one is stronger or has other advantages. Most fights last only a few seconds because that's all it takes for a buck to realize that his opponent is stronger. The fight continues until the lesser buck finds the opportunity to break off the fight and dash off without getting gored.

Two bucks warily circle each other with a sidling walk, before crashing together in a fight.

In a fight, each buck tries to throw the other off his feet and gore him.

Clash and Clamor

Bucks issue an unintended auditory signal when their antlers crash together. Although the fighting bucks don't intend to attract all other bucks within hearing, they do so. The sound of fighting bucks is a magnet to all others. They don't want to miss the fray, even if they have no intention of joining in. That response is the reason hunters use antlers taken in previous years and rattle them together to attract bucks. Rattling is an important deer-hunting tool. All told, prior to and during the fight, a lot of information has been emitted.

Hormones, Infatuation, and Foreplay

About forty-eight hours before a doe comes into estrus, under the influence of her androgen hormones, she becomes exceedingly high strung and restless, moving almost continuously. At that time, she will actively seek out the bucks and lay down a trail of pheremonal urine by secreting a small amount frequently. The estrus doe will seek out the buck's scrapes and urinate in them. The buck's odor in the scrape also helps to stimulate her ovulation. She knows where the scrapes are because she has been encountering them for three to four weeks. As each buck follows her trail he will be displaced by any buck of higher status. The doe's forty-eight-hour pre-estrus activity helps ensure that the strongest, fittest buck will find her and pass his genes to their offspring.

Testosterone is a steroid, and under its influence, the buck has "bulked up" much like athletes who use steroid, to bulk up. The most obvious "bulking" is in the buck's greatly swollen neck.

High testosterone levels also cause droplets and strings of drool to drip from the buck's mouth. The more dominant the buck, the more he drools.

All bucks test doe readiness from the start of the rut, which begins in the middle of October in the northern three-quarters of the United States, by running at them with their heads lowered but with their ears pointing forward. Mature does are experienced enough to just squat and release a little urine to prove that they are not ready to be bred. Younger does will be chased until they finally get the idea and let out a urine sample too. Although younger bucks attempt almost constant chasing, mature bucks go about the process much more methodically.

In testing for a doe's sexual pheromones, the buck will use his vomeronasal organs, doing what is known as "flehmening." The vomeronasal organs are two tiny openings in the top of a deer's palate one inch in from the front of its mouth. These tiny openings are a counterpart to the Jacobson's organ found in the top of a reptile's mouth. Similar to a buck using his vomeronasal organ, a snake will flick its tongue constantly as it goes through the world, scenting everything by the molecules it gets on its tongue and identifying what it encounters through the use of the Jacobson's organ.

This buck is flehmening. Deer have no upper front teeth.

Note the swollen neck of this buck. He is literally on steroids of his own creation.

When a buck can get a doe to urinate, he may either smell or taste the urine directly from her vulva or from the ground. Bucks almost always eat some of the urine-soaked leaves, which is a better way of ensuring contact with the vomeronasal glands in the roof of their mouth. After doing so, he flehmens, an activity seen by almost everyone

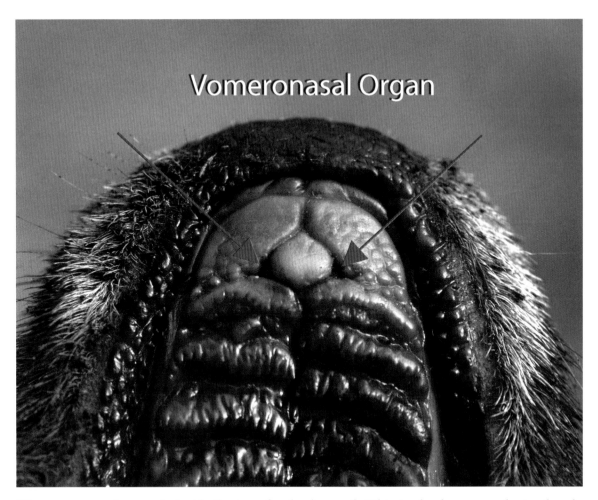

Vomeronasal Organ

The vomeronasal organ is inside the top of a deer's mouth. This is also known as the Jacobson's organ.

who has watched rutting bucks. In flehmening, the buck smells deeply of the urine, then raises his head high, closes his nostrils, and opens his mouth. Most odors are of organic origin and are released as a gas. These scent molecules are breathed in where they adhere to the epithelial lining in the deer's nostrils. There they are changed from a chemical compound to an electrical impulse and sent by a neuron pathway to the two olfactory bulbs, and thence to the brain's olfactory cortex where the scent is identified. Some of the scent is also pulled into the deer's vomeronasal organ, which sends signals to the two lesser olfactory bulbs and thence to a different part of the brain. The main olfactory system elicits immediate response to feelings of fear, and to behavioral and sexual stimulants, while the vomeronasal system regulates the physiological readiness of the deer's system to breeding.

Courting this pre-estrus doe, this buck caresses her. Mature bucks make "better lovers."

During flehmening, the scent is drawn into the mouth, the head is held high, and the upper lip is curled upward, basically closing the nostrils, devoting all of the scenting action to the vomeronasal organs. During this process you can easily see that deer have no upper teeth in the front of their mouths.

Mature bucks make "better lovers" because they court the does more assiduously.

They court and stimulate the doe by licking her head, her ears, her body, her nipples, her anus, and her vulva. She responds by licking the buck's head and genitals and being ready to stand for him sooner for breeding. All of this is communication raised to an art form.

Chapter 10

Emotions in Deer

A really good book, movie, television, stage show, or real-life situation can often cause us to laugh with joy, cry with sadness, or recoil in horror. Those are all emotional responses triggered by the stimulus of what we have just seen, heard, or read. The most commonly known emotions in humans are anger or aggression, anxiety or stress, cheerfulness, conceit, contempt, contentment, curiosity, deceit, despair, devotion, disgust, envy, fear, frustration, grief, guilt, hatred, helplessness, horror or terror, indignation, jealousy, joy or happiness, love, lust, pride, suspicion, and vanity. Emotions are usually expressed by words, actions, or body language and are expressed in such a way that most people instantly recognize the message being conveyed. There are times, however, when to get the real message we have to read between the lines or note that there is more than meets the eye, such as subtle inferences. As societal creatures, it behooves us humans to be able to recognize, decipher, and respond to all of these means of communication. Without communication it would be impossible for us to coexist. And so it is with wildlife.

The *American Heritage Dictionary* describes "anthropomorphism" as, "The attribution of human feelings to nonhuman beings, objects, or natural phenomena." Most scientists "recoil in horror" when we naturalists ascribe wildlife reactions or behaviors in terms of human emotions and denounce such observations as being anthropomorphic. They claim that our observations are purely anecdotal and cannot be duplicated in a laboratory. To many scientists, any "finding" that cannot be duplicated in a laboratory by different observers reaching the same positive result cannot be a fact. Rats, dogs, and primates can be trained and tested in labs, and dogs, in particular, are anxious to please. Most wildlife cannot be tested in laboratories because most species aren't confined and, even if they were, couldn't care less about pleasing anyone. Consequently, most observations and conclusions about wildlife emotions must, by the nature of the creatures being studied, be empirical, made by actual observation of the subject. I live with deer and this discourse on emotions in deer is based on my personal observations of deer over the past seventy-four years.

I am not claiming powers of observation that others don't have; I am claiming that I probably have had more opportunities to make these observations than most other folks. How do I know that my conclusions of emotions are correct? Can I prove that they are correct? No, I can't, but I doubt that there is anyone who has not witnessed a dog jumping with "joy," its tail wagging as if it were about to fly off, or a cat purring "contentedly" as it rubbed its cheek glands against your leg. Could you prove that either of these emotions are what you witnessed? Probably not, but then you don't have to prove them; you know what you witnessed and so do I.

The emotions I have witnessed in deer are anger, leading to aggression, anxiety or fear, as well as contentment, curiosity, devotion or love, frustration, grief, joy or happiness, pride, suspiciousness, and revenge.

This doe is as "lovingly affectionate" with her fawns as a human mother is with her offspring.

Dominance

I have just come in from filling up my deer herd's two feed troughs: shelled corn in one and 16 percent protein feed in the other. Three of my big bucks were standing on the hillside above the troughs watching me. The dominant buck was quietly walking with his ears laid back and his body hair partially erected. He was not angry, he was not being aggressive, he was merely reinforcing a message to the other two bucks that he had undoubtedly given them many times. It was a message that I know that he has physically impressed upon them several times: that he is boss and that they should keep their distance. They both got the message and walked a circuitous path around him.

Some deer, like some people, always seem to have a chip on their shoulder. They are just naturally more aggressive. Such deer usually don't live long because they are

By laying his ears back, this buck is showing his dominant status.

much more apt to throw caution to the wind during the rutting season and chase the does at any time of the day, and thus are much more likely to be seen and shot.

My friend Gary Knepp had an old buck in his herd called "Rooter" that had been the dominant buck during his prime. Even in his old age, long after he lost his high status, he was still always aggressive to everyone and everything. He was always looking for a fight, and, fought many fights that he knew he couldn't win even when he started them. But that never stopped him from starting fights.

I have long said that the most dangerous animal in North America today is a captive white-tailed buck that has been raised on a bottle and petted. Such bucks have no fear of humans and, during the rutting season, they may attempt to kill you.

I had to destroy three of my bucks that I raised on a bottle as pets when I was first starting my research herd because of their aggression during the rut. The first buck I had was tearing chain link fences apart during the rutting season and continued to be aggressive even after casting his antlers. I fully realize that anger is an emotion and aggression is a behavioral action, but it is impossible to separate the two; they are indelibly linked. No one witnessing this aggression can mistake the hostility behind it.

A buck shows his animosity by laying his ears back along his head and tucking his chin in, which projects his antlers forward. Erector pili muscles are employed to cause all of his hair to stand on end, which makes the buck look much larger and darker in color because his opponent is now looking down the erected hair shaft. The hair of the clamped down tail is widely flared and the long tarsal-gland hairs are reversed, forming huge rosettes, releasing pheromones into the air. The buck may paw the ground, throwing clumps of dirt into the air behind him. His vocalization is a deep, raspy grunting. He will walk with a stiff-legged gait, taking shorter steps than normal, approaching his adversary with his head arched slightly away. His tongue may be flicked in and out of the mouth and the tip turned upward to touch the nostrils. His preorbital glands are everted as widely as possible. If you haven't correctly decoded all of these actions as an expression of the emotion of anger and taken evasive action before more than half of the signs were given, your wife, if you have one, is about to become a widow.

Anxiety or Fear

Anxiety or fear causes stress, although a deer can be stressed without being anxious or fearful. That apparent contradiction depends upon the stimulus. A deer is easily stressed by an unexpected rise in the ambient temperature in the early fall, during the time that the hair in its winter coat is lengthening in response to the lessening of the hours of daylight and declining temperatures. A deer stressed by external heat will retire to deep shade, stand in water, pant rapidly with its mouth open to exchange its internal body heat with external cooler air, and restrict its activity until the ambient temperature declines with the onset of evening. Many times I have watched deer come out to feed in the late afternoon in September and move farther out in the field only as the setting sun caused the trees to cast longer shadows, extending the cooler shade zone.

Anxiety and fear cause hormonal stress. In response to either anxiety or stress, the deer's pituitary gland causes the adrenal medulla gland to secrete epinephrine (adrenaline) into the bloodstream. It is that hormone that prepares the deer for flight or fight, according to whichever action is needed. It does this by increasing the heartbeat rate, raising the blood pressure, causing increased oxygen consumption into the lungs and thence into the bloodstream. It also causes the liver to release glycogen sugars into the bloodstream to meet increased energy demands, slows down or stops digestive functions, increases body temperature, and causes more rapid blood clotting, if need be. The deer responds to this mobilization of internal readiness by opening its mouth and panting rapidly as already described.

Although the deer's internal resources are marshaled in the same way for both anxiety and fear, it displays its body language differently. In an anxiety situation, the deer usually extends its neck and holds its head as high as possible. The higher the head, the more intense the anxiety. The ears are usually held forward and all of the deer's senses are in overdrive. The anxious deer may stamp just one of its forefeet, stamp by alternating its forefeet, or may simply lift one forefoot off the ground like a bird dog pointing. When stamping is done, it may be performed forcefully or so lightly that it is more of a going-through-the-motions than it is an actual stamp. The tarsal glands and tail hairs are usually flared.

When fearful, deer tend to make themselves smaller, often bending their legs and compressing their body into a slinking position. The ears may be drawn forward to try to capture additional sound, or they may be held back along the head. The tail is usually clamped tightly to the body.

Most of the world's forest-dwelling deer are "slinkers," sneaking away from potential danger. We usually think of the white-tailed deer as bounding away from danger, and it most often does so if it is in an open area. However, the whitetail has evolved from a forest dweller to one adapted to more open areas to feed, although it usually reverts back to heavy cover to rest. Research has shown that most deer escape detection by either slinking off or by remaining absolutely motionless, according to the wind conditions and direction, and letting the predator or hunter walk by.

Fear will sometimes cause a deer to slink off to escape detection.

Over the years, a number of states have conducted controlled hunts to study the tactics employed by deer to escape from hunters. At the Cusino Wildlife Experiment Station, located in Michigan's Upper Peninsula, the researchers released nine bucks into a one-square-mile fenced-in area. Six hunters were allowed into the area to hunt for the bucks while the biologists watched from high towers. The six hunters went four days before they even saw one of the nine bucks, and it was on the fifth day that one buck was finally killed. What everyone thought was going to be a piece of cake hunt was actually an eye-opening hunting experience. Although many of the bucks did circle around behind the hunters, most of the time they simply remained bedded or stood motionless in the brush and allowed the hunters to walk on by. A deer's coat normally matches its background so well that the deer is hard to detect if it doesn't move, and deer seem to know this.

I can vouch for that from personal experience. Times without number, I have gone out to feed my research herd and casually glanced at the wooded hill to see where they were. Even if I took the time to carefully check out the hillside, I often did not see any deer until one of them moved an ear or tail, and only then would I be able to make out more of them bedded down.

A detailed search would reveal the entire herd, but most hunters would have just given the area a cursory glance, as I had done at first, and missed them all.

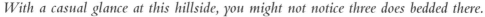
With a casual glance at this hillside, you might not notice three does bedded there.

Contentment

Contentment usually manifests itself through sound. Again, I have to mention the purring of a cat because it is a sound with which we are all familiar, and we usually acknowledge that the cat doing the purring is contented. A pair of Canada geese raise their young on my pond every year and, as I feed them constantly, they have no fear of me. When the goslings are feeding or have fed, they make soft gabbling sounds of contentment. It is only because we have raised some of our whitetail does on a bottle and have gotten them very tame that I have been able to hear the sounds of contentment made by fawns as they nurse. As the fawns suckle and the doe grooms them, they make very soft, high-pitched, whining murmurs of contentment.

It is usually conceded that curiosity is a component or indication of intelligence. It is only by constantly checking new odors, new sounds, and new objects that curiosity manifests itself into a learning experience through which deer increase their knowledge of their surroundings and thus increase their chances of survival. There is not a hunter who hasn't seen deer constantly sniffing the air for the scent of danger or the scent of a rival buck or an estrus doe. That constant investigation, interpretation, and cataloging of every scent molecule by deer is curiosity. I have seen fawns smelling every type of vegetation they pass and every inanimate feature or object they encounter in an effort to fill in all the blank pages in their olfactory notebook. There is an old saying that "curiosity killed the cat"; it would be the *lack* of curiosity that would cause the death of a deer.

Devotion

Devotion, or love, is much harder to categorize in deer, and I can't say that I have seen evidence of either of these emotions between adult bucks and does. I have, during the courtship phase, seen both bucks and does display affection and tenderness toward each other. This is apparent in the extensive mutual grooming in which they engage. It is true that the licking of the genital areas is a sexual stimulation effort, but so much of the time the couple caress each other all over the body. It is also obvious that the courting pair like to be close to each other, sometimes even touching each other. It is not only that the buck lies close to the estrus doe he is tending to keep other bucks away, but it is evident that the pair *want* to be close to each other. Yearling bucks, lacking the tenderness displayed by mature bucks, cause the rutting seasons to be much more hectic and chaotic.

Devotion, or love, is most visible between a doe and her fawns and such devotion goes beyond just natural instinct. The Bible tells us in John 15:13, "Greater love hath no man than this, than to lay down one's life for his friends." If love is expressed in humans by the willingness to die for others, why would it be different for deer? Archibald Rutledge wrote about a doe killing a diamondback rattlesnake in order to protect her fawn. I have seen a doe attack a dog that was a threat to her fawn. As discussed in chapter 6, I recovered a great horned owl that had its wing broken by a doe after the owl had attacked her fawn.

However, it is not just the defense of the fawns that denotes the devotion or love that some does have for them. Like overindulgent human mothers, some does spoil their fawns rotten. Whereas most does in the northern states have weaned their fawns by late August or September, some of the does allow their fawns to nurse as late as November or December. In a way, that may also cost the doe her life as it may cause her to go into winter in a poorer condition than she would if, instead of producing milk, she had built up the body fat needed for her to survive a harsh winter.

Frustration

Frustration is most often felt when something wanted can't be gotten. I see it all the time when young squirrels come to my porch and can't get the sunflower seeds out of my squirrel-proof bird feeder. The adults squirrels have all tried and failed, having given up in frustration, and now they no longer try. I have witnessed deer give up in frustration—and probably disgust—time after

Nothing frustrates a buck more than a pre-estrus doe that keeps slinking away from him.

time when they tried to reach apples or tree leaves growing on branches that were just too high for them, even when they were standing on their hind legs. It's why the browse line in most areas is about seven feet above the ground. That is just about the limit to which a big buck can reach, even standing fully erect. Some bucks can reach a little higher by pulling the branches down with their antlers; other deer just have to put up with the frustration. But nothing frustrates a buck more than to chase after a pre-estrus doe that won't stand for him.

Grief

Jane Goodall, one of the foremost primatologists and who has studied chimpanzees for over forty years, tells of a young male chimpanzee that simply stopped eating and died after his mother died. The young male lay for hours in the last bed his mother had used.

In Africa, I watched a mother elephant and an "auntie" try for several days to get a young five-year-old elephant to its feet after it had died. They finally left the area most reluctantly and only then because they needed water.

This past spring my wife awakened me at 3 a.m. because she could hear the frantic bleating of a fawn. We went down to our pond and discovered a two-day-old fawn entangled in a barberry bush. Getting brush cutters, I was finally able to free the fawn, only to discover that its hind leg was broken. Maggots had badly infested the wound where the skin had been torn and the little creature was so weak that it lay prostrate on the ground. That the maggots had hatched was evidence that the fawn had probably been entangled in the bush since early the previous day, but it hadn't bleated until just before it was about to die. I quickly put the fawn out of its misery. Although the doe was a tame one, it would not come any closer than 150 feet, as we could see by the beam from our flashlight. I carried the fawn away to dispose of it elsewhere. For the next two days, whenever I passed by the area, I saw the doe checking out the bush where her fawn had been trapped.

Grief is caused by the loss of something held dear. I am sure that in all of the situations just described, the mothers felt grief, but I can't prove it.

Play

All play is a conditioning for life, and all young animals engage in play that increases their chances of survival.

Fawns engage most frequently in some of the same games we did as kids. They play follow the leader, tag, and hide and seek. Occasionally they play king of the mountain, a favorite game of young wild sheep and goats. Fawns are not couch potatoes; they enter into the games, giving them all they've got, running at top speed. Such play develops the heart, making it a stronger muscle. Simultaneously, the fawns are also expanding their lungs, increasing oxygen consumption, and expanding the blood vessels needed to deliver the oxygen to all parts of the body. The running also improves the fawn's coordination between the eyes, brain, and body that allows them to successfully navigate the brushy environment in which they live. Play in deer is an expression of joy, happiness, sheer pleasure. The fawns run, they jump, they buck, they hump their backs, they kick out, and they throw themselves so wildly that they frequently lose

Fawns engage in many of the same games that children do, including tag, hide-and-seek, and king of the mountain.

their footing and come crashing down. All the fawns join in the playtimes and, if the weather is cool, the does frequently join in, too. In brisk weather, even the adult bucks may join in the play. Such play is done in the exuberance and enjoyment of life and no one witnessing the antics can take the "joy" out of enjoyment. However, play is exhibited only in well-fed deer. Deer on short rations have to conserve all possible energy.

Pride

Pride and vanity are often listed as sins. Are deer ever sinners? Could be. Is a doe ever "proud" of her two beautiful fawns? I just don't know, but I'm not discounting such an emotion and I wouldn't fault her if she was. Bucks don't stand there and look into a reflective stream and say, "Mirror, mirror on the wall, who's the fairest one of all?" but

Who could blame this buck for feeling a little proud of himself?

they are proud animals and have earned the right to be number one. If their pride is a sin as well as an emotion, so be it.

Suspicion

Acting with caution is a behavior while being suspicious is an emotion, and deer are naturally suspicious and usually act with caution. Scientists have done extensive studies on the reactions in wildlife and have termed the "approach and withdrawal phenomena." I have seen countless thousands of examples of this phenomenon in deer, as has everyone else who has ever watched or hunted them. Scientists have concluded that low intensities of stimulation cause creatures to approach whatever it is they are curious about, but the closer a creature gets, the more suspicious or cautious it becomes if it has not definitely identified the object, and then the stronger stimulation causes it to withdraw. Think of the many, many times when you had a deer approach your stand, and you could all but taste those fried loins, only to have the deer become more suspicious the closer it got until it finally turned away and you never did get a shot. Now try to tell me that deer don't have an emotion called suspicion.

There are undoubtedly other emotions of deer that I haven't mentioned, but these are the ones I have witnessed and, in most cases, documented. I don't believe that I am being anthropomorphic in relating these events, but I've been called worse. I am trying to open your eyes to how you see deer and their activities and to open your mind to the results. You will have a better time in the deer woods if you do.

Being cautious lengthens lives.

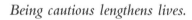

Curiosity or anxiety will cause a deer to extend its head and neck as high as is possible.

Chapter 11

Instinct vs. Intelligence

Two of the greatest areas of conflict within the scientific community today are "nature vs. nurture" in humans and "instinct vs. intelligence" in wildlife. Startling revelations are being announced in both fields. To some biologists the attribution of cognitive processes in wildlife borders on heresy. If others can't replicate an observation in a laboratory, they claim that it is merely anecdotal, and while interesting, it can't be acknowledged as fact. I have had a number of statements in my twenty-nine books questioned by biologists because they couldn't be proven. In each case, I have stated that I have recorded the observation in the hopes of stimulating someone's interest in perhaps making a further study of it. I readily admit that many of the statements made in this book are based on empirical knowledge, which I have gained by spending thousands upon thousands of hours studying, working with, hunting, and photographing deer over the past seventy-four years.

There is an endless argument over whether a deer's response to a situation is "purposive" or "reflexive" action. Behaviorists can't test deer in a laboratory because they are too wild and they aren't interested in working for a reward. Therefore, conclusions about the mental processes of deer must be made from observation in the wild.

I readily admit that most of the things that a deer does are innate, reflexive, done without thinking—but then, so are many of ours. All creatures act instinctively because so many times action must be taken long before a thought could take place; our very survival depends upon it. Yet, I believe that they often show a response to new situations that is akin to reasoning. That is the acid test, their response to a situation to which they could not have been programmed.

First, we must acknowledge that all types of wildlife are individuals just as we are, and that means some of them are smarter than others. I could never be a rocket scientist because I was never exposed to the math and electronic knowledge needed. I think that the coyote is the smartest wild animal on the continent because, despite constant persecution, it is more than holding its own. Deer are highly adaptable and are also thriving, but no one is trying to eliminate them, as some are trying to do with the coyote in so many areas. Federal predator, control men have removed over eighty thousand coyotes a year, every year, for over fifty years without ever putting a dent in their population. In my opinion, deer are nowhere near as smart as a coyote, but they are a lot smarter than most folks give them credit for.

Deer have good memories. They remember where the holes in a fence are, where they are able to get into and out of fields. They know when and where to go when the apples, acorns, and berries, etc. are ripe and have fallen. They know which dogs are loose and will chase them and they know which are tied and can be ignored. They know lots of things and they remember them.

Yearling bucks are easier to hunt than adults because they have not lived long enough to gain the knowledge they need to survive. It is a well-known fact that many of the dominant bucks do not venture out of cover in the daylight hours, even in the rutting season. That is acquired knowledge that comes with age and experience; if it was inherent, no buck would move during the hunting season.

A reader of *Deer and Deer Hunting* sent in pictures to prove the actions of what has to be one of the smartest bucks in the country. A really big buck was seen on the reader's farm all year but never during the hunting season. The mystery was solved when

Yearling bucks haven't learned all the tricks of survival that older bucks rely on.

This buck just "knew" that no one would look for him out in an open field.

his tracks were seen going into an abandoned root cellar located out in the middle of a field. A remote camera was set up that proved that the deer spent every day in the cellar, a spot in which no one would ever look for him. It is inconceivable to think of a wild deer going into a confined area, especially one with only one entrance, yet that is what he did, and he did it every year. That's intelligence.

There was another buck in one of the southern states that did a similar trick by hiding in a storm sewer that ran under a major road. Despite the roar of traffic and the vibration from the huge tractor trailers, the buck sought out that dark pipe that he had to crawl into as his place of refuge all during the hunting season. That's intelligence.

I realize that some biologists might say that the actions of these two bucks is what is known as "associative learning," that the deer had learned to associate their actions with the results achieved. I can't argue with that, but I still say it shows intelligence far beyond the norm for most deer.

When I first started to work on some of the ranches in South Texas with both whitetails and turkeys, I discovered that almost all ranchers fed both species with automatic feeders. The feeders had timers set to scatter the feed at the same time every day. Both species were accustomed to being at the feeders at the specific time. However, I was told that I could get both species to come in by taking a stick and turning the rotating blades on the bottom of the feeder. The turning would scatter additional feed and both species were keyed to come in whenever they heard the sound of the blades turning, and they were. That was acquired knowledge. A doe on one of the ranches took that one better, because she learned to stand on her hind feet and turn the blades with her forefoot, allowing her to get feed whenever she wanted it. That's intelligence.

I keep my high-protein feed in thirty-gallon galvanized barrels to protect it from the weather until I'm ready to use it. My oldest doe, Lady, learned to lift the pressure-sealed lids off with her nose whenever she wanted more feed. That was not only intelligence, that was being a damn nuisance! The only way I could circumvent her was to wire all of the tops on to the cans. Fortunately for me she never taught any of the other deer to do that. Since she passed on, the lids stay on.

Chapter 12

The Deer's Year

Spring

Let's start with spring, because in the Northern Hemisphere, almost everything in nature takes part during the resurrection. Technically, spring starts on March 21, because of the vernal equinox, wherein there are exactly twelve hours of daylight and twelve hours of darkness. The sun is rising one hour and nineteen minutes earlier and setting one hour and thirty-nine minutes later than it did on the first day of winter, but that two hours and fifty-eight minutes of more daylight may not translate into more warmth. March lived up to its reputation as a most treacherous month in the year. January 2006 was the warmest one on record, for the country as a whole, and March refused to acknowledge spring. On the twenty-first, storms dumped two feet of snow on the midwestern states, and I had never seen the wind blow so strongly, so constantly, so consistently as it did in the Northeast that year. The cold winds blowing out of Canada prevented the snow from melting, and the accumulated depths kept the deer yarded longer than usual. I heard no reports, but I'm sure that many of the northern states did find deer dying of starvation because of their extended imprisonment. February is usually known as the "starvation" month, but some years, March may also have that designation.

In spring, the first green vegetation is always found along spring runs and in swamps. The fifty-six-degree water has even allowed some vegetation to grow throughout the winter. The spathes, or hoods, of the skunk cabbage blossoms, push their way up through the mud and ice in swamps in December, and are often the very first food that the deer and bears eat in the spring. Because the amount of this food is limited, the spring runs are where the bodies of starved deer are often found.

The deer compensate for extended periods of snow and cold by moving only during the daylight hours. Where possible, they will seek out south-facing slopes where the snow depth is minimal and exposure to the sun is maximal. A recent study done by Hynek Burda at the University of Duisburg-Essen in Essen, Germany, found that grazing animals were generally aligned facing magnetic north. His study was done on cattle, red, and roe deer and were the results of photos taken from Google Earth. I don't challenge his conclusions, but that they may be more applicable to bison which roam for long distances. My personal observations have proven to me that when whitetail

Skunk cabbage is one of the first plants to grow in the spring, and hungry deer eat it readily despite its skunk-like odor and the tongue-burning oxalates in its leaves.

deer feed in cold weather they align themselves east and west because it exposes the broadside of their bodies to the sun, gaining them greater warmth. Conversely, they feed north and south in warm weather because it minimizes exposure to the sun. I have also noticed in areas where the predation is high that the deer feed into the wind to put the predator at a disadvantage, as I've noted elsewhere. The deer may have been concentrated during the winter but split up into matriarchal family groups and bachelor groups just as soon as they can do so. However, deer that have left their yards will return to them if winter returns, if only for a week or so.

With the lengthening of the hours of daylight in a twenty-four hour period, the deer's metabolism also kicks into high gear, both allowing and requiring the deer to eat more food. They start to feed earlier and stay at it longer because it takes them more time to gather the new growth. In part, this is also the result of the demands placed upon the doe's body by the fetuses that she is carrying. Up until midterm the doe's own welfare takes top priority, after which it changes to the fetuses' needs. The fetuses experience a growth spurt when the doe's metabolism increases. Does, contrary to

From bottom to top, the age of fetus: sixty days, one-hundred and twenty days, and about two hundred days.

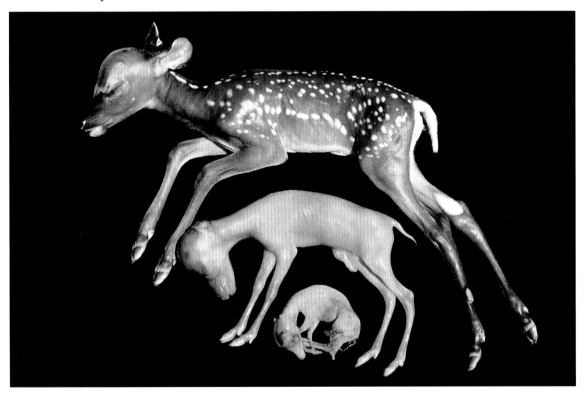

old wives' tales, are seldom if ever barren because of age. Does are often rendered barren if they do not have ample fat stores and are not able to secure enough nutrition to sustain their own lives and the lives of the fetuses that they are carrying. A starving doe will deliver dead fetuses or underweight offspring, which will probably die if they are less than five pounds in weight. Such does, not seen with fawns in the early summer, are often thought to be barren, but such is not the case.

It is not just the does that develop insatiable appetites in spring. It has been calculated that the expense of producing antlers is as costly to the bucks as producing fawns is to the does. All deer are ravenous in the spring. It must be remembered that deer are primarily browsing animals and prefer browse to all other foods when it is available. Deer are designed to be browsing animals; it is why they have the long tapered muzzle and narrow mouth. They are known as selective feeders because they carefully select each bite of food that they take, carefully removing each plant from the midst of other vegetation. However, in most areas the deer population has exceeded the carrying capacity of land, and they have long since eliminated most of their favored foods. I am constantly being told that more people are seeing deer eating grass, and that is due to the fact that the deer's preferred food is gone. I always caution everyone reading lists of food eaten by any species. Such lists only show what that particular animal was eating at that particular time in that particular place. And what it was eating may have been all that was available at that particular time.

New growth always has the highest nutrition, the value of which steadily declines as the plants mature and is at its lowest after the vegetation has died and dried. In watching deer feeding upon grass or emerging blades of wheat, oats, or rye, I have noticed that the deer prefer the two-inch sprouts to the four-inch blades of vegetation. They instinctively know that the nutrition is higher in the two-inch sprout than in the four-inch blade. When feeding upon such grass-like plants the deer average fifty-two bites of vegetation per minute. Fortunately, the maturing of the different plants occurs throughout the spring, summer, and early fall. Browsing and feeding, like the pruning and cutting of cultivated crops, stimulates new growth and, if not too severe, actually spurs the plant to higher yields. Various types of plants respond differently to browsing. Some plants can only stand light, some medium, while some actually thrive on heavy browsing.

When I was chief gamekeeper for the Coventry Hunt Club, we used to do a lot of felling of young maples in the wintertime for deer food. We never cut the tree completely off. We would just cut it partially through, four feet above the ground, and push it over. This made the tender branch tips available to the deer at once, and as the tree continued to grow, it produced browse over a period of many years. Such cuttings benefited all types of wildlife. The opening in the forest canopy allowed the sunlight to get to the forest floor, which allowed the berry bushes and grasses to grow better among the branches, creating cover for the deer, rabbits, grouse, and songbirds. Deer feed heavily upon berry bushes—not just the fruit but the leaves and twig tips, thorns and all.

Spring is always a time of catch-up for the deer. The harder the winter, the more the food that the deer eat to replenish what was depleted from their bodies by the rigors of the cold weather. As of this writing, the year 2012 was the warmest on record. So deer over most of the continent came through the winter in better shape than usual. That meant that as their bodies were in better condition, the food that they ate did not have to go as much for replacement but could go directly into antler growth for the bucks and bigger and stronger fawns for the does. You might say that this is a benefit of global warming except that unless more deer are harvested it only compounds the problem of overpopulation and habitat destruction.

Another drain on the deer's system that is not often considered is the fact that in May the deer finally shed out their worn-out, bleached-out winter hair and replace it with the bright russet-red coat of summer hair. They lose their ragged, moth-eaten coats and attain a new, sleek appearance, but their new coat comes at a cost in nutrients.

White-tailed deer are not large-herd animals and as soon as they leave their winter yards, or areas where they may have concentrated because of food sources, the does split up into familial groups and the bucks into bachelor groups. Although an occasional old buck may be a loner, that is exceedingly rare because being part of a group extends a tremendous survival factor to each individual. The more eyes, ears, and noses are employed, the greater the possibility the threat of danger will be detected long before it is more than just a threat. Of course, there is also the factor that too many animals may attract more attention, and for that reason most of the bachelor groups of woodland deer are usually restricted to no more than five animals. Bucks that live in more open spaces, as in the Midwest and western areas, tend to congregate in larger numbers. By the same token, woodland deer will often be in large concentrations when they are feeding in open areas but split up in family groups as soon as they retreat into cover.

The white-tailed deer live in a matriarchal society with each family group being led by the oldest doe. These groups are seldom represented by more than three generations because does after the age of two and a half have a tendency to go off and form their own group. While it is generally considered that each family group is lead by the oldest doe, that is true only so long as the oldest doe is physically able to be the leader. As is true with all wildlife, the oldest doe can lead just so long as she is strong enough to make the other deer back down. When she can no longer do this, because of advancing age or injury, she is relegated to a lesser role and may even be picked on by all of the other younger, stronger deer.

Except during the time of a food shortage, or when claiming a birthing territory, does get along amicably with each other. The one exception is, when about a week prior to giving birth, the does select a natal area: a birthing territory. The peak of the birthing season for most of the United States north of the thirty-first parallel is between May 26 and June 8. Farther south, the birthing occurs later and is stretched out over a longer time period.

The main purpose for a doe to establish a territory from which she will attempt to drive all other deer, is to make sure that her new fawns will imprint on just her. The young of many birds or animals will be attracted to, follow, or imprint on the first creature they see that moves after hatching or being born. This is a traumatic time of turmoil for the doe's yearlings because she drives them away too.

For a year the doe was the one constant in her fawn's lives. Every place she went with her fawns; everything she did with her fawns, everything she ate she shared with her fawns. It was the doe who was constantly on the alert for danger and who taught her fawns how to avoid it. It was the doe who taught her fawns everything they didn't do instinctively, and then instinctively, she drove them off. If her aggressive demeanor didn't do it, her flailing hooves did, and

Three deer were killed when this pregnant doe was struck by a vehicle.

usually the hooves were employed because the yearlings found it hard to overcome the conditioning they had had of following their mother for the past year.

For the yearling does the separation from their mother is a temporary experience, as most of them stay in the general area and will rejoin her and their new siblings about three weeks after the birthing. About 50 percent of the yearling bucks will also rejoin the family group, while the other 50 percent will begin the dispersal that almost all young bucks undertake, either now or in September. Collared yearling bucks have shown that the average dispersal distance is about five miles. Occasionally the young does also disperse, especially if their dam has been killed. Dispersal is a major factor preventing inbreeding in deer.

The size of a birthing territory depends upon the number of deer in the area. The higher the deer population, the smaller the territory each doe can hold, but most average about ten acres in size. Although the territories are basically contiguous there are travel corridors between or through them. Like any piece of real estate, some territories are better than others. Even with deer, the secret to survival is location, location, location. The most desired territories offer the best protective cover, lack of predators, and adjacent food and water. Naturally, the mature does will get the best territories because they know through experience where they are and, because of their size and status, they are able to force lesser does out of such areas. The younger does must utilize territories that do not contain all of the desired features, while the youngest does have to be satisfied with the peripheral areas. On average, 40 percent of all fawns die or are killed before they are one month old. The mortality rate of the fawns of the youngest does is more than twice that of the older does.

At her time of parturition the doe withdraws to the seclusion of her birthing territory. Does giving birth for the first time usually have a harder delivery than older does because they are actually smaller in body size themselves, their uterus and birth canal is smaller, and they usually give birth to a singleton, which is larger in size than an individual twin.

The norm for deer is that to be bred a northern doe must be at least eighty-five pounds in body weight. In the heartland of America, where the soil is deep and rich and the food produced on it is highly nutritious, as many as 80 percent of the seven-month-old female fawns will be bred. In my home state of New Jersey we average about 40 percent of the young does achieving the necessary weight needed to breed. In the northern New England states, few if any of the young females breed their first year. Captive fawns in New England that were fed a 16 percent protein diet, ad libitum, have proved that they would be capable of breeding if they had gotten the proper

Before birth, the doe stands up at the last moment so the fawn's weight helps pull it from her body.

Credit: Len Rue Jr./Len Rue Enterprises.

nutrition in the wild. In any case, a doe giving birth for the first time, no matter her age, usually gives birth to a singleton. Thereafter, if she has access to sufficient nutrition, twins are the norm. On especially good food, triplets occur fairly often, occasionally quadruplets, and, very rarely, quintuplets.

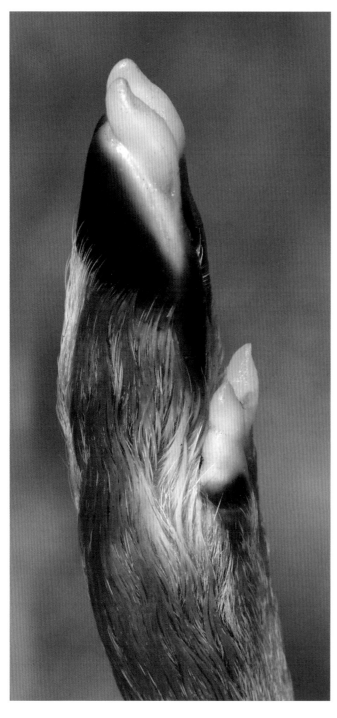

About forty-eight hours prior to giving birth, the doe's udder and four teats begin to swell and fill with milk, giving advance notice of the event that is soon to follow.

Like humans, deer go through labor pains, and the pain often elicits moans and groans. This is little noted because so few of us have witnessed the birth of fawns. The placental sac containing the fetus and the embryonic fluid breaks first, and the cascading liquid verifies that the birthing is imminent. The doe is usually lying down at this stage, straining and pushing with all of her might. There is no Lamaze for wildlife, nor is it needed; she doesn't need to be told to push, and strain is inherent.

The appearance of the soft-cartilage flexible white-tip pad of the fawn's front hooves are the first indication that the birthing is actually taking place.

With more straining, more dilation, the head appears, neatly tucked between the front legs like a diver about to cleave the water. Once the shoulders and the rib cage have emerged, the doe gets to her feet and the weight of the dangling fawn pulls the rest of its body free from its mother.

The drop to the ground tears the fawn loose from its umbilical

The soft-cartilage tips on the newborn fawn's hooves prevent puncturing of the placental sac. The soft tips wear off as soon as the fawn walks on them.

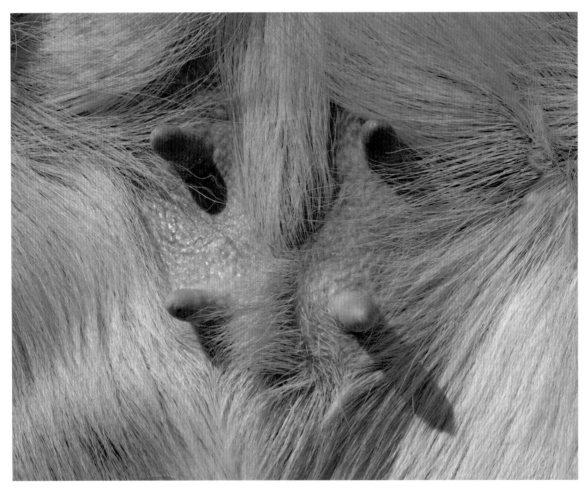

A doe's udder has four nipples.

cord and the jolt probably starts its lungs to function. The doe immediately turns around and, with her rough tongue, begins to lick and tear the placental sac from the fawn's head so that it can get air. Its ears are about the first thing that the fawn can move on its own, and they will move more or less constantly from that moment on, for the deer's entire life.

A deer's tongue has to be one of its strongest muscles, because the doe will lick the fawn, or fawns, constantly for hours without stopping. The constant licking stimulates the fawn to move, removes the odor of the blood and amniotic fluid that is a part of the birthing, and helps to imprint the doe on the fawn and vice versa.

Most fawns will attempt to stand by the time they are ten minutes old and most succeed after twenty minutes. At birth, a fawn's legs are longer in proportion to its body than at any other time in its life. And it takes tremendous effort on the fawn's part to coordinate those long legs. After getting all four of them straightened out and under its body where they belong, the fawn falls forward, backward, or rolls off to the side. When it finally succeeds in standing up, the rough licking of the doe's tongue undoes all of its efforts and knocks it sprawling to the ground again. It is the struggle to stand that develops the strength the fawn will need to reach its mother's nipples in order to get her life-sustaining milk. Just finding those nipples is a real puzzlement for the fawn at first, but through trial and error and searching Mom from stem to stern, and attracted to the extra warmth emanating from her udder, nursing is finally accomplished. Much of the time, the first nursing is done while the doe is lying on the ground. In order to nurse, the fawn gets down on its foreleg knees. Occasionally, a fawn will be too small or too weak to be able reach the doe's nipples while she is standing. Or, a young doe giving birth for the first time will not allow the fawn to nurse. Both cases contribute to natal fatality, the latter actually being abandonment.

Early research claimed that as many as 10 percent of the fawns that were handled by biologists died by being abandoned by their dams because of the human odor that had been inadvertently transferred to the fawn. The latest research has proven that this is not the case. A number of other factors, such as the age and physical condition of the doe, interrupted imprinting, etc., cause abandonment.

If the doe is giving birth to twins, the only time she stops washing the first fawn is when she has to put extra effort into straining to give birth to the second. The time varies but the second fawn is usually born about twenty to twenty-five minutes after the first one. The birth of the second fawn is a replay of the

The doe is licking her second fawn twin to remove body odor.

birth of the first one with the only difference being the doe now has to contend with the first fawn trying to nurse and getting underfoot at every turn. Within the hour both fawns are walking about, lying down, and nursing. Worn out with her exertions the doe will lie down and the fawns soon learn to get down on their front knees and nurse. But through it all, the washing never stops. The doe will wash whichever fawn is closest and will wash any part of that fawn that she can reach while bedded.

The old saying "there is no rest for the weary" is certainly true in the doe's case. Although exhausted from the strain and stress of the birth, she is soon on her feet because there is much to be done yet.

The most immediate task, once the fawns have been washed and nursed, is to eat the two afterbirths. Deer are herbivores and their teeth are designed for the grinding of rough vegetation; they don't have the carnassial teeth predators use for scissoring flesh. The process involves a lot of chewing and takes about one hour for each. Then, it's time to clean up the surroundings. The doe will eat every piece of vegetation that has been contaminated with blood or embryonic fluid. In most cases, she will also eat the contaminated soil. This cleansing prevents predators from being attracted to the area. The eating of the afterbirth also returns to her body some of the nutrients that she has lost, as the afterbirth is high in protein. The doe interrupts these tasks every so often to nurse and wash her fawns. She also consumes the fawns' urine and feces that they void as she nurses them. To stimulate their bowels, the doe constantly licks her fawn's anus as it nurses. Most does continue this practice until the fawns are at least four to five weeks of age, although I have seen some does continue to do it for several more weeks.

Finally, after a period of eight to nine hours the doe will lead the fawns away from the birthing area, hide them in separate locations, and then go about four hundred to six hundred feet farther before bedding herself. She does this so that her body odor does not attract predators to her fawns. The fawns themselves are practically odorless and, as they stay bedded all of the time, even dogs that are trained to find fawns, have a difficult time doing so.

I have been most fortunate to have witnessed and filmed the entire birthing procedure on a number of occasions. In one instance, I photographed one of my captive does giving birth from start to finish, just as I have described it here. I was shooting video and I did not turn my camera off for the entire nine and a half hours.

A newborn fawn can stand in twenty minutes, walk in one hour, run a bit in twenty-four hours, and outrun a man in five days. It is only after the first five to ten days or so that each fawn becomes reacquainted with its birthmate from whom it has been kept separate. It is those first five days that are the most perilous of the fawn's life.

The fawn's spotted coat is its first line of defense, and fawns have about three hundred white spots on a coat of bright russet red. The fawn's cryptic coloring matches the dappled sunlit pattern cast by the tree's leaves on the forest floor. At the first sound of anything unusual, and the fawns are closely attuned to all the normal forest noises, they lay their ears back along their necks and lie curled into a tight, flattened circle, motionless. Researchers, using telemetry collars, have noted that frightened fawns are even able to suspend their breathing for several minutes until the danger has passed. They then hyperventilate to make up for the oxygen depletion. I am firmly convinced that the fawn's interdigital glands do not function for the first five days. I base this on the fact that the does, when they come back to nurse their fawns, call them out of hiding with a low grunting instead of being able to track them as they can do at a later time. Because the does can't track the fawns, it is not likely that other creatures can either.

The does seek out their fawns about three to four times in a twenty-four hour period. The fawns nurse for about ten minutes, during which time they will drink about six to eight ounces of milk, later going up to about twelve ounces. Most of the milk that we humans drink is produced by Holstein cows, which have an average three and a half percent butterfat content. Most of us today drink 1 or 2 percent milk to help us control our cholesterol. Fawns don't have that problem, which is a good thing because a doe's milk averages about 10.5 percent butterfat. While nursing, the fawns often punch their mother's udder with their mouths, and this probably stimulates the milk flow. What I don't understand, nor have I heard a satisfactory explanation, is why the fawns also kick forward with their front feet while they nurse. The fawn's front feet make no contact with anything, but it is something they all do. The does spend no more than ten minutes with the fawns and then they are off again. It is the does that picked the bedding areas but it is the fawns that pick the individual spots they lie in. The fawns prefer to lie under something or up against something, such as a log, rock, or even a fence. They feel much secure with something behind them. The fawns will get up, stretch, turn around, and lie down again in the same spot, frequently. Because the fawns get up and move about more as they get older, the doe often has to hunt for them when she comes back to nurse them. I have noted that some fawns have an affinity for a certain spot and will lie in it consistently while others change the spot they bed in every time they get up to stretch. This practice is a characteristic of the individual fawn.

It is those first five days of the fawn's life that game wardens and rehabilitators hate. When any of the well-intentioned but misinformed persons encounter a fawn lying out in the woods, and not seeing a doe in attendance, they often think they have found an

The fawn's spotted coat provides excellent camouflage.

orphan. Their first impulse is to pick the fawn up and take it to someone who can care for it. Unless you know the doe has been killed, DO NOT pick up or touch any fawn you find in the outdoors. The does deliberately stay away from their fawns, and out of sight, for all of the reasons I have just given you. Just by touching the fawn, and being in the area, you may cause it or the doe to be stressed, and that may be enough to keep some young does from coming back. Then the fawn may in fact become an orphan. Unfortunately, as more of our forested areas disappear, more fawns are being born in hay fields or suburban areas where their cryptic coloration does not keep them hidden.

Fawns are not ruminants at birth but become so in a short period of time. For the first week, the milk that the fawns nurse from their dams does not go into the rumen but is bypassed directly to the reticulum. Within that first week, however, the fawns are nibbling at the surrounding vegetation and gradually increase their consumption with each passing day. They are cud chewers by the time they are two weeks of age. They feed mainly upon the vegetation that the doe is eating and at times they will actually take some of the food from the doe's mouth before the doe has a chance to eat it herself. I have also recorded on video five-day fawns employing rub-urination, balancing on their two front legs only days after they had trouble standing on all four.

Sometime around the third week of the fawn's life the does give up their birthing territories and the family groups are reunited. Basically, the fawns are capable of keeping up with their mothers and do follow them most of the time, but I have found that the does still keep apart from them for extended periods of time. I believe that the does just don't want to be pestered by the fawns wanting to nurse frequently. By four weeks of age the fawns are getting more of their nutrition from the vegetation they are eating than from the milk they get from their mothers.

It is interesting to note that the young of most mammals, not just fawns, are more flighty than the adults and run off more quickly at perceived danger. I lay that to the fact that the young are acting instinctively, as they have not become habituated to anything at such an early age. By the same token, the fawns are provided with neural stimulus filtering whereby their nerves and brains are able to ignore the sounds of scampering squirrels and chipmunks that do not represent danger to them.

I am frequently asked: at what age would a fawn be able to survive on its own? As mentioned above, most fawns are getting most of their nutrition from the vegetation they are eating at four weeks and many does are already starting the weaning process, although most fawns won't be weaned until between two to four months. For most does the weaning process is a gradual one. She allows the fawns to nurse for shorter periods of time and terminates the process by simply stepping over the fawn's head and walking off. To answer the question of how old would a fawn have to be to survive on its own, I believe it could do it at one month of age because I have seen them do it.

There is absolutely no argument that the longer the fawn is with its mother the greater its chances of survival. Not just because of the extra nursing it would get, but also because it would be taught what foods to eat, where they can be found and when, and the doe would be more alert to danger and know how to avoid it. That being said, I have seen fawns of about one month in age, or perhaps a week or so older, fend for themselves satisfactorily. They come out and feed with the other deer and perhaps may even try to nurse some of the does but are quickly rebuked. Many species do what is called "alloparenting," where an adult of the species will care for young that are not its own, but deer do not. Alloparenting female African lions will allow every cub in the pride to nurse. Older siblings of "alloparenting," gray wolves will bring back food for

Deer pay no attention to squirrels scampering about in the leaves but are instantly alert to the squirrel's alarm call.

the young pups. I saw a two-year-old coyote that had never been bred have a pseudo-pregnancy and produced milk and nursed her parents' current litter of pups. It is very uncommon for a doe to allow any but her own fawns to nurse. The does may not only refuse to let the orphan nurse but some of them may actually attempt to chase it off. At one month of age a fawn would have no trouble outrunning all but the most determined of the does. The orphaned fawn is not entirely without adult protection because, even though it may not be welcome, it more or less tags along with one family group or the other. The orphan is always welcomed in play by the other fawns, but it has less time to play as it is totally dependent on the vegetation it eats. It has been noted that orphaned bucks are not as inclined to disperse from the area in which they are born, because they are not harassed by a mother and are less likely to be harassed by any of the relatives of his former mother's group. Conversely, orphaned yearling does frequently disperse from their natal areas for a considerable distance, as they have no attachment to a familial group.

On several occasions I have seen orphan fawns that, because they had to fend for themselves from an early age and were forced to be more self-reliant, become very aggressive and dominant over other fawns their own age when those fawns wandered beyond the protection of their mothers. One orphaned fawn even chased adult does from the corn that I had put out for bait for photography.

Almost all creatures strive to be "top dog" because, as President Andrew Jackson said, "to the victor belongs the spoils." The hierarchy in the animal world is referred to as "the pecking order," wherein the dominant, or alpha, creature lords it over all of the others, while the number two, the beta, gives way to number one but lords it over all of the rest, and so on down the line. The dominant creature has the first chance at breeding, food, shelter, and all other benefits. Dominance is not hereditary among wildlife, as it is so frequently among humans; it is a position that in most cases must be fought for and is maintained only so long as it can be kept. It fluctuates constantly, and every creature knows its place in the hierarchy or is soon taught it. Every creature is also looking for the slightest opportunity to advance its own standing, and every dominant creature is aware of that fact and does its best to suppress such ambitions in any of the subordinates. Whereas the dominant buck is satisfied that all of the lesser bucks recognize that he is boss, the number-two buck seems to take great pleasure in impressing on the number three buck that he is number three, while the number-three buck relishes making sure that the number-four buck knows his ranking. On a number of occasions I have seen bucks that have displaced a dominant buck follow after that buck and continue to harass him even after the breeding season was over. It can only be revenge for all of the times that the dominant buck had harassed them before they became dominant.

No two creatures are exactly equal, and dominance in fawns starts at about two weeks of age, or as soon as the twins are brought together by the doe.

Their differences are subtle at first, but with age it becomes more pronounced with shoving, butting, forward leg kicking, and, eventually the rearing up and slashing out with the front hooves. By the time the little bucks are four months old they are playfully sparring. One little buck will often initiate the sparring by giving the "invitational bow" to another, as dogs do. Facing their playmate they bend down, keeping their front legs straight with their rumps sticking up in the air. The partner will then position himself in front of the challenger and the other straightens up and the pushing begins. The little bucks push with their foreheads because their antlers haven't grown yet.

A doe's twins are almost inseparable after she brings them together.

While all of this frenzied activity is going on, what are the bucks doing? As little as possible. They eat voraciously all spring to replenish body weight lost over the winter and to nourish their growing antlers. The antlers get off to a slow start around the first of April but experience a growth spurt as the amount of vegetation and its nutrition increases throughout April, May, and June.

The surge of testosterone that starts the buck's antler growth in the last of March or the first of April also gives impetus to the urge for the bucks to make scrapes. During the last week in March, the bucks will paw open the scrapes that they used most frequently during the past rutting season. Not having antlers, they gently rub with their forehead scent glands on the overhanging branches. The scraping is done for only a week or so, but the depositing of the forehead scent is done all year long with greatly increased activity during the rut.

Deer do tremendous damage to farm crops, such as hollowing out this pumpkin.

The fraternal group of bucks is just that, fraternal. There is no jockeying for dominance now because at this time it doesn't matter, and the status quo is maintained by memory, as it was determined last fall. The bucks reinforce their bond of friendship by mutually grooming each other. A lesser buck approaching a more dominant one usually instigates grooming, but I have observed that in the spring and summer it is often the other way around.

Summer

The daylight hours increase until June 21, and then they begin to decrease, although the summer heat intensifies all through August, waning in September. The deer's activity decreases proportionate to the heat's intensity. Folks looking for deer in July and early August might be led to believe that there are none. Activity is held to a minimum and what is done takes place under the cover of darkness. When the deer do start to feed in the late evening, their progress into the fields keeps pace with the lengthening shadows; they do not go out into the sunshine in hot weather if they can avoid it. They will feed more in the fields because most of the natural vegetation's growth peaks in early July and the plants die down. The woodland edges just "open up." It is at this time that crop damage becomes more noticeable, simply because the deer are forced to rely more upon those foods due to their high moisture content. The deer often bed down in the fields where they are feeding at night instead of going back into heavy cover.

If there are any hills in the area, the deer will spend the daylight hours bedded down on the north-facing ridges. The transpiration and evaporation of the thousands of gallons of water given off each day by the forests causes the temperature to be ten to fifteen degrees Fahrenheit cooler than in non-wooded areas. The evaporation creates air currents, and if breeze is blowing it will be up on the ridges. The deer are plagued by hordes of biting insects and, even though bedded, parts of their bodies are in almost constant motion of flapping ears, rippling skin, and feet stamping or moving in an effort get relief. The forest deer will feed more in ponds, and all deer will go to water several times a day and drink a gallon or so each time.

In the summertime, especially in the north woods, the deer spend a great amount of time in the water feeding, cooling off, or just seeking relief from the stinging and biting insects that plague the woods in warm weather. Sometimes they enter the water just to play and splash about. I have seen fawns get as much enjoyment as a human child would get by splashing the water with one of its front feet. Does frequently swim out to islands before giving birth to their fawns, thus gaining the protection of a water barrier.

Deer often take to water to elude their enemies, and in the South, where they are hunted with dogs, they use the water to extinguish their trail. They swim well and fast.

In his book *The Deer of North America,* Walter P. Taylor reports one man who was able to check the speed of a swimming deer by using the tachometer on his powerboat. The doe was frightened at first and swam about a quarter mile at thirteen miles per hour. When the deer found that she was in no real danger from the boat, she settled down to an easily maintained speed of about ten miles per hour. Whitetails have been seen swimming out in the ocean five miles off Cape Cod, Massachusetts, and 6 2/3 miles in Maine. During the 1950s and '60s, I lived along the Delaware River. The deer-hunting season in Pennsylvania always opened one week in advance of New Jersey's season. Every year when the guns started banging and the drives commenced

Deer are strong swimmers. To escape enemies, they readily take to water.

in Pennsylvania, herds of deer would swim across the river to the New Jersey side. A week later, when the New Jersey season opened, the Pennsylvania side of the river was comparatively quiet, even though the season was still open, the deer would then swim back to Pennsylvania.

The bucks' reclusive behavior is not entirely due to the heat but also is a means of protecting their rapidly growing antlers. The faster the antlers grow, the softer they are and the more easily damaged. The newer growth does not have the access to the minerals the first growth of the antlers received because the reserve taken from the buck's body is steadily being decreased. It is true that the velvet hairs on the antlers act as a radar system, silently warning the deer when they get too close to an obstacle, but sometimes the warning comes too late, as when the deer is in headlong flight from danger. I have photographed many bucks with freak antler growth, or hanging antler tips, that resulted from such accidents.

By July 1, the increased antler growth is accelerated and as much as a quarter-inch per day may be added. The typical whitetail buck ends up as an eight pointer, having three tines, with the projecting end of the main beam considered the fourth tine. Older bucks may have additional tines, and the foundation for all of them will be formed. By July 1, all of this is evident and the G-1 tines (by Boone and Crockett Club standards) will be fully grown while the others will be rapidly lengthening. By August 1, almost all antler growth will be completed and another transformation starts to take place.

It actually starts on June 21, as the daylight hours start to shorten, but the change is so gradual as to be imperceptible. However the effects are cumulative and the evidence apparent by August 1. With the minutes, then hours, of darkness increasing, the pituitary gland signals the brain to increase the production of melatonin, which activates the deer's entire endocrine system. The buck's testicles begin to enlarge, causing the scrotum to descend from the body. The testicles send testosterone coursing through the body, which has the visible effect of causing the red summer hair to start to fall out in order to be replaced by the tips of grayish-brown winter hair. It is a good thing that it will take the winter hair over three months to completely grow out, because a deer is highly susceptible to the heat stress that winter hair could cause if it grew too fast while the weather was still warm. Although the bucks start to go through their pelage change around the first of August, the does will not start until sometime in September. The nursing of their fawns puts such a drain on the does that they are in poor bodily condition until weaning is completed. The does that wean their fawns first are the first to acquire their winter coats. From the middle of August on, the fawns begin to lose their spots through a combination of some of their birth hair tips breaking off and the emergence of what will become their winter coats. By the second week in September most of the fawns will have lost their spots.

The descending of the buck's testicles is also a measure to prevent his body heat from destroying the testicle's sperm. It is a known fact that human males who wear boxer shorts are more fertile than those who wear briefs, and for the same reason: the testicles stay cooler.

The testicles now produce more testosterone, which causes the antlers to solidify through mineralization, which is not visually evident, but this begins the drying of the velvet and can be seen. The lateral grooves, created by the blood vessels that nourished the growing antlers, begin to stand out in bold relief. The antler's burr, or coronet, which by growing outward further restricts the blood flow, now becomes prominent.

In late August, the testosterone prompts the bucks to overcome the heat-induced lethargy that had been so pervasive over the past two months. According to the individual buck's physical condition, some will begin to rub their antlers free of the dried velvet covering sometime during the last few days of August and the first week in September. It is usually the oldest, mature bucks that peel the velvet from their antlers first. However, after a really severe winter, some of the younger bucks may be the first to peel. When that occasionally happens the young bucks may lord it over the older bucks but can do so only until the "big boys" peel.

The old idea that bucks made rubs just to remove their velvet has long since been laid to rest. The first rub is made to take the velvet off, but from that time on the rubbing is done for multiple purposes. We have already discussed how the rubs are used in communication. They are also made as a means of the buck working off his sexual frustration. I know this to be a fact as I have, times without number, seen a buck that was rejected by a non-estrus doe beat the living daylights out of some unfortunate bush or sapling; this is known as redirected aggression. There have been times when the buck will deliberately entangle his antlers in a bush or vine, such as the Japanese barberry, and then, with great effort, tear the entire bush out of the ground. This means of relieving frustration is common to all of the members of the Cervid family, as I have seen mule deer, elk, caribou and moose do it, too. At times these animals will run around with all types of vegetation entangled in their antlers. I have come to the conclusion that most of the time the animals deliberately want to have the vegetation tangled in their antlers because it makes their antlers look so much larger to a rival. With most wildlife, bigger is definitely better.

Sports records are being broken on an almost daily basis today, and the disclosure of performance-enhancing drugs being used by many of our top athletes is also being reported on an almost daily basis. One of the top drugs for improving performance is testosterone. Testosterone, as we have discussed, is what first determines the gender difference in the sexes and then causes the secondary sexual characteristics, such as antlers in deer, to be formed. It is a naturally occurring hormone, under the control of the pituitary gland, and is produced in different species, in different seasons, for different reasons, in different amounts. Synthetic testosterone, injected by athletes, does not increase their performance. The extra testosterone must be coupled with additional exercise to achieve the muscle mass and strength that the hormone can produce. It is the combination of those two factors that allows the bulking seen in many of our athletes and causes the neck swelling in the whitetail deer. The bucks start their workout program as soon as the velvet has been removed from their antlers but for the rest of September eating takes top priority.

There is absolutely no debating that acorns, in every section of the country where they occur, are the number one preferred food of the white-tailed deer. Deer get fat on acorns faster than on any other type of food. In late summer and on through autumn, the deer are subject to "hyperphagy" or "mandatory lipogenesis"; they must build up the fat reserves in their bodies that they will need to survive the winter.

The fat first accumulates under the skin as a sheet along the back from neck to tail that thins out as it descends toward the belly. That sheet of fat is not only emergency food but also provides a layer of warmth much as blubber does on marine mammals. This fat is often one inch thick over the hams and around the base of the tail, while wedges of fat form in front of the shoulders and the hams. A really fat deer will have its paunch and intestines surrounded by fat tissue that resembles a basketball net, while globules of a very hard fat, like a cluster of cherry tomatoes, fill the pelvic arch.

In good years, acorns make up as much as 80 percent of the food that the deer eats. It is interesting to note that deer never eat a single food diet, no matter how much they prefer one food, when it is possible for them to eat some roughage with either the high-protein or -carbohydrate diet. If only we were that smart.

Unfortunately, acorns are a sporadic crop; their abundance, or the lack thereof, depends upon many factors, many of which aren't apparent. The fall of 2004 was an exceedingly poor year for acorns in my home section of northwestern New Jersey. The fall of 2008 was even worse due to gypsy moth defoliation.

The year 2005 was the most productive year for acorns, walnuts, and hickory nuts that I have ever seen in my lifetime. It was the only year I can recall when there were still lots of nuts on the ground in December. It also coincided with an exceedingly low gray squirrel population. Starting in August the gray squirrels just disappeared, and I have no idea why. No dead squirrels were found, no evidence of disease was seen, the squirrels were just not here, and I got reports of the same thing happening in both New York and Pennsylvania. I fully realize that the superabundance of acorns, coupled with a shortage of squirrels, goes a long way to explaining why there were still nuts on the ground in December. It also brings up a point I would like to make here.

There is absolutely no arguing that the exceedingly high deer population, in many areas of the country, is preventing forest regeneration. It's happening in my own area; seedlings are eaten as fast as they sprout. I want to point out, because almost no one else seems to be doing it, that the deer are not the sole culprits. In almost all of the states,

To gain weight and fat for winter, deer compulsively eat more—fortunately at a time when fat- and nutrient-rich nuts are falling. This buck eagerly eats acorns, in competition with bear, squirrels, turkeys, waterfowl, and other deer.

the black bear population is exploding. In New Jersey, we went from a couple of dozen bears in the 1960s to an estimated population of 3,500 today.

Black bears scarf up every acorn they can find, gaining as much as several pounds of weight per day. The restocking of the wild turkey has been a real conservation success story, but those hundreds of thousands of turkeys eat hundreds of thousands acorns. It's a fact that most of the oak trees in our forests grew from acorns that had been buried by gray squirrels that were not dug up. It is also a fact that most hunters don't hunt gray squirrels anymore, and except for the fall of 2005, the gray squirrel population has exploded over most of the country. Those squirrels eat countless tons of acorns that they do dig up.

The defoliation of oak trees by gypsy moth caterpillars robs deer of acorns that are a major food source in autumn.

Black bears feed heavily on acorns.

Chipmunks also gather large stores of acorns and hickory nuts for their winter food supply.

Chipmunks seem to have a broken appestat; they store far more food than they can ever consume.

All over the eastern forests we seem to be having unprecedented numbers of chipmunks, and all fall they are all busy gathering and storing acorns. And a recent study showed that the white-footed and the deer mice carry off every acorn *they* can find. I know that the owners of every household in wooded areas always find acorns in their dresser drawers or shoes, stored there by mice. The point I'm trying to make is that while it is true that the whitetail deer do eat most seedlings as fast as they sprout, it is also true that not as many seedlings are sprouting because so many creatures are eating the acorns. Yet the deer get all the blame.

Although the deer will eat all kinds of acorns, they do have a decided preference for the white oak acorns because they have less tannic acid than any of the others, which makes them sweeter.

Also, white oak acorns start to sprout shortly after falling from the trees and are less nutritious after sprouting. The deer in my area eat the acorns of the various oaks in the following order: white, pin, red, black, scrub, and rock—or chestnut—oak. The acorns of the latter tree are the largest in actual size and weight, but the deer don't eat them until they are almost forced to do so because they have the highest rate of tannin, which makes them very bitter. The chemical components in tannic acid also inhibit the activity of the microflora in the deer's rumen, making the bitter acorns harder to digest.

The white oak acorn is the deer's favorite, owing to lower tannin levels.

It takes at least fifteen years for an oak sapling to grow large enough to start to produce acorns. An oak must be at least thirty to forty years old before it matures and reaches its peak production. Like the bucks that eat the acorns, it is only after the tree matures that it can put more of the nutrients it absorbs into acorn production than into maximizing growth. The Pennsylvania Game Commission has done extensive studies on acorn production and has found that in good years the oaks may produce as much as 528 pounds of acorns to the acre.

Because I am always interested in everything in nature, particularly as it relates to deer, I did a little research of my own. I found that six red oak acorns weigh about one ounce, or ninety-six acorns to the pound. A deer eats on the average of eight pounds of food per one hundred pounds of body weight in a twenty-four hour period. So, a 150-pound buck, having acorns as 80 percent of its diet, would eat approximately 922 acorns in a twenty-four-hour period. According to Pennsylvania's figures, if a good year produced 528 pounds, or 50,688 acorns to the acre, that acre would feed two bucks, four does, and eight fawns, weighing approximately 1,100 pounds, for seven and a half days.

So many times in autumn, I have been asked by hunters who have been watching or scouting for deer, where have they all the gone? The acorns start to fall in August and the peak drop occurs around the third week in September. When that happens, the deer forsake all of their usual haunts and spend almost all of their time in the woodlands, not venturing out into the fields where they are usually seen. Although deer often bed out in the fields where they are feeding in the summer, they usually have their bedding areas in the woodlands and on top of any hill in the area. When they are feeding on acorns they are feeding in their bedding areas and so are seldom seen.

As stated before, deer are primarily browsing animals and eagerly eat all of the tips of most of the bushes and trees that they can reach. However, I have noticed that deer do not care for the green leaves of the various maple trees when they are blown down during a storm but readily eat those of the oaks. This is despite the fact that the oak leaves contain some tannic acid. All of this changes after the maple leaves change color; they change color after the moisture has been removed from the leaves and stored in the tree's roots for the winter. This results in the sugars being concentrated in the leaves, making them sweeter. Although the deer can't see all of the brilliant colors in the maple leaves, they always eat the brightest leaves first as those leaves have the highest sugar content which the deer can obviously smell. The oak leaves are then eaten after the maple leaves have been consumed.

As mentioned, the midwestern states' rich soil has allowed them to be the bread basket of the nation, and the deer that live on those farms thrive. However, after the crops have been harvested, the deer have to move into the small woodlots because most of their protective cover is gone. A few years ago we had a particularly wet fall here in New Jersey, and many of the farmers could not get their heavy equipment into the fields to harvest their corn. The deer moved into the standing corn for the winter and found fantastic food and cover.

In addition to all of the regular vegetative foods that deer eat, one, or some, will occasionally eat meat. There are numerous examples of deer eating fish. In one case, a doe was seen wading in the riffles of a small stream, striking spawning suckers with her forefeet, which she then ate. Biologists C. W. Severinghaus and E. L. Cheatum reported five instances of deer eating fish. Robert Dailey of Yorkshire, New York, reported a buck and a doe eating bluegills and perch that had been caught by ice fishermen and thrown out on the ice. Tom Rogers of Altamont, New York, has a movie of a whitetail doe eating fish he had tossed up on the bank of Lower Sargent Pond in New York. My friend Jim Gaucher saw a doe kill meadow voles with her forefeet, like a fox pouncing on mice, and eat them. A doe that was killed in Herkimer County, New York, in 1969 was found to have a rufous-sided towhee in its stomach. The bird had probably just been killed, perhaps by a car, and the deer had eaten it as carrion. I saw a doe eat the wing off a grackle that had been killed flying into a window. Deer are not alone in these occasional instances of herbivores eating meat. I recorded video of cow elk in Yellowstone National Park killing, chewing, and eating week-old cottontail rabbits. Another friend of mine, Fred Space, saw a bison kill and eat a wild turkey—feathers and all!

Autumn

The purpose of life is the perpetuation of life, and for deer that culminates in the rutting season. Divested of all emotions, the basic reason for the existence of all living species is the propagation of that species. Without reproduction, extinction is inevitable. Among the single-cell forms of life, reproduction takes place by simple cell division, whereby two completely identical cells are produced. Among some of the lower forms of life, reproduction takes place by the organism itself, changing its sexual gender from male to female, or vice versa, according to the circumstances or even according to the ambient temperature. In others, where there are no males in the species, the female is capable of reproducing herself by replicating, or cloning, via "parthenogenesis." In most of the higher forms of creatures, reproduction is possible only through the fertilization of the female's egg, or eggs, by the male's sperm, and this involves sex in one of its many forms.

In the northern states, basically all actual body growth in white-tailed deer stops at the end of November so that mandatory lipogenesis can cause the accumulation of fat that is required for the deer to survive the severe winters. And so body growth is sacrificed for body fat. This accumulation of body fat and body size is needed in most mammals, including humans, before conception can take place. Rose Frisch, of Harvard has demonstrated that girls must acquire about 17 percent body fat before their first menstruation can take place. Girls are experiencing menarche at an earlier age today because most have a more sedentary lifestyle and an increased caloric intake. Young does must also gain a body weight of about eighty-five pounds before estrus can occur.

Those yearling bucks that do rejoin their family group after the birthing period, and about 50 percent of them do, will be forcibly driven from the group in the latter part of September or the first part of October by their mothers and other related does. Dispersal among the one-and-one-half-year bucks is mandatory unless the buck's mother was killed before he was one year old, in which case he may stay in the general area in which he was born. This forced dispersal is an innate action taken on the part of the does to prevent inbreeding, which is deleterious to most species. The offspring of incestuous mating are often smaller, weaker, and less resistant to disease and have shorter life spans. That is not to say that incestuous breeding among white-tailed deer does not take place, because it does. Because of the dispersal distance, a buck that becomes dominant in his new area is not likely to breed with his mother or her siblings or with any of his own siblings, but he could, if he lived long enough, breed with his daughters, granddaughters, and even his great-granddaughters. The likelihood of this happening is very slim. In the wild, very few bucks ever live to be five or six years old. Even the most dominant bucks in the North, where the breeding window of opportunity is very short, seldom have a chance of breeding with more than six does in any given season. During the rutting season a buck expands his home range of one to two square miles and travels up to eight to ten square miles in his search for estrus does. That being the case, there is a good chance that he would be off seeking does elsewhere when one of his own familial does came into estrus. Dominance is a major factor in the life of white-tailed deer for both bucks and does; it manifests itself very early and is constantly being reinforced throughout the animal's life. The competitive testing of strength and fitness that becomes the norm in all forms and levels of deer society begins as early as two weeks of age.

Dominance is also a very important survival factor for deer because it brings order out of chaos; it is the basis for the evolutionary survival of the fittest. In deer, the dominant bucks do the bulk of the breeding, which guarantees that their genes are the ones to be passed on. It is self-evident that the members of every species that is alive today are the finest example of that species that have ever existed or they wouldn't be here. The deer we hunt today are the biggest, fastest, smartest, most adaptable deer that have ever lived.

If the deer you hunt don't match that description, it is only because the overabundance of deer that we have in most areas is destroying their habitat, and so the deer in that particular area are not able to develop to their full potential.

Mutual grooming by bucks during the pre-rut and rutting season often leads to an invitation to spar. It is also interesting to note that, when certain parts of the body are licked, a neural reaction causes the deer being licked to flick out its tongue in synchrony with the tongue doing the licking. A deer can reach almost every part of its body to lick an itch with its tongue or to scratch it with a hoof or an antler. I am sure that some of the mutual grooming done on the animal's head is to remove ticks that are embedded there. Some researchers claim that this social grooming is part of a

Sparring prepares bucks for the fights to come.

homosexual expression, but I strongly disagree with such conclusions because I have never seen any evidence of a sexual nature being exhibited while this was being done. The social grooming done by the bucks is a bonding commitment, not a sexual overture, and there are no sexual overtones.

I was raised on a dairy farm in northwestern New Jersey and frequently saw homosexual activity among animals. Homosexuality is usually defined as sexual interest or activity between members of the same gender. We could always tell when one of our cows was in estrus because one or more of the other cows would mount her exactly as a bull would do, except that there could be no actual copulation. Although there were several cows that would act the part of the bull, there was one cow that did it much more frequently than any of the others.

There is great dissension among biologists as to whether homosexuality is genetically programmed or an acquired condition. It is the old nature vs. nurture argument. However, the noted ethologist Joseph Alcock, in his book *Animal Behavior* states,

"The fact that the development of any attribute of any living multicellular organism is dependent on both genes and environment means that no trait—not one—is 'genetic' as opposed to 'environmental' nor is any attribute environmentally determined in the sense of developing without genetic input. This claim is counterintuitive to many who want to divide the features of living things into those that are caused by 'nature,' the so-called genetically determined traits, versus those that are caused by 'nurture,' the so-called environmentally determined traits." With the deciphering of the human genome, a gene leaning toward homosexuality should soon be proven, if it has not already been done, without my having seen the evidence. There is no doubt that most homosexual activity is caused by hormonal influence under genetic control, but I will be the first to admit that I wouldn't recognize a hormone if I fell over it. There already is proof, provided by homosexuals, that their lifestyle was also influenced by other homosexuals they encountered. My knowledge of the sexual activity in deer is empirical based on my constant study of deer over the past seventy-four years.

It is androgens, the male sex hormones, which causes an embryo to develop into a little buck in the first place. It is low levels of testosterone, from the buck's testes, that cause the development of the secondary sex characteristics such as the start of the antler pedicles. It is the increased amounts of testosterone that starts his sexual drive that prompted his mounting of his mother at four months of age. In the little doe, it is her ovaries that will produce the female hormones estrogen and progesterone that, prompt later by hormones from her pituitary gland, will cause her to develop the eggs needed for pregnancy. However, both genders of animals produce the sex hormones of the opposite sex but usually in such small amounts, or they are suppressed by the dominance of their own hormones, that their effect is nullified.

Transgendered animals usually have a greater amount of the opposite sex hormones than is normal, and this is made apparent by their homosexual activity. In the case of the "bulling" cow back on the family farm, she evidently had more testosterone than any of the other cows and so was the one that most often acted the part of the bull. In all other respects she was perfectly normal, as she came into estrus at the proper time, was bred, had calves, and was a good milk producer.

Bucks communicate throughout the entire year by rubbing scent from their forehead glands on overhanging branches but, from September on, those glands enlarge and produce much more scent, and the bucks increase their usage by at least tenfold. Mature bucks are usually, but not always, two weeks ahead of the yearling bucks in antler hardening, velvet peeling, and in the making of scrapes. Sexual activity increases steadily in northern deer during the month of September, although southern deer lag behind by about two months or more. Sparring increases as the bucks constantly test one another for dominance, as well as develop the muscles and skills that they will need if they should actually have to fight during the breeding season. Sparring is also a reaffirmation of the status quo in each fraternal group and prevents actual fights from having to take place, which could cause severe injuries, if not death. A dominant buck always has to be willing to fight if he is to maintain his standing, but he is more successful if, by showing a willingness to fight, he can intimidate any potential rival without fighting.

Sparring can best be likened to the horseplay indulged in by human teenage males; a time of constant testing. The main difference being that a human teenager may excel in something other than physical sports, while a young buck that does not constantly involve himself in sparring has no chance of ever attaining any status.

Sparring is a very ritualistic endeavor that only occasionally gets out of hand. There is an obligation on the part of the dominant male to partake in sparring with the younger bucks as if to teach them the finer points of combat. And it starts at a very early age. I have documented five-month-old bucks sparring with dominant bucks while the big bucks were lying down. It usually starts with the little guy smelling the big buck's antlers. At five months of age the little buck's pedicles have started to grow but the little buck doesn't use them. He usually puts the middle of his skull against one of the big buck's antlers and starts to push. It takes almost no effort on the part of the big buck to offer all the resistance the little buck can handle no matter how hard he pushes, but the little guy is sparring and gaining strength through the exercise. This can go on for five minutes or more until the big buck tires of the disturbance. Then with a toss of his head he will deliver a whack with his antler to the little buck that leaves no doubt that the game is over. I have on several occasions photographed button bucks attempting to chew on a big buck's antlers.

Yearling bucks start to spar on the spur of the moment without going through the formality that they employ to get a big buck to spar with them. They approach a big buck head-on, but they may pretend to eat or stretch their necks out with their heads lowered, before raising them to touch noses and start to groom the big buck's head. The big buck's response is to tilt his head down and project his antlers forward while being groomed on his forehead scent glands. After several minutes the yearling buck will project his antlers forward, engaging the big buck's antlers, and the shoving begins. As the big buck usually weighs twice the weight of the yearling, the yearling does most of the shoving with the big buck offering massive, passive resistance.

Yearling bucks pester big bucks to spar even while the big bucks are bedded.

Many folks seeing the sparring believe that they are seeing a real fight, but fights are comparatively rare. Even the folks at *National Geographic* occasionally get things wrong. In their October 2006 issue they show a pair of young bucks playfully sparring, but the caption reads, "Photographer Michael Melford used a telephoto lens to catch a park-goer just feet from battling bucks." A careful look at the "combatants" would reveal that the bucks are not battling; they are sparring, and not really expending much effort. In sparring, the bucks' legs are usually pointing straight down; in a fight their legs angle sharply backward and out, as each animal does its best not to be thrown to the ground. Occasionally, what starts out as sparring may develop into a fight if one of the two bucks becomes too aggressive. Fights don't start between a yearling and an adult buck because the larger buck is quick to put the lesser animal in his place if he gets too pushy.

I have found several areas, over the years, where the ground was all torn up by sparring bucks. What was unique about those areas was that they were used frequently during the season and were used year after year. They were usually about twenty by twenty feet, about the size of a boxing ring, and used just for the purpose of sparring. I believe that the bucks were attracted to those same areas because of all the interdigital scent that was deposited by the bucks' splayed hooves. I have had other hunters tell me that they have seen such frequently used areas, too.

The beginning of the actual rut occurs around the middle of October and can readily be seen by the swelling of the buck's neck to almost twice its normal size. The swelling is the result of hormonal steroids, causing increased muscle mass built up by the constant rubbing and fighting with bushes and saplings that the bucks do. The increased muscle mass acts as shock absorbers, preventing the deer from breaking their necks when they crash together while fighting. Concurrent with this physical development is the expansion of the range over which the bucks travel in their search for estrus does during the last weeks of October. From September on, the bucks are willing to breed, but no doe is capable of accepting them. This doesn't deter the bucks in their quest and, during the rutting season, the bucks check out every doe that they encounter. A buck tracking a doe usually does so with his nose down sniffing her hoof tracks while his tail is pointed straight up in the air. The buck might also be giving a short, raspy grunt with every few steps that he takes. From about the first of November on, they usually run at the doe in a very aggressive posture, with their heads and necks held straight out below their shoulder height; their tail is held clamped down against their body. Their ears are usually held forward instead of being laid back along their necks, as they would be in an aggressive run at a rival buck.

Before starting their run, the bucks often grunt or may make a prolonged moaning grunt, about twenty to thirty seconds in duration. The purpose of this run is to get the doe to urinate so that the bucks can check for the pheromones that will indicate that the doe is about to come into estrus. As mentioned earlier, experienced does will usually squat immediately and release just enough urine so the buck can check. That way they don't have to be involved in all the running that often takes place. Less experienced does will run from the bucks, using a low slinking posture, but will be chased until they finally stop and urinate so the bucks can check them out. It is the constant seeking and chasing of the does that causes the bucks to lose up to 25 percent of their body weight, which is normal, before the end of the rutting season two months later. It also causes the bucks to experience tremendous frustration that they express in an outburst of autoeroticism. Masturbation by the bucks is a common form of self-gratification.

The bucks hunch their backs at the same time that they rub their fully extended penis against their chests and flex it back and forth, ending in the copulatory thrust that signifies that ejaculation has taken place. They also, to a considerable extent, employ oral stimulation of their own penis, sucking that organ until ejaculation is achieved.

The mounting of one male animal by another male is listed by many biologists as a homosexual act and, for a number of species, it is, I myself have witnessed it in many species a number of times. Such homosexual mountings are very common among both domestic and wild sheep and can occur at any time of the year, not just during

During the rut, bucks frequently seek sexual gratification by masturbating.

Bucks also relieve sexual frustration by engaging in fellatio.

the breeding season. I have photographed this activity many times and, although the penis is often extended, I have never seen anal penetration. Dr. Charles Roselli, of Oregon Health and Science University, has discovered that among sheep the percentage of homosexuals is about the same as humans, at about 8 percent. It is also very common, if not more so, among male bison from the age of about five months up to about four years of age. Same-sex mounting is rarely employed among white-tailed bucks and, when it is, I believe it to be more of a dominance display than an act designating homosexuality. I base that observation on the fact that I have never seen the penis extended.

Although I have photographed such mountings, I have not seen it occur more than about ten times in my seventy-four years of deer observations. In most cases, it was the dominant buck that mounted the lesser buck, which was not always the case with

One buck mounting another is not necessarily a sign of homosexuality.

other species in which there was definite homosexual activity. With yearling bucks, the lesser buck sometimes mounts the larger buck.

White-tailed deer in my area are entrained by photoperiodism to have the peak of their breeding season occur between November 7 and November 20. These dates may fluctuate by a day or two, according to some localized condition, but the variation is minimal because, through evolution, it has been determined that does bred at that time will give birth at the optimal time in the spring, approximately 203 to 205 days later. A dark, rainy fall may advance the breeding season by a day or so because less light is absorbed by the deer's eye. The dark days mimic a shortened day.

It is important to understand the proper terminology as it pertains to the breeding patterns of the different types of wildlife. Monogamy is where only the dominant male and female, holding a territory, breed. We are all familiar now with hearing about how the dominant male and female wolf, the alpha and beta, are the only ones in the pack to breed. "Monogamy" is primarily found in all the members of the canine family.

"Polygamy" is where one male breeds with three or four females and keeps all other males out of his territory on a year-round basis. The prairie dog is a good example of this, and his harem and territory are known as a "coterie."

"Polygyny" is where a male breeds with as many females as is possible but associates with the females only during the breeding season. Some members of the "Cervidae" family, such as the elk, gather together a harem of cows and fight with all rivals to keep them away from the cows until he has them all bred.

Some mule deer bucks try to maintain a harem, but the white-tailed deer bucks do not. The difference is that the elk and mule deer live in open areas where the cows

The bull elk guarding his harem of cows is an example of polygyny.

get together in larger herds than do the whitetails, which live in forested areas. It is a lot easier to keep a herd together in open country, where rivals can be seen at much greater distances.

"Polyandry" is a condition where one female has several mates. I have seen this situation with red-necked phalaropes and know of it in several other bird families. I do not know of this type of breeding pattern in mammals, although a doe may be bred by several bucks.

Photoperiodism also causes the hypothalamus gland in does to signal their pituitary gland to release lutenizing hormones, causing them to ovulate, which brings on their estrus period.

About forty-eight hours before a doe ovulates, she becomes increasingly active under hormonal stimulation and walks with her tail held up horizontally. She travels almost constantly within her home range, urinating frequently. There are no sexual stimulants in the doe's urine. The pheromones are picked up by the urine from the

Bucks travel in a fraternal herd until the rutting season commences.

doe's vaginal mucus as it is excreted through her vulva. Her scent trail is picked up and followed by every buck that crosses it. Although bucks flehmen throughout the year, they do it constantly during the rutting season as they encounter more of the doe's urine. Now is when dominance comes into play, as the biggest, strongest buck will do everything in his power to keep all of the other bucks away from the doe. And all of the other bucks will do everything they can to get to her. This is an extremely important aspect of the deer's breeding cycle, because it increases the number of bucks attracted to the doe and the competition between them. The investment costs of bearing and raising her fawns is so great that intrinsically the does want to be bred by the biggest, best bucks, and nothing proves a buck's superior genes like competition.

Ordinarily, the bucks from a fraternal group do not fight, as they have already hammered out their individual place in the pecking order.

However, dominance fluctuates as often as the temperature. Whereas the oldest buck is usually dominant because he is heavier in weight, larger in size, and has the largest antlers, there comes a time when being older nullifies the other advantages.

When that occurs, a younger, smaller, but more vigorous, buck may best the dominant buck. It happens to all of us.

Most fights take place between two dominant bucks that are meeting, perhaps for the first time, as they have expanded their ranges during the rutting season. When two bucks of equal size meet, and each buck knows exactly his own body and antler size, they try to bluff their opponent into giving way. After appraising each other they will go into the hard-stare aggressive posture. With their ears laid back along their head, they will cause their erector pili muscles to stand all of their body hair on edge, which makes them appear to be much larger than they actually are. It also makes them appear much darker in color, because the rival is now looking into the depth of their hair, instead of at the flat surface. The bucks will pull their chins back toward their chests; this will project their antler tips forward into position for fighting. Extreme aggression is shown by the buck rapidly flicking his tongue in and out of his mouth. Quite often the bucks will paw the ground, throwing dirt and sod for a considerable distance. Pawing is also a sign of extreme aggression. The bucks usually circle each other, walking in a sidling fashion with their heads turned slightly away from each other. They walk with a stiff-legged gait and a shortened stride. They will give out short, low-pitched, raspy grunts. If by this stage neither buck turns aside, a fight is imminent. The charge occurs in a blur of motion as each buck meets his rival as nearly head-on as possible. A buck's antlers are designed for just such an occasion; they are both offensive and defensive weapons. After the initial, bone-jarring impact, the two bucks keep in contact, with each trying to throw his opponent off his feet so the one that is standing can gore the one that is down. That seldom happens. Although only equal animals fight, it soon becomes apparent to both of the bucks that one of them is stronger than the other and, with that realization, the lesser buck will immediately try to break free and dash off. Most fights are over in seconds; some may last a minute, but that is rare. The longest fight that I have recorded on video lasted a little over six minutes, and I have photographed a fight that lasted more than seven minutes. When the bucks do break apart, the victor will do his best to gore the rapidly departing buck and although he would have killed him if he could have, the losing buck usually only chases him for a short distance, because he has preserved his dominant status and they both know it.

The most vicious fights take place when a doe is actually in estrus. Most fights take place to prove dominance, but when an estrus doe is the prize, the bucks throw caution to the wind, status is often forgotten or ignored, and the fights are prompted by desperation. Many times, while the dominant buck is actually breeding the doe, a rival buck will attack him viciously when he cannot defend himself. Occasionally, while the dominant buck is mounting the doe, a rival buck will mount him in an attempt to breed the doe.

Occasionally when fighting, the two bucks will lock antlers, leaving them unable to separate themselves.

We read so much about this happening that many folks believe it to be a common occurrence. In reality it is such a rare happening that it gets a great play in the media and in magazines when it is seen. I have never seen it in all my years of watching deer but I must have read about it one hundred times or more. I have seen several sets of antlers, in collections, where the locked deer had died and their antlers were found. One set of antlers I saw showed considerable wear at the contact points where the antlers were locked, showing that one or both of the deer had lived for a considerable

These are skeletons of two bucks that died because their antlers locked during a fight.

period of time after the accident. The deer hit each other's antlers with many hundred pounds of pressure, causing the antlers to spring apart upon impact and then back again. Depending upon the actual shape of the antlers, the straight tines may slide by one another while the curved tines may grasp each other securely.

Once securely locked the deer usually die a lingering death of starvation or lack of water. Some deer have been found locked up in a pond or stream where one or both of the animals died quickly. I read of one pair of bucks where coyotes ate the dead one while it was still attached to the live buck. One can only imagine the terror that the live buck must have experienced each time the predators came in to feed and it could not escape. There have been a number of reports where the locked deer were found and a person, or persons, were able to save the bucks by sawing off one of the antlers. There are also a couple of reports where a buck, after being released, has charged his benefactor, so care must be taken in any rescue operation.

What happens more often, but which is not often documented, is that while two bucks are fighting, a third buck will join in the fight, and the third buck will cause considerable damage to one of the combatants. As neither combatant can protect himself, the third buck will plunge his antlers into one of their bodies. I have recorded this on video several times and have seen it perhaps a dozen times. I have also found the bodies of deer that had been killed by the third buck and not by the one that they were fighting. In December 2006, I lost my dominant buck in just such a fight. Although I didn't see it happen, the six-inch puncture wound in his ham bore mute testimony to the cause of his demise.

In an elementary school in Black Earth, Wisconsin, where I was lecturing, I saw a mount of three deer heads, belonging to the principal. Two bucks were fighting when a third buck charged in from the side, hitting their antlers with his own. The force of his charge caused him to cartwheel over the top of the other two bucks, breaking his neck in the process. All three bucks were dead and the principal had their heads mounted together as he found them. It is the only instance that I have heard of where three bucks died with their antlers locked together.

All deer are attracted to the sound of two bucks fighting; it's why "rattling antlers" is such a successful ploy to call deer within shooting range. The big bucks come in to get into the action, the small bucks are anxious to see the action, and the does are interested in which one is the better buck. Rattling antlers was a hunting technique used by the Indians. Being expert observers of deer behavior, the forest Indians used antlers in rattling and a split reed to call in the deer that they depended on for their food.

I first became acquainted with rattling antlers a number of years ago while I was doing my whitetail deer seminar at the Dixie Deer Classic in Raleigh, North Carolina. That evening I was at a reception given by my host, Dr. Carroll Mann. Included among the guests were Fred Bear, Dr. Rob Wegner, Dick Idol, Tom Fleming, and many other knowledgeable deer people. The talk turned to calling deer by antler rattling, and Tom Fleming, who was known as "The Rattling Man," was persuaded to show us his technique. Afterward, Fred turned to me and said, "Lennie, what do you think about its effectiveness?" I replied that I still had to be convinced. At that, Tom offered to prove the technique's effectiveness if I would come down during the next hunting season. I agreed to be his student on one condition: if he were successful, I'd tell the world, if he were not successful, I'd still tell the world. Tom's technique proved to be as good as he said it was and I'm still telling the world that Tom Fleming is a rattling good man.

The sound of the big bucks fighting attracts every deer within hearing. The buck being shoved up on a rock is in a bad position.

Tom taught me that it's always best to use a set of medium-size antlers rather than the biggest set you could get. The larger the set of antlers, the deeper sound they make when banged together. He reasoned, and is right, that a big buck may come charging in to the sound of big antlers, while an average buck may sneak away out of fear of the big guys. Tom always started his session by merely ticking the antlers together at first because he didn't want a loud crashing to scare nearby bucks out of the area. After all, the buck's hearing is so much better than ours that even the ticking can be heard for a long distance. Immediately after rattling, Tom put down the antlers, picked up his bow and scrutinized the surrounding area for five to ten minutes. If no deer appeared, he would bang the antlers together and again carefully scrutinize the area. The third time he would crash the antlers together, in an attempt to get the sound out to some distant buck, and wait ten minutes or more to allow a distant buck to come in. After a third futile attempt. He said it was time to go to another spot and set up all over again. Not every buck that hears the crashing antlers will come in, but enough do to make it worthwhile. I don't know why rattling works better in the southern states than it does in the northern ones. In Texas, I have seen bucks jump fences in their response to come in.

We hear so much about the dominant buck doing the bulk of the breeding that most people don't realize the doe often makes the actual selection of the buck with which she breeds. The doe is usually bred by the dominant buck because she instinctively wants to breed with the best buck available. I became aware of this fact when my very first doe would not breed with the eight-point buck with which I had her penned. Unbeknownst to me, the doe was being courted by a big ten-point buck on the outside of her pen. The big buck was coming in at night. The night my doe came into estrus, she stretched the wire on her pen and ran off with the big buck. She returned the following day with the big buck following. My doe had never been out of her pen before and, to her, that pen was home; after being bred she was simply coming home. When the big buck saw me he stopped out in the woods while the doe walked back in through the gate I held open for her. She did the exact same thing the following year; she wanted to be bred by that big buck. This is not an isolated case but is par for the course; I've seen this happen all over the country. Her twin buck fawns also became ten-pointers.

Every year during the rut I have does come to the outside of the fence containing my research herd. My bucks are much larger than the wild bucks outside the fence because mine are older and better fed and the does want to be bred by the biggest bucks. That my bucks want to breed those does is attested to by the ruts they have walked on the inside perimeter of the fence as they follow after the does on the out-side. This occurs wherever someone has big captive bucks.

It is interesting to note that when the wild does approach my fence during the rutting season, they often do so even if I am there, close by and in full sight. Because my does are habituated to me and don't run off, the wild does are not alarmed and don't run either. Wild bucks often come to the fence to fight through the fence with my bucks. One wild eight-point buck allowed me to get within twenty-five feet, and because my bucks didn't run, he didn't either.

In Louisiana, I photographed a yearling buck breed a doe while the dominant buck was busy keeping another big buck out of the area. We know now that many does are

The wild buck outside of my deer fence didn't run when I approached, because my captive buck didn't.

bred by more than one buck because the DNA of the fawns sometimes shows different paternity. If a doe drops two fawns of the same gender they are probably identical twins caused by a single fertilized egg splitting, and they will have had a single sire. If the doe drops two fawns of different gender they are known as fraternal twins, the result of two different eggs being fertilized, and they could be the result of two different bucks breeding the doe. Researchers have found that up to 25 percent of all does have been bred by two bucks or more.

I have also recorded on video pre-estrus does standing up on their hind feet flailing away at eight-point bucks that they wanted nothing to do with; so does definitely have a lot to do with determining with which buck they breed. By the same token I have seen does that preferred to breed with a younger buck and rejected the advances of the dominant buck to do so. I also know of two does being gang raped. In Louisiana, I saw three bucks pursue a doe and all three bred her and would not let her rest. In the second incident, I did not personally see the rape occur but was told about it by two friends who did see it.

The Hercules Powder Company had built a munitions factory in my hometown of Belvidere, New Jersey, and had purchased and fenced in five farms. In the process, they had also fenced in a number of deer. As no hunting was allowed on the property the deer herd increased in size very rapidly. During the rutting season a group of the men were standing outside of the power plant during their lunch break. Suddenly, a doe ran over a nearby hill with eight bucks in hot pursuit. The doe was evidently exhausted and would attempt to lie down, but as soon as she did one of the bucks would rake her with his antlers, forcing her to get back up on her feet. When she did, one of the bucks would mount her. The men saw three different bucks mount the doe in quick succession before she ran over the hill, followed by all of the bucks, until they were all lost to view.

Ordinarily, when a pre-estrus doe pairs up with a dominant buck, the wild chasing is basically over and they settle down in some particular spot. I have never been able to ascertain who picks the spot, although I think it is wherever the tired doe decides to bed down. In my area, I have noticed that she usually selects a spot where she can lie up against a large rock or log in order to keep any buck from sneaking up behind her. The tending buck may bed down close to the doe, or he may have to remain on his feet to keep the satellite bucks out of the area. A great deal has been written about how the dominant buck will drive every other buck completely out of the area, but that's just not true nor is it possible. The dominant buck will patrol an area that has a radius of about seventy-five to one hundred feet with the doe as the focal point. He will then chase off every buck that comes closer than that and, when he does give chase, he will go no farther than that distance from the doe. To go farther than that would leave the doe vulnerable to the harassment of a buck that might sneak in from the opposite side and the other bucks are always looking for the opportunity to do just that. The yearling bucks are the ones that are usually the biggest pain in the drain to the dominant buck. The yearlings have not really been hammered enough by the dominant buck to have respect for the boss bucks.

Many times I have seen a dominant buck tending a doe with as many as five or six satellite bucks forming a circle around the breeding pair. With dominance established, the events are almost as programmed as a minuet. With the tending buck standing near the doe, one of the satellites bucks will move into the defended circle. As he does, the tending buck will take several aggressive steps toward the intruder. An adult buck, which knows his place in the hierarchy, will usually immediately stop his incursion and move back out of the defended zone. As he steps out, the dominant buck will move back to his original position near the doe. Things are quiet for a few minutes until another adult moves in. Again, the dominant buck will exhibit the aggressive threat display and hard stare which is enough to cause that intruder to retreat. Occasionally one of the intruders will use subterfuge by feeding or pretending to feed as he slowly walks into the defended area. Feeding is often used by lesser bucks as a sign of appeasement, letting the dominant buck know that they know that he is boss. Using the "feeding ruse" the intruder is sometimes able to get close enough to the doe to be able to make a run at her. If the dominant buck can intercept him, the intruder may just be chased off. If the intruder gets close enough, the doe will usually jump to her feet and dash off, and pandemonium is created as every buck in the area joins in the wild chase, which will continue until the dominant buck can get between the doe and the rest of her pursuers. When does run from any of the bucks they usually run in a huge circle. This keeps them within their own home range, which they know intimately; it also keeps them close to their fawns which may or may not run with their mother. After the doe tires and drops down, the dominant buck will immediately define the boundaries of the newly defended zone. As mentioned, the dominant buck has the most trouble with the yearling bucks, who almost constantly probe the defended zone. At each incursion, the dominant buck will walk toward the intruder and then suddenly make a very aggressive charge of five or six steps, ending with a jolting four-footed slamming on of the brakes. Whirling about just as quickly, the yearling will dash off for five or six steps, as if he knows that that is as far as the big buck is going to come. When the big buck returns to the doe, the yearling starts the incursion all over again, and again and again.

Another common misconception is that a tending buck never has the chance to eat or sleep, and that's simply not true either. He will do both at every opportunity, although admittedly the opportunities are few and far between. I have documented a tending buck getting a little shut-eye while all of the satellite bucks are doing the same thing.

As the deer are most active at night, as has been proven by telemetry, there are periods during the daytime when all of the deer are bedded and sleep for up to an hour at a time. Although they seldom do it at other times of the year, during the rut the deer become so exhausted that they sleep with their heads stretched out on the ground, as if they are simply too tired to hold them up any longer. Even in an exhausted state any deer can instantly spring to its feet, as its heart rate skyrockets, if the need arises. I have also documented older, dominant bucks becoming so exhausted halfway through the rutting season that they simply give up trying to maintain their rank. They simply retire from the fray.

Anyone who has ever owned a dog is well aware of the fact that the dog often dreams, as can be told by its twitching, whining and even growling. Deer dream, too. Deer go through the rapid eye movement that is indicative of deep dreaming in humans. They twitch, toss their heads, grimace, and curl their lips as if hissing, as though they were in the throes of a nightmare. Their dreams sometimes cause them to awaken with a start, and they look around to see what might have sneaked up on them.

Another little-known consideration is that, when a doe is in estrus, they attract every buck, young and old, in the entire area. While all of the bucks are attending to the estrus does, the other does have a comparatively quiet time. Prior to the first doe coming into estrus during the rutting season, all of the bucks are constantly testing all of the does, and none of them get any peace and quiet. Estrus does attract all of

The dominant buck, and three satellite bucks, are all napping while the doe is bedded.

the bucks like bees to honey, which momentarily takes the pressure off the rest of the herd.

It is important that we discuss the actual breeding cycle in some detail so that all of the details are known. We have already discussed how the doe sets out to attract the bucks just prior to her ovulation. The doe's pituitary gland releases a follicle stimulating hormone, which, in turn, causes a mature egg, or eggs, to leave the ovary and start the journey down the fallopian tube.

This occurs during the twenty-eight-hour period during which a doe will accept the buck and can be bred. It is the hormonal secretions of estrogen and progesterone that signal to the buck, through the doe's vaginal discharge, that she is ready to be bred. Adult bucks assiduously court the does when they finally get them to stop running. They rub their heads and bodies against the does. They lick the does' heads and bodies and especially their vulvas to stimulate them so that they will stand to be mounted. Any doe that is not ready to be mounted cannot be mounted, as she will just keep slipping out from under the buck. When the doe is ready to stand, the buck usually makes three or four pre-copulatory mounts, often without extending his penis out of its sheath. The false mountings are not evidence of the ineptness of the buck but are, I believe, a part of the ritual that makes sure that the doe's eggs are down in either her fallopian tubes or in her uterus where they can be fertilized. During the actual copulation mount, the penis tip hunts for the vaginal opening and the thrusting is done

This is a doe's entire reproductive tract: ovaries, fallopian tubes, uterus, and vagina. The bladder is the pendulous sac hanging beneath the vagina.

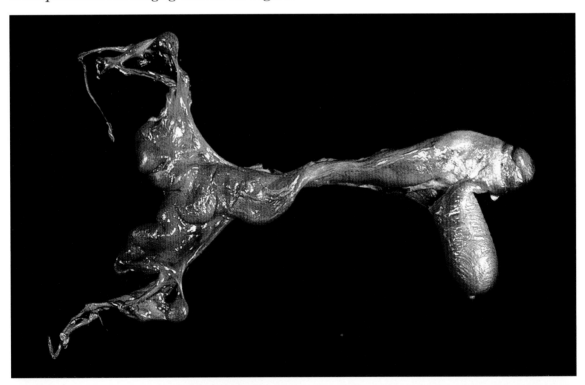

by the extension of the penis's sigmoid loop and not by the pelvic thrusting that is so common with most mammalian mountings. The searching takes from twenty to thirty seconds, whereas once the penis enters the vagina the entire ejaculatory thrust takes about two seconds. There is a tremendous pelvic thrust that accompanies and signifies that ejaculation has taken place. The thrust may be done so forcefully that at times the buck's hind feet may leave the ground and he may fall over on his back. In that length of time, the rigid penis is inserted for its full length of about ten inches, the semen is released, and the penis is withdrawn.

The buck may or may not lick his penis before it is withdrawn back into its sheath. The doe always confirms the copulation by assuming a "kyphosis," hunched-up posture with her tail raised and strains mightily as if trying to excrete the just-deposited semen. I estimate that she ejects about a tablespoon of a cloudy, viscous string of liquid. Several deer biologists have assured me that this liquid is vaginal mucous, and it must be, because the doe ends up pregnant, proving that the semen is retained. I have never been able to prove whether or not the doe experience orgasm. A friend who raises pure blooded milk goats said she was taught in the agricultural college she attended that the female goats do experience orgasm, that it creates vaginal waves that help to propel the sperm toward the uterus. I have witnessed does going through waves of shuddering, as if climaxing, while a buck licked her vulva in courtship.

I don't want to create the impression that all of the mature bucks are good lovers, because some are not. I photographed one huge buck that was absolutely stupid! The doe was willing to stand for him, but each time he approached he hooked her with his antlers and of course she ran off. This went on time after time, and as she always ran off, he never did get to breed her.

Another interesting note is that it is common for a cow elk to false mount the bull, and I believe it is done to stimulate the bull to breed rather than being evidence of a transgendered cow. In seventy-four years I have only seen a white-tailed doe mount a tending buck on two instances.

After copulation, the doe will lie down while the buck stands guard. If the satellite bucks are quiet, the buck may get a chance to rest and feed. If not, he will spend his time keeping them out of the core area, as I have already described. Often the dominant buck, after chasing the satellites, will make rubs and thrash bushes, as if to show the younger bucks what he will do to them if he gets the chance. Unfortunately for the dominant buck, the satellite bucks are most often yearlings that act like a bunch of horny teenagers. They not only harass the buck with their constant incursions into his core area, but they chase every doe that chances by. If

The buck approaches the doe gently as she reaches up to touch noses with him.

He then caresses her with his tongue.

When she stands, he stimulates her by licking her vulva area.

He presses his head and body against her.

As she shows willingness to stand for him, he begins to mount her.

As the buck mounts her, his penis hunts for her vaginal opening.

Ejaculation is attained with a deep copulatory thrust.

After being bred the doe stands with humped back as the buck's sperm travels to its destination of her egg or eggs.

the estrus doe's fawns do not stay within the tending buck's core area, the yearling bucks, showing true homosexual feelings of deprivation, will try to mount the fawns whether they be male or female. Many times I have seen other pre-estrus does lie down within the dominant buck's core area so that they will not be harassed by the satellite bucks. I have also seen the dominant buck keep the estrus doe's buck fawns out of the breeding area.

If through excessive hunting pressure all of the mature bucks are removed from an area, it is detrimental to the herd because of the chaos created by the breeding behavior of the inexperienced yearlings. The yearlings run every deer ragged and lack the courtship skills that the older bucks possess and practice. Due to the turmoil created, all the deer have less chance to eat and rest, so they go into the winter in much poorer shape than usual and may not be able to survive a really hard winter.

After being bred, the doe will usually lie down for a while. All deer get up from time to time to urinate. They can defecate while bedded but have to get to their feet to urinate. The doe will get up, turn around or just walk for a few feet, and then bed down again. The buck will go over to the doe and caress her by licking her head and ears, and she will usually reciprocate by reaching up and licking his head. After about four hours (and you can usually set your watch by it), the doe will get to her feet and walk or slink off for a distance of several hundred feet, although she may go in a small circle when she does it. That is the signal for the buck that it is time to breed again and he will immediately go through the series of mountings already described. The timing is definitely set by the doe. On several occasions, I have seen a dominant buck tend two does at one time and breed both does within twenty minutes of each other. That proves that the bucks are capable of breeding more frequently but are limited by the doe's timing. I have witnessed that four-hour timing far too often for it to be happenstance.

Because of the four-hour interval, a buck will breed the doe five to six times during her estrus period. He is with her for twenty-four to forty-eight hours before she comes into estrus and for the twenty-eight hours or so that she is in estrus. He then stays with her for another twelve hours to prevent other bucks from breeding her. Even the most dominant buck will not have the chance to breed more than five to six does in any one season. The post-breeding guarding is to prevent sperm competition. The testicles of a buck are only a fraction of the size of those of a wild sheep ram, although the animals are similar in body weight. A buck physically keeps all competitors away from the female, while the ram cannot do this. The ram has to produce far more sperm to "flood" the sperm of lesser rams that may have copulated with the ewe after the first insemination.

The buck does not leave the doe until her estrus period is over, but that doesn't say that he is not tempted. Times without number, I have seen a tending buck lying close to his estrus doe only to have another buck chase a pre-estrus doe somewhere within the area. The buck may not even be able to see the doe that is being chased or the buck that is doing the chasing; all he can hear is the crunching of the dry leaves, but he is instantly galvanized. Springing to his feet and watching the satellite bucks go tearing off in hot pursuit is sometimes more temptation than he can stand. I'm not sure if he has ever heard that a bird in the hand is worth two in the bush or something to that effect, but not to dash off takes all of the willpower that he can muster. Sometimes it's just not enough, and off he dashes.

It was just such an occasion that I witnessed when three does in the area were in estrus all at the same time. Does in family groups tend to synchronize their estrus periods, mainly through odor. Chaos reigned as all of the bucks dashed off after the three does. Luckily for me, the does usually run in a big circle so they stay within their home range and close to their fawns. From a hilltop vantage point, I was able to record on video one doe being bred four times in one hour and twelve minutes by four different big bucks, including the dominant buck. She was actually bred six times in two hours and thirty-five minutes. How many more times was she bred that day? I actually don't know, as a downpour forced me to take shelter to protect my expensive video equipment.

The peak of the rut is of about ten days duration while the so-called window of opportunity is about three weeks in length, but most does are bred in a shorter span of time than that. It has been proven that wherever a large number of women are housed together, within a very short period of time their menses periods synchronize. And so it is with many mammals, including deer, whose estrus period, also synchronize. This synchronization is of a tremendous survival value, because it means that not only are all the females bred at about the same time, but that their young will all be born about the same time. The multiplicity of births means that more young will be born at one time than the predators can possibly eat, raising the possibility that more of the young will survive.

The so-called second rut occurs about twenty-eight days after the regular rut because does are on a lunar cycle, just like a human's menses. If for some reason a doe is not bred, or is bred but does not conceive, she will recycle again and again until she does conceive. It is in December that any of the doe fawns that have achieved a body

In northern states, the rutting season is basically over by the middle of December, when the buck's testosterone drops and the swelling goes out of his neck.

weight of about eighty pounds will also breed. In areas that produce lots of highly nutritious food, such as Ohio, Indiana, and Illinois, 60 percent or more of their seven-month-old fawns will breed. Almost none of the little doe fawns in New Hampshire, Vermont, or Maine breed because they just don't have access to the food they need to reach the required body weight.

For the northern tier of the United States, the rutting season is over by the middle of December, when the buck's supply of testosterone drops as his testes shrink and the swelling goes out of his neck.

Over a period of the next six weeks most of the bucks will cast their antlers. However, with or without their antlers and despite their shrunken testes, some bucks are still capable of breeding throughout the year.

Several years ago, I had a two-and-a-half-year-old doe that I did not want bred because I really didn't need to build my herd any larger. I kept the doe in a separate pen from October until the following April. The dominant buck had cast his antlers in January, yet on April 8 he bred the doe, and she gave birth 198 days later, on October 23. This proved a number of things. The doe's gestation period was shortened by about six days because she had not had to contend with the rigors of winter and had access to unlimited nutritious food. Despite the fact that the buck's testosterone level was down, he was still capable of producing viable sperm. It also proved that the doe had gone through six complete estrus cycles and would probably have continued to recycle until she was bred. It is common for tropical deer to breed at any time of the year because they are not entrained to a photoperiodic cycle, as they have twelve hours of daylight and darkness year-round. Although it is most uncommon, I do have records of white-tailed fawns being born in every month of the year, even in the northern two-thirds of the United States. In many of the cases, the fawns that are born out of sync with the rest of the deer don't survive, and it is better for the species if they don't. After all, it has taken the deer thousands of years to get the timing of the breeding and birthing just right. Fawns that are born out of sync with most of the herd, whether early or late, tend to be smaller in size and weight. I have found that, even if they have access to nutritious food, they will be smaller in size and weight all of their lives and will never reach their full growth potential.

Deer do not experience the population-controlling factor of life cycles that are common to so many other species. Mice, lemmings, and many of the other small rodents are on four-year cycles of "boom and bust." It is the lack of these small rodents that send the snowy owl on its predictable invasion of the lower forty-eight states. Hares, ruffed grouse, and other species are on a basic ten-year cycle. Deer do experience a little-known population control. On overstocked ranges, where the does are in poor nutritional health, they tend to conceive later in their estrus cycle, which results in their producing a preponderance of buck fawns. Fewer does, for any reason, means fewer offspring. No species can increase its population when it has outgrown its food base.

Winter

On the calendar, winter starts on December 21. However, despite global warming, in Canada and across the northern tier of states the cold weather has already drastically altered the activity, or inactivity, of the white-tailed deer, often starting at the end

Without antlers, the big bucks protect themselves by flailing with their forefeet.

of November. All body growth stops and the young are about two-thirds the size of their mother.

The rutting season, for the northern three-quarters of the country, winds down around December 15, as the buck's testosterone level drops and the swelling goes out of their necks. Within a month most of them will cast their antlers with the better-fed bucks retaining theirs longer. Ordinarily, the dominant bucks grow their antlers and remove the velvet before the lesser bucks because they are in better condition. Due to the stress of being dominant and the breeding season, the dominant bucks are usually the first to cast their antlers. This occurrence causes the entire dominance factor to change, if only momentarily. Once the biggest bucks lose their antlers, the lesser bucks still with their antlers become dominant. As if to make up for the all of the times they were chased, the lesser bucks will now chase the big bucks almost constantly, trying to gore them. Not having their antlers, the only defense the big, antlerless bucks have is to rise up and strike out with their front feet. Their slashing hooves are formidable weapons, but if the younger bucks are really aggressive, the big bucks have to give way to escape the punishment of the other's antlers.

This chasing usually lasts for only a couple of days, because when the lesser bucks have established their dominance, things quiet down for a while. But as soon as the lesser bucks lose their antlers, the big bucks reassert their dominance. The dominant bucks desperately need to regain the 20 to 25 percent of the body weight that they lost during the rut and those that don't are seldom able to survive a severe winter. This temporary reversal of dominance could be a factor in some of the big bucks being unable to regain their needed body weight.

A number of years ago I was told of a twist on this situation. Joe Taylor had a spike buck that removed the velvet from his antlers several days before the two big bucks in his herd. Giddy with his feeling of dominance, the little buck chased the big bucks, jabbing them whenever he got close enough to do so. He made their life a living hell. The morning after the big bucks removed their velvet Joe found the spike buck's body with twenty-eight puncture holes in it.

I don't believe Bill Haley and the Comets had deer in mind when they sang "Whole lotta shaking going on," but losing one antler causes the bucks to do a lot of head shaking. Bucks don't experience a lopsided feeling until one antler is cast, and the larger the antler, the more pronounced the sensation. In many cases, the extremely vigorous, circular rotation of the head helps to dislodge the remaining antler.

In response to increasingly cold weather and diminishing food supplies, most creatures face three choices: migrate, hibernate, or tough it out. Before cold weather, most small birds and a few mammals migrate to warmer climes. The metabolism of the small birds that stay in the northern part of the country speeds up in order to produce more heat. That means that their consumption of food has to increase, and so long as they can find enough dried berries and over-wintering insects, they can withstand the cold. Many birds flock to our feeders. Some mammal—such as woodchucks—some bats, and some mice hibernate, whereby their body temperatures drop dramatically and they spend the winter in a state of torpidity. Bears, raccoons, skunks, etc. become somnolent with some lowering of body temperature and long periods of sleep. The gradual dropping of the temperature causes the deer to become more inactive or their metabolism

If the snow is not crusted, deer will push it aside with their heads to feed on underlying grass.

to decline. This is a tremendous survival factor; faced with a diminishing food supply, they counter the problem by needing far less food. They wouldn't eat it if they had it. Although my research deer herd is offered an unlimited supply of food, I have found that from around the first of December until the first of March they voluntarily reduce their food intake 40 to 45 percent.

Don't get me wrong, deer will eat-need to eat-throughout the winter, they just need to eat far less. Studies done by Penn State University have proven that well-fed deer going into the winter with a good layer of fat can survive sixty-five days without eating. All of this depends upon whether or not the deer are disturbed. Caloric expenditure is minimal for a resting deer; it skyrockets when the deer are pushed out of their beds by predators or sightseers on snowmobiles, etc. That expenditure can be deadly when the deer exists on what is known as a negative energy balance. That occurs when the deer expend more energy in gathering and processing the food than they get in calories from the food consumed. Deer will frequently paw down through the snow to reach grass and leaves until the snow gets to a depth of about ten inches or if the snow gets crusted over.

Ordinarily, deer feeding on browse or twig tips eat twigs up to the diameter of a wooden matchstick, which have a twelve-millimeter-circumference covering of bark. The food value is in the bark, not in the cellulose of the wood. In times of starvation, a deer will consume twigs up to the size of a wooden pencil, which have twice the bark covering but four times as much cellulose. Plus, the twigs are frozen and must be thawed out by the heat in the paunch, which consumes more calories. In many cases, it would be better if the deer didn't even try to eat. Because of deer overpopulation, in most areas browse has become very scarce, forcing the deer to consume many of the dried fallen leaves. When feeding upon either browse or leaves, the deer's feces will be hard, individualized pellets.

In the northern Border States and southern provinces of Canada, the whitetails may migrate up to twenty-five miles to traditional yards although ten to fifteen miles is the usual distance. If after a series of mild winters, when the deer did not migrate and the adults were killed or died, the youngest deer may not know how to get to what had been traditional yards. Deer are what we call "conditional migrators;" migrating only when they are forced to do so by environmental conditions. Biologists use a formula called the "winter severity index" to gauge the likelihood of deer yarding. They keep track of the number of days where the temperature was below zero degrees Fahrenheit. They add those days to the number of days where the snow depth was more than fifteen inches, the total giving them the winter severity index.

Getting to the yards is a learned experience that the young deer acquire by following the adults. These yards are usually in dense white cedar swamps or other protected areas where the vegetation breaks the force of the wind. A well-fed adult deer can withstand bitter cold; they will not stay out in the wind. Another advantage to dense conifer stands is that their branches will hold up as much as 50 to 75 percent of the snow cover, making it easier for the deer to move about beneath them. The yarded deer soon walk out a network of trails, which allows the deer to move about more easily. It has been found that in most yards the bucks usually stay on the outside perimeter of the yards while the does and their young occupy the center. The major disadvantage to the yards is that, as they are traditional, most of the preferred food has already been eaten years ago. Although the yards do provide protection from the elements, many become death traps in severe winters when the deer die of starvation.

Deer that depend upon yarding are facing two major threats today. Many of the huge lumber companies that own thousands upon thousands of acres of woodland containing many of the yards are selling off the areas to developers. The lumber companies are finding they can make far more money as real estate companies than they can by being lumber companies. With the increased emphasis on harvesting more does to control the burgeoning deer population, many of the younger deer are not being taught the routes to traditional yards. Whereas elk and mule deer usually don't start to migrate until they are forced to by deepening snow, whitetails usually migrate when the temperature gets down to freezing and the first snow starts to accumulate. Eighteen to twenty inches of snow usually puts a stop to most whitetail movement, because the snow is up to their chests and they have to move by bounding.

The deer south of the northern Border States usually don't yard, but, change their activity routines. They may seek dense shelter during severe storms; those in my area seek out red cedar or rhododendron stands because such vegetation breaks the force of the wind. The cedar stands will also hold the snow aloft, but the rhododendron bushes do not because their leaves curl up tightly as the temperature drops. The deer will be found on the south-facing slopes, near the top of the hills; the hollows are avoided because the cold settles there. I have found that there is as much as a ten to fifteen degree Fahrenheit difference in temperature between a sunlit hilltop and a shaded hollow on even a slight hill. When possible, the deer will lie down in front of a rock ledge or large fallen tree. The backdrop deflects the northern wind, reflects the sunlight, and absorbs the sun's rays, creating a microclimate beneficial to the deer. The deer do not move during the night or early morning until about 9 a.m. They feed for only short periods of time because there usually isn't much feed available. By 4 p.m. they are bedded for the night.

Deer lose body heat through convection, conduction, evaporation, and radiation. Their first line of defense against such loss is their extremely efficient coat of guard hair and wooly undercoat; their erector pili muscles allow them to stand their guard hairs on end, increasing the depth of insulation and their body fat. Deer always paw a hole in the

snow in which they bed. That the deer is a southern species that is moving northward is seen in the fact that they do not use snow efficiently, as do the cold-evolved species, such as moose and caribou. The latter species always lie down in a fresh expanse of snow so that the snow envelops their bodies, providing the insulation of the snow itself, which basically contains much dead air. Dead air is the basis of almost

Melted snow in this bed shows that the deer lost body heat where its hair was compressed and therefore was unable to insulate well.

all insulation. Deer always paw a hole down through the snow and then lie down in the hollow.

It is true that the hollow does protect against wind and it does create a microclimate of trapped sunshine on sunny days, but it does not provide the advantages that a blanket of enveloping snow would provide on cold nights. Quite often a dominant deer will kick a subordinate out of its bed and lie down in the hollow that the other had dug.

In warm weather, a deer usually lies down with its legs extended for heat dissipation. During cold weather, a deer lies down with its legs folded beneath its body to keep them warmer. The folded legs raise the body up from the snow or frozen earth so that its body hair is not compressed, thus resulting in less loss of body heat through conduction. Although deer lose very little body heat through their winter coats, they do lose enough to cause the snow beneath them to melt while they are bedded. The bottom of every bed will be slightly iced over after the deer leave them, proving the loss of heat. Upon arising the deer immediately shakes its hair to increase its insulating value.

In the left-hand pocket of my camo pants I always carry a ten-foot by quarter-inch tape measure, because I am always measuring something. By measuring a deer's bed, whether in snow or leaves, you can guesstimate the size of the deer. A forty-inch bed will be made by a deer that is in the 125-pound range and may be either a small buck or a good-size doe. A forty-eight-inch bed will be made by a deer in the two hundred-pound class, and you can be sure that it was made by a buck.

The deer cannot prevent the loss of some body heat through evaporation because with each breath that it takes it also exhales carbon dioxide and moisture. To replenish the moisture the deer will drink additional free-flowing water, eat snow, or lick ice; all three are necessary but are calorically expensive as the liquid ingested is warmed to body temperature.

Global warming is a fact; I have seen it occurring over my lifetime in the range expansion of myriad creatures, as already mentioned. An additional effect of the warming is that our country is now experiencing many more ice storms than previously. Ice covering bare ground makes it treacherous for deer to walk, as already mentioned. Ice covering snow puts the deer at a tremendous disadvantage, as their small hooves usually break through crusts that will support the larger feet of their lighter predators, such as wolves, coyotes, and lynx. Ravens are increasing their populations in most parts of the country, as the wolves are making a comeback in the West and the coyotes are increasing in the East. Both predators are killing more game species and leaving more scraps

Deer that die provide food for the predators, or scavengers, such as this black vulture. Nothing in nature goes to waste.

for the ravens, allowing for their expansion. And it is not just a one-way street; the ice storms bring down uncounted tons of tree branches that provide excellent food that the deer could never normally reach. Although unsightly, the broken branches have the same effect as pruning, actually stimulating tree growth.

To many Indian tribes, February was known as the "starvation month." More deer starve in March, if they have utilized their body reserves and no new food is available. The loss of some of the deer through starvation is not a total loss to the deer herd because of what is known as compensatory mortality. Wherever deer are found you will also find predators that feed upon them. When deer are dying of starvation, many of the predators, particularly the coyotes, change from being hunters to being scavengers. Every dead deer the coyotes scavenge is one less deer they have to kill. This makes it easy on the coyotes and is compensation for the deer.

What is particularly devastating is for the deer to start to move out of their yards: As the temperature rises to above freezing, their appetite kicks into high gear and then a late-season snow storm will sweep in that prevents them from acquiring food. Barring a late-season storm, the deer move out of their yards faster than they moved into them.

The Eastern coyote is a major predator of the white-tailed deer.

A late spring can be disastrous for the deer.

The deer that didn't survive the winter—mostly the young of the year and the oldest bucks—will usually be found dead along spring runs. Even in the coldest weather, the warm spring water, fifty-six degrees Fahrenheit, will allow some green vegetation to grow. It is this vestige of vegetation that lures the deer to such spots, but unfortunately for some of them, spring itself will come too late.

Chapter 13

Deer and Man

In 1956, Pete Seeger wrote a song that asked the question, "Where have all the flowers gone?" He answered it a few sentences later with, "Young girls picked them, ev'ry one." The song was a great hit throughout the nation, at a time when folk songs were at an all-time high in popularity. However, his answer was wrong. It wasn't the young girls or the young men that picked them, although I have to admit that when I was young I picked some of them, too. It was deer that ate them, ev'ry one.

Carrying Capacity

I was raised on a small dairy farm in northwest New Jersey where we had about fifteen cows, milking about twelve on a regular basis. We couldn't keep more cows because we didn't have enough land to raise the crops needed to feed more cows; the land just wouldn't support them. That was basic; that was the carrying capacity. I was brought up knowing the relationship between the sun, rain, and soil, what could be grown and what could not.

Nowhere can more of anything be raised than the habitat can support, and our farm was our cows' habitat. My roots were, and still are, in the soil. I grew up learning and living with those basic facts. Today, over 90 percent of the populace in the United States lives on concrete, in urban or suburban areas, and most haven't the foggiest notion of the interrelationships of everything on this planet Earth that we share.

I was hired by some of the heirs to the Pittsburgh Paint Co., who lived on a family compound of about ten square miles northwest of Philadelphia, to lecture on my white-tailed deer program and to make suggestions about managing their deer herd.

Good deer habitat in my area of New Jersey consists of farm fields adjacent to hardwood forests.

As I mentioned earlier, I didn't have to census their property. Just by looking, I could see there were far too many. Everywhere was devastation. Every forested piece of land had a browse line up to seven feet above the ground; there was no understory of plants anywhere. Every shrub or garden that wasn't fenced was decimated. And this is typical of what is taking place over much of North America—overabundance of white-tailed deer.

The family member that hired me was a hunter and hunted on his section of the estate, as did some of the other members. Some of the family were not against hunting but didn't hunt, while a third faction was adamantly against anyone hunting on their portion of the estate. Sound familiar? Naturally, the deer retreated to the no-hunting areas when hunting occurred elsewhere on the estate, but they wreaked havoc over the entire estate at other times.

The family wanted me to explain the basics of deer biology and why I felt the herd had to be drastically reduced for the good of the deer as well as the entire ecosystem. I don't know if I won any converts that night, but that was just one of the many contested presentations I have experienced over my lifetime of trying to educate folks. The white-tailed deer is one of the most adaptable of all creatures, and it is that very adaptability that has caused the deer to be its own worst enemy.

Later, I was hired by a group called the Deer Protection Society. My deer presentation addresses the life history of deer and how to benefit them. When I got there, to my chagrin, I found that this society wasn't interested in "protecting" deer. They wanted to know how to get rid of them. The "damn" deer were devastating the shrubbery on their estates. No, they didn't want hunters on their land; no, they didn't want to put up fences. They just wanted "no deer." I didn't win any converts that night, either, for I just didn't know how to make the deer disappear.

The Social Carrying Capacity

We have a unique system in the United States wherein most of the deer's habitat is owned by private individuals, even though the deer themselves are owned by the state. Large landowners may keep the public off their land via "no trespassing" laws, which give them the right to hunt their land exclusively, subject to the hunting laws of the state. Or some of those landowners may not want any hunting on their land. Many landowners may not have extensive holdings, but laws preventing anyone from hunting within set distances of a home effectively bar all hunting. This has brought about a new concept in game management known as the "social carrying capacity." To serve the needs of the general public, most of state game commissions are now composed of members of the general public and not just representatives of hunter's organizations. "Social carrying capacity" is roughly the deer population that the public will tolerate in their locale. On that, the number of conflicting views would tax a Solomon to resolve. Because no single answer could please everybody, policy becomes compromise.

I am no Solomon but can offer suggestions on what will be best for deer.

Some History

The 1890s saw the nadir of the white-tailed deer population in North America, with an estimation of fewer than five hundred thousand whitetails remaining from a population of more than twenty million when the pilgrims landed. Witmer Stone, of the Philadelphia Museum of Natural History, estimated an 1890s population of fewer than two hundred whitetails in the entire state of New Jersey. During those decades, various states responded to the crisis with curtailed hunting, new laws, better enforcement of existing

The "social carrying capacity" refers to the number of deer landowners are willing to tolerate on their land—or porch.

laws, and the importation of deer from other areas to bolster local herds. Extinction was prevented when hunting clubs and individuals joined in the preservation effort.

Naturally, most game departments and sportsmen wanted to restock their areas with the largest deer possible. Fortunately, the northern tier of states had enough deer that some could be exported. Coincidentally, northern states also had the largest subspecies. Researchers soon learned that they had to import does as well as bucks. Importing big bucks to breed with the existing does did not really improve the strain. In fact, in just four generations, the imported bucks' genes were diluted. I was thoroughly shocked when I first started to photograph deer in the 1970s on some of the private ranches in South Texas, along the Rio Grande.

This large Texas eight-pointer clearly inherited genes from translocated northern whitetails.

The deer were not the little goat-like deer I had earlier seen on Texas's Edward Plateau; these were as big as the deer that I photographed in the North. With good reason: they were descended from northern deer. Because most of the native subspecies of deer had been wiped out, the area was restocked with bucks and does of the northern subspecies. That tremendous amount of restocking in the United States is another reason that our deer should be reclassified taxonomically. Most of the original criteria for subspeciation simply do not apply today.

Professional Management

First and foremost, the management of deer and all wildlife should be done by professional wildlife biologists, people who have the knowledge and training. Wildlife management should not be politicized. The decisions must be made for the good of the environment, as well as the species, although most decisions can never please everyone.

There are simply far too many deer in most parts of the country. I have been a hunter all of my life and I, too, like to see lots of deer. But I also like to see lots of other wildlife. Deer overpopulation is destroying the habitat in most areas, causing a drastic decline in many species. Depending on habitat, biologists usually suggest that sixteen to twenty deer per square mile allows the herd to stay in balance with their habitat, without significantly degrading it. Of course, some isolated areas have fewer than that per square mile. But in such cases, the habitat must not be able to support more deer. Even in hunted areas, there are often thirty to fifty deer to the square mile. In protected areas, those figures often soar to two hundred or more deer to the square mile.

Overpopulation is detrimental to the deer themselves. It leads to habitat destruction, which can cause death by starvation, reduced deer size, increased deer-vehicle

Here is a mature forest with only tree canopy and understory of hay-scented ferns. No forest regeneration. No deer food available.

collisions, and the spread of diseases among deer weakened by poor nutrition and close bodily contact with diseased animals.

Deer overpopulation also prevents forest regeneration. It takes decades for a habitat to recover, if ever.

For people, the economic and health impacts of deer overpopulation are almost incalculable. Deer threaten vegetative plantings of every kind, and the loss is beyond calculation. Family farming is an iffy business at best, so excessive crop damage can push some farms into disaster. Vehicle-deer collisions are mounting, and so are the repair costs. What can't be calculated is the human suffering and deaths resulting from such collisions. Besides, some deer are reservoirs for diseases that ticks can transmit to man—such Lyme disease and ehrlichiosis. What is to be done?

Hunting Perspectives

Regulated hunting by sportsmen and -women is the most efficient and effective tool for managing our burgeoning white-tailed deer population. I realize that some people are against hunting for various reasons, and they are entitled to their opinions. But antihunting opinions should never be allowed to take precedence when detrimental to deer themselves or to a habitat.

I realize that many hunters are unhappy with some regulations that biologists put forth. Some hunters think the new hunting seasons are too long, too liberal, too restrictive, too much of other things. They long for the "good old days" not realizing that, today, deer hunting in most areas is better than anything they have ever encountered. For good hunting to continue, we must employ the science that will allow it.

Some hunters and antihunters fail to realize that in some areas deer populations need to be reduced to below the land's carrying capacity if the habitat is ever going to recover. The hunters should commit to this for the long haul because the forest

A poacher is a thief. Here a poacher took just the head and antlers from this big buck, leaving the meat to spoil. To me, that's sinful.

regeneration will not happen overnight; after all "generation" is an integral part of "regeneration."

In populated areas where deer need to be controlled and firearm hunting is not possible, alternatives means are being tested. Live trapping is no longer feasible because there are no places left that are devoid of deer in which to release the captured animals. Sterilization of the deer simply does not work as yet and would be far too expensive if it did. Some communities are allowing qualified bow-hunters, for a fee, to help reduce the deer in their parks and residential areas. Communities that will not allow hunting have had to resort to hiring marksmen from such organizations as White Buffalo to reduce their herds. Such reductions are very expensive but very efficient, and the meat goes to shelters for the homeless.

Although the overall deer herds must be reduced, we cannot allow poaching. The poacher is a thief. Unfortunately, as mentioned, big bucks bring big bucks and poachers are depriving many law-abiding hunters of the opportunity to harvest a trophy buck legally.

Most states have hotlines for notifying the authorities when they witness game-law violations. Having worked as a deputy game warden for the state of New Jersey, I know that the wardens and conservation officers need and deserve all the help that they can get. It is estimated that less than 5 percent of game violators are caught, mostly because there are not enough officers to do the job. Those officers are dedicated to protecting the wildlife we love, to enhancing the sport we love. Let's give them all the support we can.

Options for Land Stewards

Every individual or hunting club that has enough land should plant supplemental food plots for deer. The deer can get as much, and sometimes ten times as much, nutrition from a food plot as they can from an equal-size forested area.

Cornell University recommends planting birdsfoot trefoil because it is self-sustaining and highly nutritious. I also recommend a winter blend of rape, sugar beet, turnip, and brassica, because all of these plants will stand upright under all but the heaviest snows, allowing the deer to reach them. Clovers, alfalfa, rye, and corn are also good deer foods. In the wooded areas of my land, where no machinery can be used, I plant rye using a chest seeder that broadcasts the seeds.

I plant this crop just as soon as the frost is out of the ground, which gives it about two months of sunshine before the tree's leaves shade out the forest floor. I do no soil preparation, nor do I have the ability to cover the scattered seeds. I plant the rye just before a rain, and the water washes the seeds into contact with the soil and provides the moisture needed to sprout them. As fast as the deer eat the tender shoots I plant more and continue to do this until October. This is the cheapest, most efficient way I know to grow good deer food in a wooded area.

To ensure that your money, effort, and time in planting food crops are not wasted, it's important to know which crops deer prefer at different times. For this, ask your local county agriculture agent which deer-preferred crops grow well in your locale. But before planting anything, ask your agent or county extension to conduct a soil test. Alternatively, low-cost do-it-yourself soil-testing kits are available at garden and farm suppliers. At the very least, test for soil acidity, known as soil pH. Generally, a pH level between six and seven is best for most crops. Anything below six is usually too acidic, requiring that the soil be "sweetened" with lime to raise the pH so the plants can grow better.

To create food for deer, I use a chest seeder when planting tons of rye and wheat throughout my woodlands.

For soils that need lime, plants often aren't able to absorb enough beneficial minerals, including the phosphorous, potassium, and calcium that deer need for general health, strong bones, and better antlers. Based on pH, the county agent should also be able to advise on fertilizer combinations and amounts to apply.

If your land is forested and thus unsuitable for planting crops, you can still increase the amount of deer food by selective timber cutting. Opening the forest canopy allows sunlight to reach the forest floor, thereby increasing growth of new vegetation. Native berry bushes and seedlings of most types make excellent deer food. Avoid planting invasive aliens, which native insects can't digest, thereby reducing populations of insect populations—caterpillars, for example—on which native birds depend, especially during nesting time. A great source of information on native plants and flowers that deer don't eat is provided in Neil Soderstrom's book *Deer-Resistant Landscaping* (www.neilsoderstrom.com). He also explains a variety of measures on how to keep deer away from your plants and out of your garden.

Such food patches will entice deer to feed on your property but will not hold them unless protective cover serves as a safe haven. Of course, the size of your refuge will depend upon the amount of land available. When I say refuge, I'm talking about an inviolate piece of land, which—after preparation—you DO NOT ENTER. For deer, if you have land with a south-facing slope and freshwater spring or stream, all the better.

This doe is feeding on the rye I planted in the woodlands.

Although a deer refuge can be as small as two or three acres, five acres and more serve better. To prepare the refuge, all you really need is a chain saw. Don't harvest any of the trees you cut because they will form the structure of the refuge. Using what is known as a hinge cut, cut the tree about four feet above the ground. But cut through the trunk only far enough to cause the tree to fall. Try to drop the next tree across the first one to make a jumble of branches. Don't fell all trees, especially if you have oaks, because their acorns are a favorite deer food, and oaks serve literally hundreds of species of wildlife for food and cover. Just cut enough trees to make an almost impenetrable barrier to people and larger predators. Even though such an area seems impenetrable to people, the deer will squirm their way through. The jumble will also provide a windbreak, offering protection from the elements, especially during winter when deer most need it. *Note:* If you succeed in felling trees while cutting the tree trunks only about two-thirds through, the felled trees will continue to produce leaves where deer can reach them. And by opening the canopy, exposing soil to sunlight, all sorts of vegetation will sprout.

Deer prefer newly sprouted browse to all other foods. After you have felled the trees, stay out of the refuge. Do not enter it, even after the hunting season is over, and try to prevent dogs from entering at any time. If deer feel safe there, they will stay. If you are a hunter or wildlife photographer, install your tree stands between the refuge and wherever the deer come to feed.

A most worthwhile organization, and one to which every hunter and hunt club should belong, is the Quality Deer Management Association (QDMA), headquartered in Bogart, Georgia. They can be contacted through their website www.qdma.com or by calling 1–800–209–3337. Some folks have the mistaken notion that this organization is mainly about raising trophy deer. It's true that by following their suggestions you can help produce trophy deer. But their main mission is to help people better manage land for all species, which in turn will be highly beneficial for the deer.

Most of the state game departments are funded solely by the sale of hunting license fees. Hunters have always been in the forefront of the conservation efforts. Unfortunately, the number of hunters is declining as more of our nation is paved over. It is time for all of the folks who want a say in deer management to step up and put their money where their mouth is; game departments need additional funding.

Recruiting Youth

Today, one of the most important tasks for hunters is to recruit more youths, both girls and boys, into their fraternity so that there will be sufficient hunters tomorrow to help in the managing of our deer. A local farmer friend of mine suffers thousands of dollars in crop damage each year and so needs to have a deer depredation permit because there are not enough hunters in the area to reduce the population.

The recently founded National Archery in the Schools Program was designed to be part of each school's physical education curriculum. Today, the program has been adopted in forty-seven states, some Canadian provinces, and other countries. And the list is growing. As I write this, the latest year's student participation topped two million, its participation eclipsing even Little League Baseball. Although the program was not set up to produce deer hunters, untold thousands of the students are doing just that.

In Closing

There are many solutions to managing our deer herds, and I have only touched upon a few.

With good management, the future for whitetails is bright, and may those flashing tails remain beacons to all of us.

I want to end this book on a bright note because I honestly feel that the future for our beloved whitetail is bright, and I know that is what most people hope for. To save the deer we love, we must learn all we can about them, and that is the knowledge I have tried to provide in this book.

Index